INTERIBERICA, S.A. DE EDICIONES

WORLDS APART
Nature in Cities and Islands

Doubleday and Company Inc.,
Garden City, New York, 1976

© 1976 Interiberica, S. A. - Madrid
© 1976 Aldus Books Limited, London
SBN: 385–11347–1
Library of Congress Catalog Card No: 75–13113

Also published in parts as Island Life and
Nature in the City

WORLDS APART

Part 1
Island Life

by John Sparks

ISBN: 84-382-0021-4 Dep. Legal: S.S.116-1976

Printed in Spain by TONSA - San Sebastián

Series Coordinator	Geoffrey Rogers
Series Art Director	Frank Fry
Design Consultant	Guenther Radtke
Editorial Consultant	David Lambert
Series Consultant	Malcolm Ross-Macdonald
Art Editor	Douglas Sneddon
Editor	Allyson Rodway
Copy Editors	Maureen Cartwright
	Damian Grint
Research	Barbara Fraser
Art Assistant	Michael Turner

Contents: Part 1

Editorial Advisers

DAVID ATTENBOROUGH Naturalist and Broadcaster

MICHAEL BOORER, B.SC. Author, Lecturer, and Broadcaster

Foreword by David Attenborough

The sea boils. Fountains of cinders explode into the air. Red hot lava rises above the waves in clouds of steam. A new volcanic island is born, and for a short period the earth has acquired a very exceptional patch of ground— one that is totally devoid of life.

But that state of affairs does not last for long. Almost immediately windborn spores and seeds drop onto the ash. Drifting larvae from the open ocean settle on boulders on the black beach and turn into adult shellfish and barnacles. Minute spiders float down on gossamer parachutes and seabirds begin to fly over the cooling lava crags prospecting for nesting places. So the island, with astonishing rapidity, acquires the foundations of a flourishing population.

Modern cities can, initially, be almost as unwelcoming. Tarmacadam, concrete, and glass are even more hostile than lava, and cities, unlike volcanic islands, have human inhabitants who do their best to discourage indiscriminate colonization by wildlife. Yet wildlife, in the end, establishes a home here too, and by similar methods. Seeds germinate in cracks. Sparrow hawks find ledges of buildings as accommodating as those of mountain cliffs. And just as passing ships often unwittingly carry animals to islands, so the trucks and airplanes bringing goods to our cities introduce all kinds of exotic invaders.

The similarity between the two environments does not end there. Animals in cities may be almost as isolated by the surrounding countryside as island creatures are by the sea.

Both are therefore compelled to breed largely among themselves and both develop races of inhabitants with their own peculiar characteristics. Many a Pacific island has a race of butterfly patterned in a way that makes it distinct from those on any other island. London pigeons are already substantially different from the rock doves that were their ancestors. Island-dwellers also change their behavior in order best to exploit their new environment. So the leaf-eating iguanas that strayed to the Galápagos have learned to crawl on the seabed in search of seaweed, and great titmice in British cities have discovered how to tear open the metal tops of milk bottles in order to sip the cream.

The island world John Sparks describes so vividly may seem more "natural" to us and therefore of greater interest to a naturalist. Indeed, there can be few more thrilling places for anyone interested in animals than such islands as the Galápagos. But the urban world that John Andrew Burton surveys in such a comprehensive way shows the same processes at work, if we are perceptive enough to recognize them, and it has an added fascination. This world apart is man's own creation and he, like the rest of its inhabitants, is being molded by it.

David Attenborough.

The Romance of Islands

If Paradise be on earth, it is as likely as not on an island, because islands can be places of exceptional beauty, charm, and peace, remote from the busy mainstream of world events.

Most of us have at some time dreamed of escaping to an island in the sun where we could enjoy the simple life of a beachcomber, perhaps reliving some of the best-known adventures of all time, because our views of islands have been molded by classic adventure stories. Our island retreat would thus teem with the fascinating (if impossible) mixture of wildlife found by *The Swiss Family Robinson*. Readers of *Treasure Island* would also expect buried treasure, for they know that every respectable island should have a chest hidden somewhere, full of doubloons and pieces of eight. Bold daydreamers might even welcome the prospect of pitting their wits against scurrilous pirates like Long John Silver, *Treasure Island*'s peg-legged arch-villain, decorated with swearing parrot and cutlass and come to retrieve ill-gotten booty.

Not all fictionally famous island visitors arrived of their own accord, like Silver, to find the spot marked "X" on a treasure map. Many escapists perhaps picture themselves as that best-known of all castaways, Robinson Crusoe, a character inspired by the real-life adventures of Alexander Selkirk, who sailed to Brazil in 1704 and was put ashore on uninhabited Más a Tierra Island, off the coast of Chile, where he had to stay for over four years. Daniel Defoe's Crusoe was shipwrecked during a storm, and found his island barren except for a few wild birds and beasts conveniently placed there for the pot, together with Man Friday, a solitary, helpful savage. Most of us like to think that we, too, could rise to Crusoe's level of practical skill, and survive by improvised methods of tool-making, crop raising, and husbandry. That perennial cartoon character the shipwrecked survivor reinforces our notion that life on a desert island is easy if not always idyllic. Sun-

Fading sunlight silhouettes palms and shines upon the Indian Ocean, here in the Seychelles Islands. Scenes such as this seem like paradise to countless city-dwellers, who see island life as a carefree escape from urban pressures and routines.

shine, enough sand to sit on, and a few coconut palms would seem to suffice for survival.

The appeal of the island Garden of Eden makes itself felt in various ways. For instance, it underpins the success of a long-running British radio program called *Desert Island Discs*. Guests are asked to choose eight pieces of music to be marooned with, which would make their lives as castaways more bearable. Even birdwatchers have played this game, and a long correspondence in at least one serious ornithological journal has built up on the subject of which 10 species of birds would bring the most pleasure to the hapless stranded birdwatcher. Predictably some showed great concern for scarce and vanishing species, and selected pairs of such rarities as Kirtland's warbler, which breeds only in Michigan. They felt that a fresh start on an island haven would bring the warblers into good breeding fettle and that a big reservoir population would spring up to safeguard the species. One ornithologist with a sensible eye on his own survival, and who also clearly appreciated his birds well roasted and handsomely stuffed, opted for breeds such as chickens and turkeys.

His taste matched that of many of the mariners who made long-distance voyages in the days of sail. Seamen once avidly sought out islands rich in edible seabirds because these provided bountiful stocks for ships' larders. Such islands were especially valuable chandlery stores when strategically placed on the sea routes of the world. Indeed, without the help of prolific penguin rookeries and other seabird colonies at the southern tips of Africa and South America, it is doubtful whether long-haul explorers such as Bartholomew Diaz and Ferdinand Magellan could have made their journeys.

Sailors found not only food supplies but spiritual and other kinds of refreshment in many of the more exotic island ports of call. Indeed the romance of tropical islands probably stems from the Age of Discovery when intrepid navigators were forging trade routes across the oceans in search of spices and slaves. To their surprise, they found they were spared the dangers of sailing off the edge of the world; instead, people such as Magellan, Álvaro de Mendaña de Neyra,

Driven ashore in a storm, a ship breaks up under the powerful impact of waves, but some of her crew may have scrambled onto dry land. Many a seaman became an unwilling islander because his vessel was wrecked or his fellows left him marooned.

and Samuel Wallis managed to add another hemisphere to the known parts of the planet: a hemisphere that was largely sea but included the "new" continents of Australia and Antarctica. More important to us here, the voyagers also discovered thousands of islands. Some were barren, but others held attractions beyond the imagination of the hardened seadogs! Many a mariner must have believed he had discovered Paradise in the middle of the Pacific.

Anyone who has been privileged enough to have visited a tropical island will have experienced a taste of Paradise. Whether in the West Indies, or in the middle of the Pacific or Indian Ocean, the stresses and strains of a civilized city life are all too easily borne away on the warm sea breezes. The comings and goings of

political leaders in Washington, London, or Moscow seem far away and of little relevance. Bad news of strikes, inflation, and other commonplace stories of doom and gloom that fill the papers and clog the wavebands are diluted by distance. On islands in the sun, the urgency is taken out of life; the rhythms lengthen, the pace slackens. There really is time to gather seashells on the Seychelles shores of coral sand, to listen to the whispers of palms swinging out toward the satin-smooth sea, to watch the dazzling-white fairy terns fishing beyond the fringing reefs, and to soak in the golden light of equatorial sunsets. The sense of isolation that comes from being surrounded by the sea loosens the spirit; inhibitions evaporate. Adventures seem to lie around every corner, and romances flourish (and fade) at the drop of a coconut. Advertising copywriters have made full play of the carefree and unrestrained way of life that goes hand in hand with island living, and—as if to prove the point—some of the highest incidences of diseases that are passed on by lovers have been recorded on islands. Love and let live has been an important ingredient in the life style of tropical island societies for some time, as the first European seamen discovered.

Since the Spaniard Mendaña de Neyra reported his discoveries about Polynesian life in 1595, the Polynesians have enjoyed an unrivaled reputation for free love. Shipload after shipload of seamen sailed from island to island, becoming increasingly more impressed with Pacific warmth and hospitality. The naturalist Commerson, a

Women of Tahiti by *Paul Gauguin*. Proclaiming that civilization makes man suffer but barbarism revives him, the artist spent most of the 1890s painting bold, colorful scenes of idyllic native life on Tahiti. (Already, though, Tahitians were adopting European dress.)

companion of the 18th-century French explorer de Bougainville, wrote of the Tahitians: "They know no other God than love. Every day is consecrated to him. The whole island is his temple in which all women are idols and all men worshipers." European seadogs had no difficulty adapting to such surroundings, as even the un-shockable Captain Cook recorded with disapproval. Later visitors to Polynesia told about their experiences in books with such tempting titles as *Isles of Eden, Daughters of Joy,* and *The Island of Desire.*

Love was not quite so free, even on Tahiti. There were still rules to observe, but the rules were different from those the sailors were used to back home. Love was just more open, uninhibited, frankly pleasurable, and considered of no more nor less significance than eating or drinking; nothing to feel unduly guilty or sinful about. It is little wonder, then, that the crew of the good ship *Bounty* found feminine friendliness so much to their liking in 1787 that they were persuaded by the mutinous Fletcher Christian to set their hot-tempered Captain Bligh afloat in an open boat, thus allowing them to settle on the islands for a life much more agreeable than the British Navy could offer.

The *Beagle*, in which the English naturalist Charles Darwin traveled, put in to Tahiti in 1835. He, too, was delighted with "charming Tahiti." Although he had heard rumors that missionaries had turned the Tahitians into a gloomy race living in fear of the Christian God, he thought them cheerful and merry. Paul Gauguin, the French Postimpressionist painter, was equally captivated at first. He quit Paris and spent most of the latter part of his life living on Tahiti.

But by Gauguin's time, at the end of the last century, things were not what they used to be. The missionaries had imported Christian guilt and grass skirts. Polynesian society had crumbled and the "Noble Savage" was humiliated.

According to one myth, the forbidden fruit that was used to tempt Eve in the Garden of Eden and to bring about her downfall grows on an island. To be precise, according to the writings of General Charles Gordon, the Garden of Eden was none other than the island of Praslin in the Seychelles. Better known as the gallant "Gordon Pasha," and "Hero of Khartoum," Gordon was highly impressed with the British Seychelles in 1881, and with the heart-shaped fruit of the coco-de-mer palm, which flourished

on Praslin and a few other islands. Now, the double nuts of this tree had been coveted objects long before Europeans had entered the Indian Ocean. Occasionally the empty shells would be washed up on the Indian or Arabian shores, where they commanded prices worthy of only royal purses. No one knew where they had come from until the discovery of the palms and their fruit during the middle of the 18th century. The attraction was their shape, because, enclosed within the heart-shaped fruit, the nuts have an uncanny resemblance to a female body. Thus the general concluded that if Eve had been tempted by any tree, this was surely the one.

At the end of the 19th century, another public relations operation was being carried out on behalf of islands by Edmund Banfield, a Liverpool-born journalist working in Australia. On the verge of a nervous breakdown, he was ordered rest and isolation by his doctor. After much searching he settled for Dunk, a fairly large

and beautiful island set in the Great Barrier Reef just off the northeast coast of Australia. In 1897 Banfield wrote *The Confessions of a Beachcomber*, the first of four such genial books. So appealing were his descriptions of life on a tropical isle "entirely free from the traces of the mauling paws of humanity" that his books were read avidly around the world by people suffering from the inhumanity of industrialization. Going a-Dunking became the rage. Many were inspired by Banfield's pen to travel from England to live a dream-life beachcombing on Dunk. But the invasion of the island's privacy quickly turned into a retreat, as disillusioned Robinson Crusoes quit the peace and the palm-gilded landscape for the busy mainland. The sad fact is, that solitude needs monumental self-discipline, even in Paradise. Living alone, off even a lush tropical island, also calls for survival skills that most of us do not possess.

Yet the cult of the "Noble Savage" in his Gar-

den of Eden persists even today. Glossy brochures advertise get-away-from-it-all island vacations. New York's jet setters have their West Indian beaches for mental refueling, and the very rich increasingly scour the Pacific and Indian oceans for tropical retreats.

Needless to say, not all islands conform to the picture of sun-soaked havens of bliss. Such names as Inaccessible and Desolation are descriptive enough in themselves. Some islands must rate as the worst, windiest, and remotest places in the world. One such is Macquarie Island, which lies southeast of Tasmania in the path of the westerly winds that lash it with rain and gales for much of the year. Bouvet Island in the South Atlantic is where the most retiring recluse should live, being the most isolated piece of land in the world, inhabited only by a few seals and seabirds.

Of course some people can cope with such rigorous solitude better than others, and even

succeed in making it part of their life style. Holy men of various orders inhabit favored island retreats where they can devote themselves to prayer away from the distracting influences of normal living. Islands around Britain are hardly congenial to a lazy, idyllic existence, being wild and windy places, and yet many have been taken over by monks at some time or another. In the year A.D. 563 St. Columba, a prince and monk, set off from Ireland in a skin-sided open boat. On 12 May he landed on an island in the heart of the Hebrides, and turned it into a center of Christian teaching. Iona became a springboard for the conversion of northern England. The island is still a famous Christian retreat. In A.D. 635 St. Aidan, a monk from Iona settled on Holy Island off the Northumberland coast. Holy Island became famous later that century under its sixth bishop, St. Cuthbert, who gave his name to St. Cuthbert's ducks—more widely known as eiders—which supposedly nested wherever he

15

trod. So many devout followers made the pilgrimage to St. Cuthbert's monastery that the saint escaped from the crowds to the desolate island of Farne. Monks still inhabit Holy Island, but instead of withdrawing they now meet the tourists and relieve them of their money in return for the honey drink mead. Tresco in the Isles of Scilly, off southwest England, used to support an order of Benedictine monks, which no amount of prayer prevented Henry VIII from breaking up. To live and die on the Welsh island of Bardsey was said to guarantee immortality. It is also said that 20,000 martyrs, saints, and holy men are buried there.

Islands provide natural sanctuaries, but isolation makes them equally useful as jails. Many an important prisoner has been shut away on some island fortress. Napoleon Bonaparte, best-known of such captives, was exiled to remote St. Helena in the South Atlantic after his defeat at Waterloo. Less distinguished criminals in the USA were once housed on rocky Alcatraz in San Francisco Bay; and in South Africa, there is little chance of escaping from Robben Island, just off Cape Town, where many a prisoner has had time to contemplate his crimes along with the jackass penguins. There was a time when selected lawbreakers from the United Kingdom were exported halfway round the world to Botany Bay, on the island continent of Australia; now the Isle of Wight, just off the English mainland, is considered far enough.

The security that islands afford is important for many of their wildlife occupants. Seabirds in vast numbers nest upon islands, safe from mainland predators. Some of these seabird cities are among the great wildlife spectaculars of the world. For instance, a million or more murres (guillemots) nest upon Walrus Island, one of the Pribilof group in the Bering Sea. To visit even a small island such as Grassholm, on which 14,000 pairs of gannets breed, is an experience not easily forgotten. Grassholm is a mere tooth of rock off west Wales, but its top is smothered in white birds and their white guano (seabird excrement) like the icing on a cake. You climb up from sea level over turf clustered with sea pinks and honeycombed with puffin burrows, to the highest point, where the view over the gannet conurbation is staggering. The air is filled with gannets, the sheer volume of their creaking and grating calls makes conversation difficult, and the smell of stale guano and

fish is suffocating. But the excitement of the nesting gannets is infectious. Wherever you look these big ocean divers with a wingspread of six feet are coming and going, bill-scissoring, sky-pointing, regurgitating fish cocktails to their young. In such a colony any sensitive human being feels an intruder, but the experience is exhilarating. It also inspires awe, for this is a spectacle that man has had no part in creating.

Places such as Walrus Island and Grassholm seem self-contained. Perhaps that is why small islands are so satisfying as places to visit. They

Below: Alcatraz seen from San Francisco. Dangerous criminals were imprisoned on the rocky island's 12 acres from 1933 until the federal penitentiary closed in 1963. Any convict escaping from his cell had to swim a mile through the cold waves of San Francisco Bay to reach the mainland. Some tried, but all drowned or were recaptured. Right: gannets soaring over an island nesting site. Tiny islands set in fish-rich seas and free from landbound predators provide sanctuaries upon which gannets, murres, puffins, and other seabirds nest in colonies of millions of individuals.

are packages in the broadest sense and thus easy to come to terms with and to comprehend in the whole. And yet this description begs the basic question of what an island actually is.

Put very simply, an island is a piece of land surrounded by water. This definition excludes such structures as buoys or ships, although supertankers such as the *Globtik London*, at about 500,000 tons deadweight, are far larger than islands such as tiny Rockall in the North Atlantic Ocean. Whether a seabird would differentiate between a heap of shingle or a ship's superstructure to rest upon at high tide is doubtful. Indeed at Plymouth, in southwest England, large flocks of oyster catchers, dunlin, and turnstones rest on lighters at high tide, and the superstructures of cocooned frigates and aircraft carriers, once busy with seamen, now support dozing cormorants. These ships are not islands, but biologically are used as such. Man

does make genuine islands, though, in the form of spoil heaps. For instance, rubbish tipped into piles below low tide on the west coast of Florida now supports offshore mangrove swamps. Even land surrounded by the sea, however, may not always deserve the title of island. With small stacks such as Rockall or Alcatraz there is no problem in recognizing their island status. Australia is also surrounded by sea, and shows many features of island life, yet because it occupies 3 million square miles, geographers prefer to call this landmass a continent. Clearly the upper size limit for an island is arbitrary. Greenland (840,000 square miles) is usually considered the world's largest island. This book will be on the whole about smaller places, although many of these have an importance out of all proportion to their size, politically, economically, biologically, or philosophically.

Rockall is a good example of a tiny island

with a potentially big political and economic value. This jagged nub of granite, just over 70 feet high, sticks out of the Atlantic Ocean some 250 miles northwest of Ireland. The fearsome North Atlantic swell occasionally breaks over the islet; landing is hazardous and has only been achieved a few times. On the face of it there seems little point in laying claim to the place, and yet on 18 September 1955 a boarding party from the Royal Navy's survey vessel HMS *Vidal* formally took possession of Rockall for Britain. This full-scale naval operation may have seemed absurd at the time, but we now know that there is oil locked away beneath the seabed in the area. Britain can thus lay claim not just to more territory, but perhaps to more oil and other seabed resources because of her farflung islet outpost.

However, the short-term national interests served by islands are nothing when weighed against the role these remote places have played in revealing to man his relationship to earth's other life forms. The credit for making this immensely important discovery goes to Charles Darwin, who, in 1835, was aboard the *Beagle* when it cruised among the Galápagos Islands. Lying some 600 miles west of Ecuador, the islands were deserted except for a handful of prisoners stranded there by the Ecuador government, and strange forms of life unlike anything anywhere else in the world. This very uniqueness helped to crystallize Darwin's thoughts about how life appeared and developed on earth.

It is difficult for us to appreciate how heretical were the notions going through Darwin's head in 1837 when he started to compile his notebooks about evolution. At that time, most Christians took the Bible's account of creation quite literally. In the West few people seriously doubted that the earth and everything on it was formed in six days by God, who rolled up his sleeves, as it were, and started work at 9 A.M. on Sunday 23 October in the year 4004 B.C. according to the calculations of Archbishop Ussher and Dr. John Lightfoot of Cambridge University. What Darwin saw on the Galápagos Islands convinced him that living animals are products of a process of change, not of static creation, and he set out his argument in 1859 in his book *On The Origin of Species by Means of Natural Selection, or the Preservation of Favoured Races in the Struggle for Life.* Darwin's revolutionary explanation of evolution came as a cataclysm to mankind, and the reorientation of our view of ourselves as part of an organic process that the theory impelled us to make is still taking place today. Such was the impact of Darwin's visit to the otherwise insignificant equatorial archipelago off the South American coast.

Because of what Darwin discovered, people are less sure than they were that God is in his heaven and well pleased with his work of creating man in his own image. Perhaps we must be content with finding Paradise on earth—on an island, perhaps. Such a paradise would not be permanent, though, because islands—like life forms—undergo change.

The Birth of Islands

The shallow sea off Iceland is rich in life, and fishing fleets from many nations vie with each other to fill their trawls with fat cod. It is an eventful, and sometimes downright hostile, part of the world in which to make a living. Freezing storms frequently whip the waves into an angry white foam, plastering ships' superstructures with a deadly covering of ice. At other times fog blankets the area. As if all this is not enough to contend with, icebergs float through that part of the North Atlantic and create a hazard to shipping. On 14 November 1963 something other than fish was stirring on the seabed. A cook on a trawler plowing past southwest Iceland came out on deck for a breath of fresh air, looked down into the angry gray water, and saw that the sea was boiling. Within a week or two the sea had parted, and a heap of volcanic cinders nearly a mile long had reared its head below a plume of flame, smoke, and steam four miles high. Icelanders named the new island *Surtsey* in honor of a fire god from Norse mythology, and Iceland's territory was extended overnight.

So another speck was added to the world map, the seas of which were already profusely decorated with bits and pieces of land. No one really knows how many islands there are. The British Isles alone are supposed to contain about 5500 islands and islets, but this figure is hotly disputed. The Philippine archipelago consists of more than 7000 islands, of which only 2400 have been named. Even in a relatively small cluster of islands such as the Seychelles, the precise number of reefs that jut from the sea is anyone's guess. Whatever the count, the world figure for respectable islands must run into hundreds of thousands, if not millions.

Just take a moment to turn a globe of our planet to view the situation—I have one in front of me. As I rotate it from right to left, big islands such as Madagascar, Sri Lanka, and Borneo pass through my field of view, looking like fragments of neighboring continents, as indeed Sri Lanka

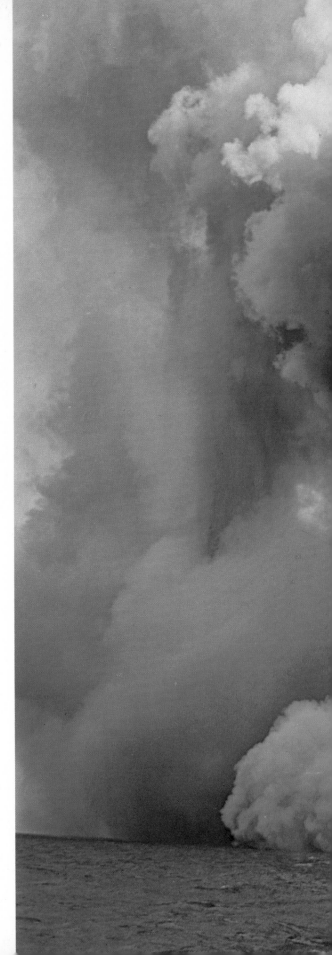

Flames spurt and colossal clouds of vapor, smoke, and ash billow from the sea as a submarine volcano surfaces to form an island. This photograph of Surtsey's birth in 1963 off southwest Iceland shows the way in which many oceanic islands began.

Bora-Bora, in the Society Islands of the Pacific Ocean, is one of the thousands of tiny islands scattered across the globe, seemingly at random. In fact, a close study of the world map shows us that many islands fall into well-defined groups. Only recently have geophysicists proved that these groups overlie deep-seated disturbances, where vast segments of the earth's crust collide or separate.

and Borneo are. If I stop my miniature earth spinning at longitude 120 degrees east an incredible muddle of islands of all shapes and sizes confronts me. In the far north stands the mainland of East Asia, in the far south is Antarctica, and between the two lies the island continent of Australia and chain after chain of lesser islands, including the Aleutian and Kuril islands, Japan, the Philippines, and Indonesia. As I turn the globe through a further quarter revolution, Asia and Australia begin to disappear, and the Americas are for the most part only just breaking the eastern horizon. Almost all that is visible is sea—the huge expanse of the Pacific Ocean, relieved only by a sprinkling of dots like stars in the sky. Many groups in this island galaxy appear to be placed at random, but constellations such as the Hawaiian Islands are strung out like necklaces of pearls across the blue Pacific. Some of the individual Pacific Islands shown on the globe are large enough to draw the eye. New Zealand's North and South islands are in this category, with such Atlantic islands as Cuba, Spitsbergen, and Ireland. The largest islands of the Solomon, Hebridean, Fijian, Samoan, and Hawaiian groups are also sizable chunks of dry land. The majority of Pacific islands, however, are too tiny to register at all on my basketball-sized globe.

By now, you may well be wondering why islands come in so many sizes and shapes, and how they got where they are. Most of our oceans have an average depth of several miles, so it seems particularly puzzling that Ascension Island managed to break surface in mid-Atlantic and even more wonderful that Tahiti appeared roughly halfway between Australia and South America. There are three basic ways in which islands are formed. Some islands—the British Isles, for example—clearly belong to continents from which they have become isolated by the sea. Other islands have been slowly built up by living organisms. Both of these types we shall deal with later. But perhaps most oceanic islands, like Surtsey, were spewed from the bowels of the earth by volcanic action. Let us first look at these.

It takes the dramatic birth of an island such as Surtsey to bring home to us the fact that we are living on a dynamic planet. Relief maps may appear reassuringly similar from year to year, or

The rocks of Himalayan peaks that now tower above all other land on earth once lay beneath the sea. Collision of the Indian landmass with mainland Asia, perhaps 50 million years ago, squeezed the submarine sediments and forced them up into the world's highest mountain range. Besides producing mountains, the clashing and rifting of landmasses has thrown up chains of oceanic islands.

even from century to century, but the truth is that the surface of the world is a dance floor on which the blocks of land are waltzing around in slow motion. Our problem of appreciating the movements is one of time scale. Over hundreds of millions of years, solid rocks underfoot can flow like treacle, continents can open up and allow oceans as broad as the Atlantic to form in their midst, and islands can come and go in the mere wink of a cosmic eye.

A nice way to grasp a sense of planetary time is to collapse our Mother Earth's 4600 million years to 46, each year representing a megacentury (or 100 million years). On this telescoped time scale most of the animal and plant life around us evolved during the last five or six years. Until then our maternal lady was largely naked. Modesty came at 40, when her bare continents acquired a soft green mantle of vegetation. She did not blossom out until well into middle age, when flowering plants jeweled her clothes for her 45th birthday, a mere year ago. That recently, dinosaurs roamed the land. Our ape-history goes back perhaps 10 days and the last ice age started three days ago. Modern man appeared as Mother Earth's promising prodigy just four hours ago. Jesus talked of selfless love a mere 10 minutes ago. You and I will do very well if we manage to spend a fleeting 20 seconds enjoying the company of Mother Earth. It is therefore little wonder that we see virtually no change in the geography of our planet during a lifetime that gives us no more than a glimpse of a moment in time.

Yet science tells us that the face of our earth is always—if imperceptibly—changing, and that islands are often the products of powerful forces involved in this change. Look at any map of the world and you will see evidence that the continents are crashing around like cars in a congested street with impatient, undisciplined drivers at the wheel. The damage is spectacular. The Himalaya, which once lay under the sea, were lifted more than five miles high when the Indian landmass collided with mainland Asia, about 50 million years ago. In another collision, Europe gained a leg in the form of Italy. When this happened, the impact created the Alps and wrinkled the land as far north as England, where it rippled the chalk to produce what became the North and South Downs.

Although collisions have been common enough, some blocks of land are at the moment being wrenched apart. Anyone who is skillful at completing jigsaw puzzles will quickly recognize the fact that the major continents can be made to fit together with uncanny accuracy. For example, the bulge on the coast of Brazil can be placed into the Gulf of Guinea in Africa. With a bit of juggling around, India, Antarctica, and Australia can be made to lie close to the east coast of Africa. Of course these snug fits could be purely coincidental. Nevertheless, there are striking geological resemblances between South Africa, India, Australia, and Antarctica that need explaining. Such puzzles began to be solved in 1912 when the German scientist Alfred Wegener wrote a book called *The Origin of Continents and Oceans*. Wegener suggested that the continents had once been part of a mighty supercontinent that he called *Pangaea* ("All Earth"). He believed that over the course of time Pangaea slowly broke up and the pieces drifted apart. For a long time this theory of continental drift was laughed out of court, partly because, as one writer has put it, Wegener belonged to the wrong labor union—he was a meteorologist, not a geologist. The views of geologists were unfortunately as fossilized as the animals and plants that, from time to time, they found entombed in the rocks, and many firmly held to the notion of fixed continents until the second half of this century, when new theories and new ways of studying rocks proved Wegener's point conclusively.

It was the occurrence of fossils in the form of coal and coral in unlikely places such as Antarctica that had started Wegener thinking. Coal

and coral both come from warmth-loving organisms, and Wegener assumed that the polar coal must have been formed from plants that lived in a tropical climate. Although the earth's climatic bands may shift slightly, the extreme north and south would have stayed too cool to support tropical forest, even when the world was in a sweltering phase. He therefore concluded that the coal- and coral-bearing land of the Antarctic had once been near the equator instead of astride the South Pole. Today no one would seriously disagree with the idea. The scientifically accepted fact is that most of us live on continents of comparatively light granite that float on a hot, yielding layer of rock called *magma*. Once, the continental landmasses that we recognize on our modern maps stood close together, but, perhaps partly due to the spin of the earth, parts of the supercontinent formed by these landmasses tended to slip past each other and pull apart. Major oceans opened between them, leaving gaps in the earth's crust that somehow had to be filled by the creation of seabed material. This process of continental drift is still going on, and—as we shall see—producing not only new ocean floors, but islands.

St. Paul's Rocks are five uninhabited little black peaks that lie just north of the equator, 500 miles from the northeastern shoulder of Brazil. Because they stood far from any continent their origin had always been a puzzle. Perhaps they were the last remnants of a sunken land; otherwise there seemed to be no possible reason for isolated crags to project from the ocean like that. In 1873 St. Paul's Rocks were one of the ports of call of the famous British research vessel H.M.S. *Challenger*, and the results of the scientific work carried out on her worldwide cruise went some way toward explaining the relationship between many oceanic islands. The credit for the whole operation went to the marine biologist Charles Wyville Thomson, professor of natural history at Edinburgh University. But the Royal Society also helped, by persuading Prime Minister William Ewart Gladstone to lend a naval steam corvette for a purely scientific enterprise. The *Challenger's* task was no less than plumbing the depths of the world's oceans and discovering what life, if any, inhabited our planet's inner space. Over the course of 69,000 miles, 362 soundings were made, and all manner of creatures hitherto undescribed were dredged up from the bottom. The *Challenger's* scientists also discovered the surprising fact that the seabed was not flat, but that the oceans concealed mighty submarine mountain ranges.

Only recently has the extent of these mountain chains been fully appreciated. Thanks to modern echo-sounding equipment for mapping the seabed, we now know that if the oceans could be emptied, a fantastic chain of mountains would be revealed, sweeping for nearly 40,000 miles around the oceans, and greater in extent than the Rockies, Andes, and Himalaya combined. In mid-Atlantic, this range swerves and curves southward from Iceland for an incredible, unbroken 10,000 miles. The peaks of the Mid-Atlantic Ridge, as it is called, break the surface in places and appear as islands, including the Azores, St. Paul's Rocks, Ascension, and Tristan da Cunha. Strangely enough, the submarine mountain range is cleft all the way by a central rift or crack on the scale of the Grand Canyon. In places this submarine gorge is 30 miles wide with precipitous walls a mile or so high. The

rift is literally a crack in the earth's crust, caused by the Americas gradual drift away from Eurasia and Africa. This moving is still happening, at a steady snail's pace. If you are a regular transatlantic commuter, each year you will have to fly about one inch farther. The widening gap is hardly likely to keep airline administrators awake. Nevertheless, over the course of time this slow continental creep adds up. Christopher Columbus sailed some 13 yards fewer on his first voyage of discovery than a ship retracing his course would travel today. If he had set off a million years ago, his journey would have been shorter by 30 miles. Two hundred million years ago, he could have walked from Europe to the West Indies.

The engine that provides the power for widening the Atlantic Ocean and causing Europe and America to drift apart seems to be the slow upwelling and spreading of magma beneath the earth's crust. The Mid-Atlantic Ridge may overlie an area where sluggish currents of subterranean magma collide, then rise, reach the base of the crust, and diverge, taking with them continents and attached slabs of sea floor that float like rafts on the magma. Deep in the rift valley, then, part of the earth is turning inside out, and new seabed is being formed to fill the widening gap. Here, lava wells up like hot tar, healing the scar in the earth's surface by building up the edges of the crack as the mountainous cliffs of the Mid-Atlantic Ridge. Surtsey and all other mid-Atlantic islands sprouted from the crest of this ridge, which explains why all these islands are volcanic.

As the upwelling lava hardens, some sticks to the sea floor on one side of the rift and some sticks to the other. As the two slabs of sea floor drift apart, the sea mounts upon them are gradually borne away from the active ridge. As you might expect, the age of the Atlantic islands increases with increasing distance from the Mid-Atlantic Ridge. The Bahamas stood on the ridge crest 120 million years ago, when the Atlantic was much narrower; now they are far to the west of the ridge. It took 150 million years to carry the Cape Verde Islands to their present position well to the east of the ridge. Bermuda and the Canary Islands are nearer to the ridge and younger, being only a mere 30 to 36 million years old. Bermuda has lost its volcanoes in drifting away from its geologically unstable birthplace, but the Canaries still have volcanoes capable of singing deep guttural tunes. On the island of Lanzarote the last eruption happened in 1730, lasted six years, and covered much of the surface with black, white, red, yellow, pink, and blue lava. Other legacies of Lanzarote's fiery past

The pioneer oceanographic research ship HMS Challenger *at St. Paul's Rocks in 1873. Soundings taken by later surveys made it clear that these tiny, waveswept isles off Brazil are visible peaks of an immense submarine mountain chain extending along the middle of the Atlantic Ocean throughout its entire length.*

include big volcanic bubbles, some of which have been turned into luxurious cellars.

The Atlantic's youngest oceanic islands are on the ridge itself. For example, Tristan da Cunha and Ascension are coming up to only their 1-millionth birthday, and their volcanoes still rumble and fume. In 1961 Tristan da Cunha's 269 inhabitants had to be evacuated hurriedly when the Peak—a dormant volcano—suddenly woke up and belched fire. The Icelandic volcanoes of Heimaey and Surtsey provide evidence for the continuing action of the ridge. Indeed, since the last phase of the Ice Age, there have been more than 150 eruptions in Iceland. Iceland itself is still being formed by an upwelling of molten material through a wide gash in the trench over which it sits. Great wedges of new rock are coming up beneath the middle of the country and spreading out sideways. Scientists

Ox-carts shifting stores landed on Tristan da Cunha, a young oceanic island on the Mid-Atlantic Ridge. This comprises volcanic rock that welled up to fill the gap caused by the drifting apart of crustal slabs carrying Africa and South America. Eruption in 1961 proved Tristan still volcanically active.

have actually measured the rate at which Iceland is spreading by looking at the relative movement of pillars planted into the rock. Apparently the island is widening by about a quarter of an inch each year.

From what we have said you can now picture our planet rather like an egg. The outside is cool enough for rocks to solidify and form a rigid shell that rests on a hot semi-fluid layer. The shell is cracked, however, into a number of pieces that scientists call *plates* (most comprising a slab of seabed attached to all or part of a continent). The plates slowly grind and jostle against each other as they float on the mobile magma. Regions where plates meet are areas of great geological instability. The Mid-Atlantic Ridge is one such line (the Great Rift Valley in Africa may be another) where adjacent plates are moving apart. In California, the infamous San An-

Long lakes mark the San Andreas Fault in a haze-penetrating infrared aerial photograph of San Francisco. The fault marks the edges of two slabs of earth's crust that make earthquakes as they grind past each other. Beneath oceans, islands emerge where one such edge dips below another or two edges separate.

dreas Fault runs down the west coast, marking the edges of two plates that are grinding past each other in a series of juddering earth tremors that threaten San Francisco and Los Angeles with utter destruction. When plates collide, the leading edge of one generally buckles under the other and dives steeply down into the earth's hot interior, causing earthquakes and a great deal of volcanic activity. The best examples of plate destruction of this kind are to be found in the Pacific Ocean, and where plates are gradually nibbled away underwater, islands are often born.

The blue waters of the Pacific hide one of the world's largest holes. Great trenches are scattered throughout the oceans, but none compares with the Tonga–Kermadec Trench, which is no less than 6·6 miles deep at its deepest point and 1600 miles long—big enough to hold half a dozen Grand Canyons. The tops of the almost sheer walls project above sea level as the Tonga and Kermadec islands. This deep rift is caused by the leading edge of the Pacific plate (the one that

floors most of the Pacific Ocean) sinking down into the interior of the earth. Wherever the seabed is nibbled away like this, the heat caused by friction as the leading edge of the plate is forced downward melts some of the rock, and the molten material erupts to the surface to produce a series of volcanic cones, usually about 100 miles beyond the trench where the edge of the dipping plate disappears. Sometimes the volcanic action is extensive enough to give birth to big islands, as in the case of Japan, which flanks a particularly

deep trench, where a nose-diving plate periodically shakes the land and causes the volcanoes Fujiyama and Sakurajima to erupt. Usually, however, the destruction of the edge of a plate produces curved strings of volcanic islands that sit beyond the deep trenches.

The Pacific region is especially rich in such island arcs. Indeed, the whole ocean is girdled with volcanoes that form the so-called Ring of Fire. Between the Bering Sea and the Pacific Ocean lies the Aleutian Archipelago, a clear-cut example of an archipelago thrown up by volcanic activity—here caused by the Pacific plate diving to destruction at an angle of 45 degrees into the earth's interior. As recently as 1912, Mount Katmai exploded and blanketed Kodiak Island, 100 miles away, under a 12-inch mantle of ash. Southwest of the Aleutians, a line of volcanic activity runs down through the Kuril Islands to Japan, and a branch line takes in the Philippines, where the volcanoes Taal and Mayon have repeatedly erupted over the past century. A descending edge of the Indian Ocean plate has produced western Indonesia, with its particularly active mountains of fire. Krakatoa, the most notorious of all, blew its top in 1883, pulverizing and scattering 4·3 cubic miles of mountain, and generating a 100-foot wave that smashed against the coasts of Sumatra and Java, killing 36,000 people. Now Krakatoa's place is taken by Anak Krakatoa—literally, child of Krakatoa—a new volcano that may one day emulate its mighty mother. In the central Indonesian island of Celebes (also called Sulawesi), the Pacific Ring is close to the northern end of another island arc. This swings southeast through New Guinea toward New Zealand via the Solomon Islands. The Pacific Ring of Fire even extends into the frigid Antarctic regions, where Mount Erebus, athwart Ross Island, shows a plume of steam. At the eastern rim of the Pacific, most of South America's west coast overrides a small oceanic plate that plunges down into the Atacama Trench, lying off Peru and Chile. As the plate is consumed, a great deal of volcanic activity is produced in the Andes, and death-dealing earthquakes strike Chile and Peru from time to time.

Fujiyama, Japan's tallest mountain, is an almost perfect volcanic cone more than 12,000 feet high. Its occasional eruptions are reminders that Japan borders a deep oceanic trench, where a dipping crustal plate produced volcanic action that helped to build Japan and still frequently sets off earthquakes.

31

In the West Indies, too, there are island arcs linked with volcanoes. Here an island arc nibbling away at the Atlantic floor has produced a number of Caribbean cones such as Mount Misery on St. Kitts, and Mont Pelée on Martinique. Pleasant places such as these have been slowly built from lava gushing from the earth's crust, but the building process itself can occasionally threaten everyone living on top of the infernal cauldrons. This happened on Martinique. On 8 May 1902, Pelée unexpectedly destroyed the port of St. Pierre and its 30,000 inhabitants in a holocaust of superheated steam and sulfurous fumes, when a rift opened up on the mountain's flank.

Not all volcanic islands are formed where the edges of plates are being pulled apart or consumed. The Hawaiian Islands, for example, emerged from the sea floor in the *middle* of an oceanic plate. Another strange fact about mid-oceanic archipelagoes such as the Hawaiian Islands is that they appear to have been planted in the sea along fairly straight tracks. The Hawaiians themselves have a nice story about how their 28 islands were made by Pele, the Polynesian goddess of volcanoes. She was a deft hand at wielding a magic spade and, traveling across the Pacific, built first one island, then another, until she finally settled in her fiery palace of Kilauea crater on the big island of Hawaii. As myths go, this one comes very close to the truth, because the Hawaiian Islands were thrust up 3.8 miles or more above the seabed, one by one, at roughly 1-million-year intervals. The oldest island is in the northwest, and the chain gets progressively younger, with Hawaii itself, the newest island, with the active crater of Kilauea at the southeast corner, 6.2 miles above the seabed.

There is a theory about how a chain like the Hawaiian Islands could be built. The theory rests on the assumption that a number of fixed "hot spots" lie just beneath the earth's crust where very hot material is welling up much as convection currents bring near-boiling water to the surface in the center of a heated kettle. The crust is fairly thin beneath the oceans, and where a mid-ocean plate is moving slowly over a hot spot,

Above: Anak Krakatoa ("Child of Krakatoa"), a volcanically active island formed where Krakatoa blew its head off in 1883, in the most immense volcanic explosion of modern times. This scene is in the Sunda Strait in western Indonesia, where notoriously violent volcanoes are fueled by molten rock thrust up as an edge of the Indian plate dives below a corner of the Eurasian plate.

The small town of St. Pierre nestles uneasily below cloud-capped Mont Pelée, on Martinique, part of a West Indian island arc associated with volcanoes. In 1902, Mont Pelée split open and belched ash and fatal fumes that killed all but two of the 30,000 inhabitants of St. Pierre, which was formerly the chief port of the French West Indies.

Molten lava at Kilauea crater on Hawaii, youngest of the Hawaiian Islands. They arose by volcanic eruption at million-year intervals, perhaps as molten subterranean rock punched a succession of holes in the slowly drifting Pacific crustal plate.

the surging molten magma may punch a series of holes in the crust and ooze through in sufficient quantity to produce a row of lava islands aligned in the direction in which the overlying plate moved. Apart from the Hawaiian chain, two similar lines of islands—the Tuamotu Archipelago and the Austral Islands—occur in the Pacific, pointing to the presence of at least two other hot spots beneath the Pacific plate. Perhaps Iceland too is over a hot spot.

Volcanic action is also needed to explain the puzzle of how coral islands such as Aldabra and Bikini appear far out in the Indian and Pacific oceans. (The Atlantic boasts only the remains of one such group of islands—the Bahamas.) This type of coral island is known as an *atoll* and it consists of a ring of coral reefs, surrounding a shallow, green lagoon that contrasts sharply with the clear blue oceanic water in which the atoll sits. Some of the reefs may support a healthy cover of mangroves, scrub, and palms.

Atolls owe their existence to many millions of tiny coral-forming organisms that are masterbuilders in limestone. Ever since the Ordovician period, between about 500 and 425 million years ago, coral organisms have raised massive calcareous ramparts in shallow water in warm, clear seas, fortifying the shores of rocky islands and indirectly making islands themselves. Today, the Great Barrier Reef off Australia's east coast is the greatest product of coral construction. It runs for 1260 miles from Torres Strait in the north to just below the Tropic of Capricorn in the south, and encloses the immense area of 100,000 square miles. Colonies of different kinds of coral organisms form the basic framework of the reef. Spiky, branched staghorn corals, massive mounds of brain coral, and corals in the form of delicate fans are cemented together by a mortar of calcareous red algae, called *Porolithon*. On one two-mile slab of reef alone, scientists estimated that there were 3,600,000 clumps of coral. Another great barrier reef sits in the west Caribbean, protecting the coast of Belize.

Anyone who has swum above a coral garden could be forgiven for thinking that it is landscaped with colorful plants, because the limy

In warm, clear seas, many islands consist of low-lying coral reefs built up by countless tiny living polyps. Greatest of all formations of living coral is the Great Barrier Reef, extending for 1260 miles along Australia's northeast coast. Above: looking across part of the southern section of the Great Barrier Reef toward Heron Island, the top 400 feet of which are made of coral, overlying sand. The circular structure in the center foreground consists of a stony type of coral found in rounded forms. Left: subaquatic view of a big school of small fish swimming near staghorn coral, one of a number of coral forms found in the Great Barrier Reef.

Below: Raised "mushroom" coral island in Aldabra Lagoon, Aldabra, in the western Indian Ocean. Such features owe their shape to marine erosion. The sea undercuts the old, dead coral, wearing bits away until the result is a top-heavy island that collapses, leaving only a submerged platform secure from the waves' battering attacks.

skeletons of living corals are covered with tiny barrel-shaped blobs, or *polyps*, many of which are brightly colored and very beautiful. When active —usually at night—these polyps are crowned with outstretched tentacles and look like bouquets of jeweled underwater flowers. In fact their true nature was revealed in the 18th century by a French surgeon, Jean Peysonnel, and an English gentleman, John Ellis. The polyps' beauty belied their real business, because each of these coral organisms, like their sea anemone cousins, turned out to be a carnivorous animal superbly designed for preying upon small fish and crustaceans swimming around in the water. Deadly batteries of minute harpoons on their tentacles are one solution to the coral animals' difficulties in snaring and stunning their active prey; the stony ramparts that the creatures lay down are another, because they help these delicate, but deadly, animals to live and to snatch food in places that take a heavy battering from the ocean swell. But scientists have recently discovered

that the coral builders need a bit of help from some house guests to build at speed.

Coral animals often owe much of their color to the presence in their body tissues of large numbers of single-celled algae called zooxanthellae. A single polyp may harbor up to 6000 algae, a sizable force of house plants to maintain. But they pay for their keep. During the day, the zooxanthellae are removing the polyp's waste materials, such as carbon dioxide and noxious nitrogenous products, and liberating oxygen into the polyp's tissues. The waste of one becomes a raw material needed by the other, thus forming the basis of a mutually beneficial partnership. But there is more to the relationship than that. In about 1960, a marine biologist found that coral polyps kept in the dark (where their algal partners cannot thrive) secreted limestone at only a small fraction of the rate at which normal polyps work. Somehow, the zooxanthellae must help in the process of extracting calcium carbonate from the water and laying it down as solid foundation

material for the coral skeleton. The coral builders are therefore formed into a coral cooperative, involving an animal and plants working together.

The presence of algae and the formation of limestone offer clues as to why corals grow profusely only in tepid seas and close to the surface. Near the top there is still sufficient light to allow the algal partners to thrive. Most reef building takes place in the upper 150 feet, and no coral forms more than 300 feet down, even in clear water. Coral polyps need temperatures of at least 70°F so that their body chemistry is running fast enough to keep their building activity at a high rate. This is why the major coral areas are in the tropics.

Many present-day coral reefs extend way down to the depths, however, well below the limit at which coral can grow. Oil prospectors drilling down through the Great Barrier Reef have repeatedly bored their way through 1800 feet of coral. Moreover at least some Pacific Ocean atolls are the tops of coral walls rising from even more considerable depths.

The problem of how isolated atolls arose exercised Charles Darwin's mind when he was cruising in the Pacific during the 1830s. Before this, the illustrious geologist Sir Charles Lyell had also had ideas about atolls. Lyell had proposed that these rings of reefs had started on the crater rims of submerged volcanoes, when the peaks were within 100 or 200 feet of the surface. Then the floor of the ocean started to sink, and, as it did so, the coral continued to grow upward fast enough to keep pace with the subsidence. Lyell argued that the atolls' volcanic bases were hidden from view hundreds, perhaps thousands, of feet down in the depths. Darwin obtained the proof of this and at the same time improved on the theory. Visiting the Cocos Islands, southwest of Java, he sailed to the edge of Keeling Reef in a small boat equipped with tools including a plumb line. Darwin's observations convinced him that the coral was dead below 120 feet, but had once been alive and close to the surface. He decided that atolls had started as reefs fringing the shores (not the crater rims) of volcanoes at a time when these projected as islands. The islands slowly sank until the reefs encrusted their summits, building tall masses of limestone as their volcanic bases vanished into the depths. Darwin noticed that palm trees fringing the shores of many islands leaned at a crazy angle, indicating to him that the process of subsidence was still under way. Careful measurements made with modern instruments show that Darwin was right. Coral reefs are still building upward on foundations that are subsiding—for instance, off the east coast of Australia, where the foundation rock is slowly sinking.

Above: four cutaway views of an island show Darwin's theory of how atolls form. First (far left) coral begins growing in shallow water on the flanks of a volcanic island. Next, the coral has grown upward to produce a fringing reef; meanwhile the island is slowly being submerged. Later, the ocean has covered the island, but upward growth of coral has kept pace with submergence to produce a coral atoll enclosing a lagoon. Later still, the island is drowned even more deeply and coral has grown over it. The upward-growing coral rim still clears the sea as an atoll. Below: Bora-Bora's volcanic peak and fringing reef suggest that this is an atoll in the making.

If Darwin's theory of atoll formation is correct, there should be volcanic rock beneath coral atolls. Proof that this is so has come from several islands, including remote Eniwetok in the western Pacific. This atoll's chief claim to fame is that its coral surface has been scorched and blasted many times by nuclear explosions. In 1954, the US Atomic Energy Commission decided to look at Eniwetok's foundations to see if the island could stand being shaken to the core by nuclear bombs. A bore sent down passed through four fifths of a mile of coral limestone before it reached volcanic olivine basalt. No coral grows at that depth, and scientists believe that the lowest limestone came from coral that lived in the Eocene period, some 50 million years ago, when the top of the basalt must have been close to the ocean surface. Thus the volcano on which Eniwetok sits has sunk nearly a mile; but its submerged top still stands about two miles above the seabed.

Sometimes volcanic islands are submerged faster than any fringing coral reefs can grow upward. Since World War II, hundreds of such submerged islands have been discovered in the Pacific Ocean through the use of echo sounders. These seamounts are called *guyots* to commemorate the 19th-century Swiss-born American geologist Arnold Henry Guyot. All guyots are curiously flat-topped, as though someone has taken scissors and snipped their heads off at levels between several hundred and several thousand feet below the surface. The guyots once stood above the sea, but were "topped" by the erosive force of the waves. Since then the sea has risen and the guyots have subsided. Rocky beaches surrounding the rims of many such seamounts provide additional proof of their island past.

Most of the islands we have been discussing have no geological connection with major continental blocks. They arise from the seabed, and are surrounded by deep water. Like Surtsey, when they emerge from the sea they do so as new land. But another class of islands clearly has a continental origin. These islands are separated from a nearby continent merely by the shallow seas covering the submerged shelf of land from which rise both the islands and their continental neighbor. One such continental island is Trini-

Port of Spain, the capital of Trinidad, an island off the northern coast of South America. Unlike oceanic islands produced by volcanic action, Trinidad began as part of a continent, from which it was eventually severed by the erosive Orinoco River.

Unless land rises or sea level drops, islands survive only until the sea beats down their defenses. Below: Atlantic Ocean breakers battering rocks at Land's End, the southwesternmost tip of mainland Britain. Right: waves have breached this peninsula on Pagan, one of the western Pacific's Marianas Islands.

dad, a lump of land bigger than California, and located just off the northeast coast of South America. Trinidad owes its island status to the fact that it lies close to the many mouths of the Orinoco River. The river's flow, particularly during the rainy season between May and November, is so strong and erosive that the patch of land was severed from what is now Venezuela by the power of water. Were it not for the fact that the spine of Trinidad is formed of durable limestone, the island would have been washed into the Atlantic aeons ago.

More usually, the action of the sea itself hews islands from the continents. The pounding force of a wave on a beach may be as high as $6\frac{1}{2}$ tons per square foot. It is little wonder that Zeus or Neptune, god of the sea, was also known as Earth Shaker. With that kind of force, and with seaborne stones as missiles, even staunch bastions of hard granite tremble and fall. In the end, the volcanic peaks of oceanic islands are entirely scoured away by the sea, as one can see from the Hawaiian archipelago, where old islands such as Kure and Midway, which once stood as loftily above the Pacific as Hawaii stands today, now

can be seen on any beach. Most of us at some time or another have built a sandcastle by the sea, and have watched the tide slowly creep in until only the top of the castle projected above the waves. Waves ultimately destroyed the fortress, but until its sand turrets toppled, the castle formed an island. This process has taken place on a much larger scale throughout the world, because the general level of the oceans has altered over the ages. Any significant rise in sea level not only helps to drown existing islands (as we saw with guyots), but also creates new islands from uplands left high and dry when sea engulfs their surrounding lowlands. Many of today's islands were born because we happen to live in an age when the seas are, as it were, in flood. They have not always been so.

Northern Holland and northwest Germany offer striking examples of islands produced by a rise in sea level. Here, the coastline has drastically changed over the last 2600 years or so. A chain of giant sand ramparts used to protect the low-lying marshes of Holland and Germany from the depredations of the North Sea. Then the sea level rose, and salt water punched through the natural dune defenses, flooding the area behind to form the shallow Wadden Sea. What was left of the dune-lined coastline became the Frisian Islands. To the east, the rising sea gradually flooded low-lying land, isolating higher patches to create the Halligen island group, where—off the west coast of the German state of Schleswig-Holstein—hardy farmers now make a living. Long, low, sandy islands strung out along the east coast of the USA have been similarly isolated from the mainland. The cause of the geologically recent fluctuations in sea level that created these islands is the fact that our planet is passing through a feverish period of climatic instability: parts of it shivering with cold one moment in geological time, and flushed with heat the next.

Over the course of the past million years or more much of our planet has been severely gripped by cold perhaps nine times. During these glacial times a great deal of what we now regard as fertile land in northern parts of Europe, Asia, and North America was turned into boggy and rocky treeless wastes, fit only for musk oxen, caribou, and mammoths to graze on. Millions of tons of water evaporated from tropical oceans and fell near the poles as snow that piled up and became compacted as ice. Scandinavia, Scotland, and much of Canada were accordingly weighed

barely stand above the waves. Many a war of attrition is waged where sea meets land. Peninsulas suffer particularly badly from the fury of the waves. Day and night the battering goes on until, grain by grain, stone by stone, the sea forces its way through a neck of land, leaving perhaps an isolated stack or tooth of rock, itself destined to be implacably dismantled by the elements. But until this happens, many a doomed offshore islet serves as a safe nesting place for innumerable seabirds.

The sea can also assemble islands by collecting coral or other debris into underwater sandbanks that gradually emerge as low-lying islands. Some just escape flooding at high tide and become colonized and consolidated by land plants. Such so-called *cays* or *keys* include Heron Island in Australia's Great Barrier Reef. The Florida Keys, and, farther west in the Gulf of Mexico, the cluster of Dry Tortugas were also formed as sandbars in this way. A sprawling fort sits on top of one of the Tortugas, which are now preserved as the Fort Jefferson National Monument and support hundreds of thousands of nesting seabirds.

The elements of another kind of island-making

down under ice sheets thousands of feet thick. As a consequence of the big freeze, so much water was locked away in the ice caps that sea level was reduced by up to 300 feet—the amount varying with the severity of the cold. A lot of offshore seabed must have been exposed, and the detailed outlines of the continents were very different from those of today. The famous port of Boston and the popular seaside vacation center of Miami would have stood miles inland. At the peak of the last major advance of ice, some 16,000 years ago, you could have walked from Ireland to France via London, with only a river or two to cross. Also, much of the South China Sea and Java Sea was dry land, so that Borneo, Sumatra, and Java joined the Malay Peninsula to form a mighty arm jutting out from Southeast Asia, and known to geologists as Sundaland. Australia was likewise part of a greater continent that incorporated New Guinea. At that time, there would have been no secure offshore island for the defeated Chinese Nationalists to retreat to, because Taiwan was within walking distance of the mainland. A seaborne invasion from the USA into Cuba's Bay of Pigs like that of 1961 would also have been unnecessary, because some 16,000 years ago Cuba must have been an integral part of the North American mainland. Sri Lanka would have been firmly joined to India. We also know that by 20,000 years ago ocean shrinkage was permitting Mongoloid people from Asia to cross what is now the Bering Sea by means of a land bridge as broad as Alaska. These emigrants settled in America, which remained the undisputed home of their descendants until Europeans arrived from the east.

The ice retreated between 10,000 and 12,000 years ago, and since then our planet has, broadly speaking, become progressively warmer. Much of the ice that weighed down the north of Europe, Asia, and North America has melted and drained into the sea. The shallow basins that connected Britain with the Low Countries of Europe became flooded, producing the fertile North Sea. The force of the sea itself opened up the English Channel, completing a marine pincer movement that divorced Great Britain from continental Europe several thousand years ago. Sundaland was submerged, too, leaving only the higher land as islands, joined beneath the surface of the shallow seas by the Sunda Shelf, upon which stand the western Indonesian islands and the long thin Philippine island of Palawan (the rest of the Philippines do not stand on this shelf). We shall see later that the eastern edge of the Sunda Shelf not only represents the eastern end of drowned Sundaland, but also follows the so-called Wallace Line that separates Asian and Australian fauna and flora.

Our islands have been formed. We can now look at how they became alive.

Like some stranded Noah's Ark, a farmhouse perches above flood level on an island in the Hallig group. The group lies off the mainland coast of Schleswig-Holstein in West Germany, and originated when the level of the North Sea rose. The sea drowned the flat areas, isolating the high areas as strings of islands fringing the coast from the northern Netherlands east to Denmark.

Below: Fort Jefferson gives an artificially high profile to Garden Key, one of the Dry Tortugas in the Gulf of Mexico. The Dry Tortugas just peep above the sea, and are largely made of sand and coral debris. At first, ocean currents piled the debris into submarine sandbars, but some eventually emerged above the sea. Land plants colonized them, and today many thousands of seabirds nest there.

How Life
Reaches Islands

It has to be said that, more often than not, islands are rather impoverished places. Few of the smaller and more remote ones would provide happy hunting grounds for naturalists who keep tally lists. Two weeks in the Seychelles would yield perhaps two dozen species of birds, and most of those would be seabirds or introduced aliens from India or Africa; a similar period of single-minded bird watching 1000 miles away in East Africa would yield several hundred species.

Early global travelers were unimpressed by what they saw on many islands. In March 1774, Captain Cook called at Easter Island, and thought it a God-forsaken place. "Nature has been exceedingly sparing of her favors to this spot." With South America about 2000 miles to the east, and the nearest vegetated island—Ducie Island in the Pitcairn group—1000 miles to the west, the marvel was that Easter Island should be clothed at all; it had only 50 kinds of native plants, and a small scattering of indigenous land animals including a fly, a weevil, a water beetle, a dragonfly, and a snail. Yet even Easter Island has more to offer on its land surface than Rockall, the lonely nub of granite northwest of Ireland.

There was never any shortage of ideas to explain how islands got their clothes. The most popular notion was that islands in general were remnants of large landmasses and had been linked by land bridges to the continents. Accordingly, people supposed that island plants and animals represented the hardy relics of drowned lands, like survivors clinging to a sinking ship. We now know that some islands were indeed joined to one or other of the major continents at some time, and that when large islands such as Great Britain were "launched" they carried with them a good complement of passengers derived from the parent landmass.

The variety of wildlife in such places is partly dependent upon the size of the island. Small islands have little scope for a diverse fauna and flora. For example, rocky stacks are rarely big enough to support large predatory animals throughout the year. Even predators no larger than foxes would rarely survive if stranded on such islets. Small islands therefore often make safe refuges for colonies of nesting seabirds that would be vulnerable to wholesale slaughter by land-based predators if sited on the mainland. The larger the predator, the more territory it needs in order to survive. Even on the sizable South American island of Trinidad at the mouth of the Orinoco River there have never been jaguars, and it seems likely that the island is not large enough to support a viable population of these big jungle cats, although they thrive on the nearby mainland. Significantly, the ocelot, a smaller predator, does live in Trinidad. On the other hand, Java, Sumatra, and Bali (which is not much larger than Trinidad) have all proved big enough to support tiger populations.

By their very nature, small islands also have far fewer habitats than large places. An extreme example is a shingle bank cut off from the mainland, and comprising nothing more than a pile of sand and stones heaped up by the sea. Its back may be covered only by a turf of salt-resistant grasses, mosses, campions, and thrift. Such a place would provide little scope for a rich wildlife community. On the other hand, Madagascar's 227,000 square miles of land, rising at one point more than 9400 feet above sea level, has enormous potential for animals and plants. There are desert areas, zones with plentiful rain, coastal plains, and mountain slopes—in fact, enough habitats to support a very varied wildlife.

The coming and going of land bridges has had a marked effect on the populations of islands. The British Isles offer some clear-cut examples of this. Most people know that there are no snakes in Ireland, supposedly because St. Patrick banished these reptiles. But, nice though the story is, the credit cannot possibly be given to St. Patrick. Ireland and Great Britain lie together on Europe's continental shelf, and were once joined to the mainland. As the glaciers retreated from northern Europe at the end of the last Ice Age, the warming climate allowed the spread of many animals north from their warm refuges in

A young coconut palm and other plants find rootholds on harsh granite rocks off Mahé, chief island of the Seychelles in the western Indian Ocean. How plants and animals cross seas and create island life is one of nature's most intriguing stories.

the south. However, the Irish Sea opened up before grass snakes and adders reached Ireland. But snakes were not the only laggards. During the height of the last glaciation, European moles survived only in Spain; from here they burrowed north, across the bridgehead between Britain and France, but were too slow to beat the Irish Sea. Weasels also failed to make it, together with short-tailed field voles and a handful of residential birds such as tawny owls and green woodpeckers, as well as migratory species including the wood warbler. All of these are common enough on the mainland of Great Britain, which was severed from the continent at a later date.

If Ireland has a poorer tally of wildlife because of this, Britain, too, has some notable omissions from its checklist of birds and mammals compared with the neighboring areas of Europe. The English Channel has proved an effective barrier to crested larks, great reed warblers, and icterine warblers, all of which breed in northern France. Disappearance of a land bridge between Britain and Europe has stopped beech martens and garden dormice from becoming British citizens. Even today we can see how a stretch of water isolates the British Isles from invasion, because, at the moment, raccoon dogs are heading west across Europe. This raccoon-like member of the dog family comes from East Asia, but was introduced into European Russia. Finding conditions to its liking, it has since spread implacably westward, perhaps helping to carry the deadly rabies virus that has now passed through Poland and Germany into Holland and Belgium. The raccoon dog will be stopped by the North Sea, leaving the British Isles poorer than the neighboring mainland by one more species.

Ever since its land bridge was submerged, England has been protected by a moat against

Since Great Britain became cut off from mainland Europe, the English Channel has acted as a barrier, limiting some kinds of animal migration and totally preventing others. Accordingly, Great Britain has fewer species of animal than nearby continental Europe. Neither of the European animals on these pages is likely to settle as a British resident. The handsome queen of Spain fritillary (right) sometimes flutters across the English Channel and turns up in England, but local conditions stop this butterfly from establishing itself there on a lasting footing. Below: the raccoon dog (unrelated to the North American raccoon) has never been seen in the British Isles and probably never will be. This mammal has been spreading westward through Europe, but it is ill-equipped to swim across the English Channel.

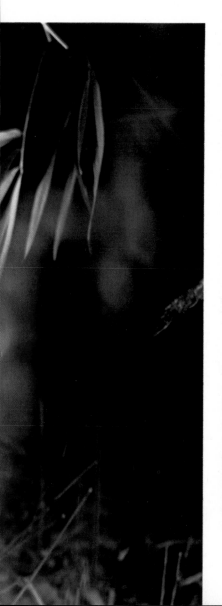

The ancestors of this Sumatran tiger probably reached Sumatra from mainland Asia by swimming or perhaps by walking across a now-drowned land bridge. Similarly, some tigers managed to colonize the Southeast Asian islands of Java and Bali. But hunting pressure and the destruction of their forest habitat has now reduced the tigers' populations. By the mid-1970s, naturalists believed that Bali's tigers had been wiped out.

Below: Wild hogs on Samosir Island in Lake Toba, on the Indonesian island of Sumatra. These dwellers on an island in an island come, like the Sumatran tigers, from stock that entered Indonesia from mainland Asia. In fact almost all of the wild animals and plants that occur in Malaysian Borneo and western Indonesia, as well as most of the Philippine species, derive from Asian ancestors that took to island-hopping. Some approached Australia and its associated islands.

the invasion of many insects, too. Cross the Strait of Dover from England to France in late summer and you will hear the chirps of a grasshopper with blue hind wings. It has no British name, and neither has another common field grasshopper, *Chorthippus biguttulatus*, because in each case none has reached the lush coasts of southern England. Although the Strait of Dover is only 20 miles across at its narrowest, so far as these species are concerned the gap could be 2000 miles wide. Occasionally the queen of Spain fritillary—a large and rather beautiful butterfly—makes the crossing and turns up as a visitor to British shores, but not very often. Along the continental seaboard, as far north as Norway, this butterfly is common. So are a host of other fritillaries (for instance, the lesser marbled and the violet), a lovely swallowtail, a copper or two, and a gorgeous blue butterfly called the *alcon blue*. All these might reach Britain if a land bridge emerged to reconnect England with the mainland.

A similar story could be repeated for other islands that are fragments of continents—Sri Lanka and Taiwan, for example. A gap of only 30 miles separates Sri Lanka from India, and from time to time this has been closed by a land bridge. Accordingly, Sri Lanka's wildlife is

Above: tree kangaroo, a marsupial living in Australia and New Guinea. Below: Australian king parrot. Some Australasian animals have island-hopped westward and share certain islands of Indonesia and the Philippines with Asian species. But deep-sea channels prevent mass migration between Asia and Australasia.

The babirusa, one of the ugliest inhabitants of Celebes and neighboring Buru Island. The male's canine teeth have become exaggerated into tusks, which disfigure without apparently serving any useful purpose. In spite of its formidably ugly appearance, this wild Indonesian swine is a timid creature that nests by day and sallies out at night, seeking plant and animal food in soft, damp mud.

basically Indian, but slightly poorer than India's, lacking rhinos, tigers, wild dogs, wolves, and numerous wild cattle. Sri Lanka also lacks the torrent fishes that are found in southern India but never made it across the lowland land bridge. Taiwan, hardly 100 miles off the Chinese mainland, has a slightly impoverished Chinese fauna and flora, but includes the Asiatic black bear, the clouded leopard, three kinds of deer, a wild pig, and a serow (a goat antelope).

The origins of island populations are more complex where land bridges have repeatedly come and gone as the sea level varied over the ages. Let us take as an example the frogs of Borneo and the Philippine Islands, east of Borneo. Frogs are not averse to swimming, providing the water is fresh; the salty sea, though, is quickly lethal to these moist-skinned amphibians. Now the Philippine frogs have all come from Borneo, but slowly and by way of land routes that have opened and closed between the islands. There are 89 species of frogs on Borneo, 15 of which have managed to move north to colonize the long, thin Philippine island of Palawan. From there, only seven continued on to Luzon, nearly 600 miles from Borneo. Each bridge therefore acted as a "filter" through which only a proportion of the frogs managed to emigrate.

Each narrow neck of land and each sea crossing—no matter how short—offers resistance to some kinds of potential colonizers. The effect of such "filter" bridges can be seen in the archipelagoes strung out between Southeast Asia and Australia. Animals and plants from Asia and Australia have island-hopped and crossed now-drowned land bridges, moving toward each other along these island chains and in places mixing. From both continents, emigration began from what are now big island stepping stones—Sumatra, Java, and Borneo off Asia, and New Guinea north of Australia. The three big Asian islands all have basically Southeast Asian animals. For example, there are leopards on Java, and banteng (a type of wild ox) on Java and Borneo. Rhinos live or lived on all three islands, and orang-utans thrive in the tropical rain forests of Borneo and Sumatra (they also inhabited Java early in the Pleistocene period). Other Asian primates, including macaques and langurs, are well represented. To the east, New Guinea, the largest fully habitable island in the world, is Australian, with none of the big Asian mammals, but plenty of Australian parrots and frogs. It also has a few marsupial mammals, including the tree kangaroo, the spotted cuscus (a monkeylike creature), and the marsupial rat.

Between New Guinea and the major Southeast Asian islands is a steeplechase route where animals—especially birds—have island-hopped across strait after strait. In Java and neighboring Bali there are about 200 kinds of oriental nesting birds, but nearly 70 have failed to cross the ancient 30-mile-wide Lombok Strait to Lombok Island. From Lombok eastward through the Lesser Sunda Islands species totals of oriental birds fall still further, and only 78 of a theoretically possible 200 kinds of Asian birds live on Wetar, more than 600 miles east of Lombok. No less than 122 have been stopped by five narrow sea crossings. The easternmost islands of the Lesser Sunda group possess Australasian birds such as cockatoos and honeyeaters, and a few kinds moving westward have actually reached the Lombok Strait, passing Asian birds going the other way. Mammals and amphibians have crossed the Lombok Strait far less readily than birds. On Bali most animals and plants are Asian, but on Lombok—within sight of Bali—most wildlife is Australasian. A mere thread of water separates the flora and fauna of two continents.

Celebes, to the north of the Lesser Sunda Islands, is well and truly in a no-man's-land, with a unique and delightful mixture of animals from Asia and Australia. There is a strange crested black "ape" (really a macaque), a small ox (the anoa), and the many-tusked babirusa—allegedly the ugliest pig in the world. All these are placental mammals, but there are also marsupials, including a cuscus. Farther north, the Philippines have also received a few immigrant species, including a small but fearsome ox—the tamarau, of Asian ancestry—and a cockatoo that could have come only from Australasian stock.

When a continental island is cast off, it bears a Noah's Ark cargo, representing the wildlife community of the area before surrounding lands became drowned. Thus, islands that have been separated for a long time may be a refuge for kinds of animals and plants that have died out on the mainland. As such, every island is a potential storehouse of zoological treasure, and some islands give us unique glimpses into the past. For example, in New Zealand, where agricultural wealth is largely measured in sheep, there are lower and—to man—less tasty forms of life that have inestimable zoological value. There is a primitive frog with a tail, and a hairy-looking bird without wings: the kiwi, sole living kin of the giant, flightless moas. But the most interesting of all is a reptile.

In 1831 a two-foot "lizard" was received by the British Museum and formally named by Dr. John Edward Gray as *Sphenodon punctatus* (although people usually call it the *tuatara*, from a Maori name referring to its spiky crest). Over three decades later, Dr. Gray's successor, Dr. Albert Günter, realized that this was a living fossil representing a group of reptiles that had flourished at the same time as, and supposedly had died out with, the dinosaurs. Tuataras are curious in all sorts of ways. The males have no penis, but this has not prevented them from surviving in New Zealand for 70 million years. Both sexes have a well-developed opening on the roof of the skull, known as a "third" or pineal "eye," and—more importantly—parts of the skull are joined together by bony arches. In this respect the skull resembles a crocodile's skull rather than that of any modern lizard. From its overall design, the tuatara appears to be the lone survivor of a very ancient group of reptiles—the *rhynchocephalians* or beakheads—that flourished throughout the world more than 100 million years ago. Until the middle of the 19th century these little dragonlike beasts lived on New Zealand's North and South islands, but today tuataras are confined to a few rocky islands off the northeast coast of North Island, and in Cook Strait between North and South Island. In these refuges about 10,000 live in burrows, from which, it is said, you can lure them by singing a rousing song—especially "Soldiers of the Queen." In fact, because these reptiles

croak as part of their social signaling, they do respond to vocalizations. Another interesting feature of tuataras is the slow working of their body chemistry (or *metabolism*). Although they usually breathe once every seven seconds—itself a slow rate—they may breathe as seldom as once every hour at low temperatures without coming to harm. This has survival value in their cool damp refuges. In fact tuataras are so well adapted to chilly conditions that they move around most at night when the temperature is sometimes only 52°F, the lowest temperature recorded for any reptile activity.

Giant tortoises (land turtles), too, have managed to survive on a number of islands, immune from the competition on the continents. There are healthy populations on some of the Galápagos Islands (*galápago* is an old Spanish word for "tortoise"), and on Aldabra in the Seychelles group. Only during the last 2000 years have they been exterminated on Madagascar.

Another two animal antiques live in the West Indies on the islands of Cuba and Hispaniola. Solenodons look like rather ungainly and gigantic shrews, and are the sole survivors of a family of insectivores that was widespread in North America 30 million years ago. These 12-inch mammals are nocturnal, and use their big claws for digging, and their pointed snouts for grubbing around after insects, which they dispatch, shrew-fashion, with venomous saliva dribbling down grooved teeth. The females' two teats are placed not beneath their bellies or tucked away in their groins, but on their behinds. Solenodons are

Above: New Zealand's lizardlike tuatara is not a lizard but the only survivor of the beakheads—an ancient group of reptiles once with a worldwide distribution. Competition from more "modern" types of animal wiped out beakheads everywhere except New Zealand. Separating from nearby lands, New Zealand bore its beakheads to safety before their destroyers had set foot upon its islands.

A solenodon, a shrewlike mammal about one foot long that belongs to a family of insectivores that was widespread in North America some 30 million years ago. Evolution produced animals whose competition killed off all members of the family except the two species of solenodon that survive on island havens in the West Indies—one species on Cuba, the other in Haiti on Hispaniola.

representative of a very primitive insectivore stage in mammalian evolution, long since extinct except on these two islands in the West Indies where they have managed to survive because of the absence of serious enemies.

The most primitive members of the order of primates, to which we belong, have also persisted to the present day on island sanctuaries. Tarsiers are strange little creatures that superficially look like a cross between a flat-faced, goggle-eyed squirrel and a tree frog. They are designed for leaping and clinging, and have suction pads on the ends of their fingers and toes for getting to grips with branches and twigs. Tarsiers live in Sumatra, Borneo, the Philippines, and Celebes, where they hunt insects at night in the jungle.

The lemurs, which, like the tarsiers, branched out early on from the main trunk of the primate family tree, are confined to the giant island of Madagascar. Madagascar is an island of oddities, and one of the world's finest museums of wildlife. Its flora and fauna all derived from Africa tens of millions of years ago. The lemurs are descendants of a kind of prototype monkey that lived in Africa 50 million years ago and from which the higher monkey, baboon, and ape stocks may well have evolved. These advanced kinds gradually superseded their more primitive lemur cousins except on isolated Madagascar, where lemurs persist in splendid isolation. The 18 existing species vary in size from the four-inch mouse lemur to the two-foot ruffed lemur. Some species are basically ground-dwellers, including the ring-tailed lemur, a beautiful animal with a graceful, long, ringed tail, and commonly kept in zoos. Other lemurs, such as the leaping sifaka, are almost entirely arboreal. A recently extinct species was extraordinarily similar to an ape, and the rare aye-aye could be mistaken for a strange squirrel.

Besides the lemurs, there is another strange group of animals peculiar to Madagascar, called *tenrecs*. Like the Cuban solenodons, they are members of the Insectivora, a large order of mammals that includes the shrews, bats, hedgehogs, and moles. The insectivores are fairly primitive for placental mammals, and were scurrying around in the undergrowth when the mighty dinosaurs were making the ground shake, 100 million years ago. Like the lemurs, the ancestral tenrecs were gradually phased out by competition from more advanced insectivores everywhere except on Madagascar, where they have flourish-

The goblinlike tarsier is yet another animal curiosity that survives only in island sanctuaries—in this case Sumatra, Borneo, the Philippines, and Celebes. This primitive primate catches insects. It leaps nimbly from tree to tree and clings on with the help of touch pads on the tips of fingers and toes.

55

Among islands rich in oddities extinct elsewhere is Madagascar —home of the lemurs. Lemurs' ancestors branched out early on from the main trunk of the primate family tree, and living lemurs resemble fossil creatures widespread 50 million years ago. Right: sifaka, an almost entirely arboreal lemur, shown here in Ankarafantsika Forest, northwestern Madagascar. Below: ring-tailed lemur, a handsome animal that roams in groups. This one is climbing in a river forest in southeastern Madagascar.

ed in the absence of more efficient competitors. Modern tenrecs come in a variety of shapes and sizes. Some are very similar to small shrews; others resemble a cross between a mole and a shrew; and *Echinops* and *Setifer* are clearly convergent in design with the European hedgehog, and even roll up into spiny balls. Many tenrecs are unpleasant little animals to deal with, because they are covered with detachable, barbed quills. *Hemicentetes* is warningly colored in a not unattractive pattern of black and white or black and yellow, depending upon the species. Would-be predators who ignore these danger signs will be met by a very effective pattern of defense behavior. When threatened, an individual raises its quills, and a particularly offensive little bouquet of sharp quills appears on the head, the spines projecting forward over the nose. The animal then bucks up and down, trying to drive the spines into the nose or paws of the enemy. But the spines have another function. On *Hemicentetes'* back, rows of interlocking hollow spines can be rubbed backward and forward to make impulses of ultrasonic sound by which the animal can communicate with its fellows.

The tenrecs are armored against beasts such as the fossa, an animal with the reputation of a forest ghoul. Superstition has it that fossa scent kills poultry; that no babies are safe with fossas around; and that you sleep in the open at your peril, lest a fossa licks your face, putting you into a trance—and just as well, because it then disembowels you. Fossa facts are more interesting to zoologists than the fables, especially the fact that this catlike animal is descended from the ancestors of the cats and civets. In some ways it is very similar in structure to the modern cats. Like them it has retractile claws, yet walks on the soles of its feet, as bears do. The fossa survives in Madagascar by virtue of the sea moat that keeps out the more recently evolved cats.

You may now well ask how the ancestors of tenrecs, lemurs, and the peculiar fossa got to Madagascar, because—unlike the other islands we have been discussing—most available evidence suggests that this huge island was never joined to the continent. It is therefore likely that nothing colonized the place by walking there. The same holds true for volcanic islands that pop up out of the sea, such as Surtsey. These places are launched scalding hot and lifeless, and yet after eruptions have subsided and acrid, sulfurous fumes have drifted away, the bare cinders and lava rock become settled surprisingly quickly. Let us look at the ways in which land plants and animals populate islands. We shall start with Surtsey, a brand-new island where scientists could almost literally see life forms arriving.

Surtsey was still erupting when the first birds landed to rest on its warm cinders. Kittiwakes, herring gulls, and fulmars were soon prospecting the cliffs for nest sites, and waders such as oyster catchers were soon hunting the shoreline. Only six months after the first eruption, bacteria and molds were present on Surtsey, and these were

The aye-aye is justifiably placed in a family of its own, for this is the strangest of lemurs, with its large ears, elongated middle fingers and big, bushy tail. It dwells in bamboo forests, where it feeds nocturnally. Aye-ayes are rare. When photographed, this individual was the only living captive specimen, and the species is unlikely to persist outside its new island reserve off Madagascar.

Two more mammal curiosities from Madagascar. Above: a tenrec, a beast with a larger mouth in relation to its body than any other mammal. Tenrecs range from shrew-size to rabbit-size, and some closely resemble hedgehogs. All belong to one insectivore family. The emergence of more effective kinds of insectivore helped kill off tenrecs everywhere except Madagascar, where rivals failed to gain a lethal foothold. Right: a fossa, Madagascar's largest carnivore. Fossas are fierce predators, assaulting pigs and climbing trees after lemurs. They are probably descended from fossil ancestors of the modern cats and civets. Fearsome though it is, the fossa would probably succumb to competition from Africa's more recently evolved predatory cats if these could cross the sea.

quickly followed by patches of moss at the edge of the highest crater. More than two dozen kinds of insects have been collected there, together with flowering plants including sea rocket. Already the shores have been colonized by algae and by marine animals with planktonic larvae. Surtsey was once uncomfortably warm, but it has cooled, and now stands as a windswept island in a cold part of the North Atlantic—by no means a hospitable place for advanced land-based life. Surtsey will never be covered by forest.

At the best of times, living astride a volcano is potentially suicidal because eruptions have a tiresome habit of sometimes sterilizing the slopes. This makes hard work for colonizing animals and plants. We have the example of Krakatoa to show what must have happened time and time again to wildlife communities living on volcanic islands. After Krakatoa blew its head off in 1883, everything was obliterated under hundreds of feet of scalding ash. And yet within half a century—which is admittedly nearly a lifetime to you and me, but nothing on a geological time scale—the devastated slopes were clothed in a luxuriant and maturing jungle inhabited by 1400 kinds of animals. Of these, 720 species were insects; of 47 kinds of vertebrates, 30 were resident birds and there was a handful of reptiles and mammals, all derived from neighboring Java. Once a rich fauna and flora like this is established it can still be literally wiped out in a multi-megaton flash, and so renewal starts afresh. The dice of fate are very much loaded against island immigrants anyway.

Gough Island is a not particularly hospitable island that sits atop the Mid-Atlantic Ridge about 230 miles southeast of Tristan da Cunha. Nothing lives there apart from seabirds, seals, a couple of kinds of dingy buntings, and a flightless rail. In May 1968, however, it had a visitor from across the Atlantic, because a South American gray heron was seen fishing by one of the streams that tumble down Gough's volcanic gullies. Unfortunately that heron was probably doomed to starve, because no fish swim in the island's rivers. The life of pioneers is perilous. On neighboring Tristan da Cunha, moths from Brazil are often recorded, but they have no future there. Even if some were egg-bearing females, and fertilized at that, their caterpillars would need special food plants that are absent from Tristan. One of the first animals recorded on the still-warm slopes of Krakatoa was a carnivorous

Leaf-tailed gecko, a tree-climbing lizard species that occurs only on Madagascar. Big jaws help to explain its nickname of "tree crocodile." Spots and squiggles provide the gecko's camouflage, as it clings to bark with toes that end in "suckers."

spider that drifted in on its silken drag line. Like Gough's gray heron, it probably starved to death on the barren cinders. Settlement on oceanic islands has to take place in an orderly fashion.

Plants are the primary food producers and these must gain a foothold before any landbound animals can take up residence. And only after herbivores have settled in can predatory creatures take up residence. Very often, weathering breaks down sterile volcanic rocks to make soil that is enriched with minerals from the body wastes of seabirds and seals. Fungi and bacteria, lichens, and mosses then start to settle, and the quantity and quality of the soil eventually improves to the point where large types of plant that chance upon the scene can put down roots. Meanwhile the first successful land-animal colonizers tend to be small creatures such as worms, mites, tiny spiders, and springtails. Higher forms of landbound animal life may follow. But even arrival at the right place in the broad sequence of colonists is no guarantee that a plant or animal will survive and perpetuate its kind. Many species have highly specialized requirements. For example, spiders need insect prey, and herons require fish; some plants must have alkaline soil to settle on, whereas for others the soil should be acidic. Then, too, every male animal needs a mate, and many a bloom needs another for cross-pollination to take place. With so many difficulties, the wonder is that remote, volcanically formed islands become settled at all.

The obvious way in which the pioneers reach the islands is by air. The air may look clean and transparent to you and me, but in fact it is full of microscopic spores, pollen, tiny insects, spiders, and mites. Some of these can be swept to great heights and transported thousands of miles across continents and oceans by the winds. It is not surprising, then that ferns, mosses, and fungi are among the first settlers on islands, because their spores are less than 1 thousandth of an inch across. A single fern plant can liberate about 30 million spores in one season. For this reason alone, lower plants are particularly well represented on islands. Flowering plants whose seeds are adapted for dispersal by winds also stand a good chance of getting to islands. Members of the Compositae family, to which daisies, sunflowers, and black-eyed Susans belong, have seeds equipped with feathery parachutes that are easily dragged along by the wind. *Olearia megalophylla*, a relative of the asters, has just such seeds. Launched from mainland Asia, and perhaps borne on hurricanes tracking across the Pacific, some of its seeds have reached and germinated on Hawaii, one of the remotest islands on earth. Orchids have seeds as fine as dust and these, like the spores of ferns, can be dispersed a long way by wind. They colonized Krakatoa soon after loamy soil evolved there to provide a roothold.

The seeds of some plants are designed for

hitchhiking. They are either sticky—for instance, tarweeds—or decorated with barbs and hooks, and thus ideal for becoming entangled in the plumage of birds or the fur of bats. The hooked seeds of *Acaena milliflora, Acaena variabilis*, and *Uncinia kingii* have all been extracted from the feathers of a yellow-nosed albatross caught on Gough Island. Between nesting seasons this bird had probably circumnavigated the earth in the Southern Hemisphere's higher latitudes. Birds can also carry small seeds in dirt adhering to

Waved albatrosses displaying on Hood (Española) Island in the Galápagos group off Ecuador. Such wide-ranging seabirds are often the first higher animals to reach islands, and may bring seeds that germinate in the soil enriched by their droppings.

their legs or bills—a fact used by Charles Darwin to help prove that life upon islands began elsewhere, and was thus part of the worldwide process of evolution and not an independent creation. He once grew no less than 83 plants of five different species from seeds contained inside a ball of mud that he had taken from a bird. Darwin knew that the seeds of many species such as figs and papayas can be carried hundreds of miles inside a bird's intestines, through which they can pass unharmed.

But Darwin conceived of even more complex journeys. He fed aquatic grass seeds to fish at the London Zoo, then gave the fish to storks. After a time, the birds excreted the seeds, which were still intact and later germinated. Freshwater snails have also managed to bridge oceans of salt water in which they cannot survive. This puzzled Darwin considerably until one day he noticed ducks with dirty feet emerge from a pond. Darwin knew that water snails can live for hours high and dry on water plants. He took a duck

Two species representing types of land birds that have colonized islands far from their homelands. Left: purple gallinule, a water hen with long toes that spread its weight as it walks on water plants. The species lives from the United States to northern Argentina, but turns up on Tierra del Fuego, much farther south. Right: Cape white-eyes feeding on grapes. White-eyes are warblerlike Old World birds. Some species colonized Indian and Pacific ocean islands when windblown flocks made chance landfalls and remained to breed.

covered in duckweed, and dangled its feet in an aquarium where hundreds of water snails were just hatching from their gelatinous egg masses. Many of the baby snails climbed onto the duck's legs. Some survived out of water for nearly a day, enough time for the duck to have flown 700 miles to a freshwater lake on some distant island.

The arrival of birds with such convenient plant and animal freight would be no everyday occurrence on remote islands, yet it would have to happen only once every few million years to account for the vegetation now present in such far-away islands as Hawaii and Gough.

Animals that can fly or make use of the air for transport are often the first, and sometimes the predominant, members of island faunas. Rockall's rotifer—a microscopic, filter-feeding animal—was doubtless carried there as a lightweight spore. Even tiny, flightless insects such as springtails reach islands by wind drift. Insects

that actively fly have a greater chance of extensive dispersal. Aphids, so light that they drift as they fly, arrive in remote corners of the world on the winds. Powerful aeronauts such as dragonflies also turn up on islands—one species has even landed on Easter Island. But weak fliers such as stoneflies, caddis flies, and earwigs do not usually occur in island faunas.

Among the higher vertebrates, many birds are strong fliers. Seabirds are invariably the first to set foot upon virgin island rock. Many land-based birds make extensive migrations, however, and when drifted off course by foul weather, individuals come down in places far beyond their normal range. We can see the process happening today. South American gallinules do not give the impression that they are capable of hard traveling, yet these big-footed, heavy, purple birds often arrive on Tristan da Cunha, at least 2000 miles away from their normal habitat. They have

Flying fox or fruit bat on Mahé in the Seychelles, which perhaps recruited these flying mammals from mainland Asia. Bats have populated remote oceanic islands including New Zealand, where they were the only mammals of any kind before man came.

targets for airborne invasion by land birds.

White-eyes show just how successful small and relatively weak flying birds can be in island-hopping. White-eyes are warblerlike, greenish, well-camouflaged, and difficult to observe when feeding on insects and fruit in the canopies of trees. They appear to be always on the move. Their mainland range extends throughout Africa south of the Sahara, across southern Asia to China and Japan, and down to Australia. They have pushed out into the Pacific to the Carolines, Fiji, and Samoa, and the Indian Ocean has white-eyes in the Seychelles. In the 1850s the common white-eye of Australia suddenly appeared in New Zealand, where the species now occupies both main islands and many of the nearby islets. One group has even managed to settle on Macquarie, a subantarctic island. Man introduced white-eyes into the Hawaiian Islands, which became a center for the dispersal of these birds in the central Pacific. Their great success seems to stem from the fact that they are strongly gregarious. When a flock of white-eyes is whisked out to sea on the wind, the chances are that the flock is large, with plenty of individuals of both sexes. Should they make landfall, the probability is that there will be sufficient to form breeding pairs.

Like birds, bats are powerful fliers, and have been highly successful island colonists. Before the Macris introduced rats, New Zealand's only indigenous mammals were two kinds of bat, at least one of them derived from Australian stock brought in on the winds. Bats of the genus *Lasiurus* have been blown across the Pacific from South America to the Hawaiian Islands. A similar species derived from South America lives in the Galápagos Islands. Bats are also well represented in Madagascar, the Canary Islands, and the Azores, and east of Australia in New Caledonia, and Lord Howe Island, and Norfolk Island. In the Seychelles, the only native mammals are bats that may have originated in Asia. On Mahé, biggest island of the Seychelles, giant fruit bats can be seen ponderously flapping their way into the darkening sky, as they leave their roosts high up on the central mountains for feeding grounds in the plantations. Magnificent fruit bats are also among the five bat species on Aldabra, north of Madagascar.

Even continental islands have their wildlife continually enriched from the air. Recently, serins (wild canaries) have moved northward in Europe, and in 1967 started breeding in England,

not yet established themselves, but one day they may breed. Two barn swallows—the North American equivalent of the European swallow—have been recorded there, utterly off course. Not surprisingly, all of Tristan's endemic (or native) land birds have been derived from South American stock brought in on prevailing winds.

The land and freshwater birds of the Hawaiian Islands came from different directions. Biologists generally reckon that Hawaii was fertilized by the winds, which brought about 14 separate influxes of bird species. The famous honeycreepers, a crow, a hawk, a duck, the ancestors of the Hawaiian goose or néné, an owl, a stilt gallinule, and a heron all came from America; two genera of honeyeaters flew in from Australasia; and an Old World flycatcher arrived from Polynesia. Hawaii and Tristan da Cunha are both about 2000 miles from the nearest land, and these isolated islands offer perhaps the most formidable

Collared doves are among the bird world's most successful island settlers this century. In 1955 individuals from mainland Europe crossed the North Sea and began colonizing the British Isles. From there, some braved the Atlantic to reach Iceland.

having made the short flight north across the English Channel. In 1955 the collared dove, a species that has been spreading westward across Europe this century, reached the Norfolk coast of England and within a decade established itself as a common species. Launching out across the North Atlantic this enterprising species reached Iceland. In 1937 fieldfares similarly invaded southern Greenland, where they are now established as a breeding species.

A great deal of wildlife reaches islands by sea, by swimming or floating. Many higher vertebrates can swim and have sufficient stamina to cross stretches of sea. You might think that amphibians would be among the first wave of island colonists, but they cannot tolerate salt water. Reptiles fare much better; big lizards and snakes, such as monitors and pythons, are able to swim strongly for miles, and within 50 years of its explosion had become re-established on

Krakatoa. Iguanas have even colonized the western Pacific islands of Fiji and Tonga, although they may have obtained assisted passages from nearby islands. Crocodilians have made substantial sea journeys. The wide-ranging Nile crocodile has reached Madagascar. The saltwater or estuarine crocodile of Southeast Asia and Australia occurs in the Philippines, the Palan Islands, and Fiji, and skeletal remains indicate that it once reached the western edge of the Tuamotus, halfway between Australia and South America. In the Caribbean, the American crocodile has reached Cuba and Jamaica.

Apart from the truly aquatic or amphibious mammals such as manatees and seals, some species are capable of swimming considerable distances. Hippos managed to reach Madagascar. Tigers and jaguars, which often have to swim estuaries, could take the plunge and make for islands. Some have doubtless been swept out to sea by flooded river torrents. Deer and wild cattle may also suffer similar fates, and have become washed up on island shores. Most terrestrial animals, however, could make only relatively short sea crossings before becoming exhausted and being in danger of drowning.

Anything that has the ability to float, however, is likely to be carried for thousands of miles by a combination of wind and water currents. The practice of sealing messages into bottles and casting them into the sea depends upon this. Christopher Columbus, when his ship was in danger of foundering in mid-Atlantic, consigned an account of his discoveries to a cask, and committed it to the storm-bound sea. But perhaps this story is apocryphal, because the floating parcel was never delivered. Dr. Bruce, a member of the Scottish Antarctic Expedition of 1902–4, released a barrel east of Cape Horn. Fifty years later, it was found lying on a sand dune in New Zealand's North Island, having traveled about 10,000 miles. To take a final example, sponsors of a radio program sealed a bottle containing a note offering $1000 to the finder, and set the bottle adrift outside New York harbor. A beach-combing boy in the Azores, 2500 miles away, successfully claimed the money.

Of course, beachcombers are not usually so lucky, but any accomplished naturalist can verify for himself the ability of the sea to carry biological flotsam for great distances. On the west coast of Wales, many people believe they owe their good teeth and gums to the fact that, as babies, they were given hard, black, tropical bean seeds to bite on. The seeds belong to a climbing shrub *Mucuna urens*, and reached Wales by floating all the way from South America. Seeds of a Caribbean climbing plant, *Entada gigas*, are also commonly washed ashore on the west coast of Great Britain and Ireland. So, too, are seeds of a mangrove, but they never prosper in the cool climate of the North Atlantic's eastern seaboard. In the South Atlantic, "sea beans" are stranded on Tristan da Cunha's stormy shores; these belong to the South American bonduc-nut shrub. Beans are particularly well designed for dispersal by sea. The embryo and its food store are well protected for at least three years against salt water by a hard, resistant jacket, and the seed itself contains enough air to keep the whole package buoyant. *Sophora*, a member of the sweet-pea family, has been particularly successful in colonizing islands throughout the Pacific, and has even established itself on Gough Island in the South Atlantic, and Réunion in the Indian Ocean. *Sophora* is a native of Chile, where it lives on river banks.

Green tree python, characteristically looped over a branch. One of the most handsome of the constrictors, this seven-foot-long snake lives among the tree tops in forests on the island of New Guinea. There are several other island-dwelling pythons, and some of their populations may derive from snakes that migrated across the sea. Pythons often live near water, and are strong swimmers. Thus some are probably swept out to sea by floods, stay afloat for days, and land on islands where their kind was hitherto unknown. A female containing fertile eggs could start an entire python population where she came ashore. This may partly explain how the reticulated python—one of the world's longest snakes—arrived on some of the Southeast Asian islands it inhabits.

Many sizable trees, as well as shrubs and herbs, have buoyant seeds and fruits that can easily ride on the ocean currents. For example, the seeds of the tropical and subtropical *Casuarina* and *Calophyllum* trees often float ashore.

Two kinds of palms do especially well in harnessing the sea to help them to spread. The nuts of the nipa palm—a species found from Sri Lanka to the Solomon Islands—float for several months, during which each seedling slowly sprouts. The germinating fruits are a common sight in the seas off Malaya. The second palm is the ubiquitous coconut. To many people no tropical shore would seem complete without a healthy fringe of these palms rustling in the light sea breezes. As coconuts have floating fruits, their widespread occurrence on islands seems natural. Yet the surprising fact is that most modern coconuts grow where they do largely because of cultivation. It seems likely that coconut palms were originally natives of the Pacific, where they were undoubtedly spread by ocean currents before man lent them a hand. Coconut palms are certainly prolific. Each tree produces up to 100 nuts annually, and there are

so many palms in the world that about 10 nuts are produced for every living person. Each nut is a sealed flotation package. The mature trees often lean out at crazy angles over the sea, and as the nuts ripen, they drop directly into the water, where they float because of the air trapped both inside the nut and in its fibrous coat, waterproofed by a smooth, green, waxy cuticle. A coconut can float for at least three or four months, traveling as much as 3000 miles (if the currents are favorable) before it becomes waterlogged and sinks. During this period, however, the embryo is growing, and with luck the nut is cast well up on shore before the seedling breaks through. (Should this happen at sea, the salt will kill the tissues of the young palm.) If all goes well, the young palm will escape the depredations of crabs, hungry for the succulent plumule (the primary bud), and will be able to put its roots down well away from salt water, and start its slow growth upward.

The fruits of the screw pine (*Pandanus*) are rather like pineapples, and these, too, can tolerate immersion in salt water. Originally found only on Madagascar, they are now wide-

Crocodiles and hippos are among the large amphibious animals capable of colonizing islands by swimming there across the sea. Left: crocodile on Malaysian river bank. The estuarine crocodile of Southeast Asia and Australasia established itself in the Philippines, Palau Islands, and Fiji, and got to the Tuamotus, halfway from Australia to South America. Below: pygmy hippos, a West African species. Long ago, a small species of hippo settled Madagascar, evidently after swimming there from Africa.

spread on islands throughout the tropics. So is the seaside shrub *Heritiera littoralis*, whose fibrous air-filled fruits are highly buoyant, and keeled so that they float aligned with the current.

Mangroves are also important pioneers of shorelines. Their seeds have specialized flotation tissue, making possible long-term transportation by sea. The seeds of the red mangrove are between eight and 15 inches long, and germinate while still inside the fruits, so that, when trapped in shallow water, they can quickly take root and send up shoots. Within a year or so, each seedling produces a dozen or more stiltlike prop roots and several leafy branches. Whole forests have been derived from just one mangrove seedling. Growing on the fringes of shores, the red mangrove's twisted mass of prop roots traps sediment and floating debris, and may slowly raise the land level by 6.5 inches a century. As land builders, mangroves have doubtless helped to turn shallow reefs into islands. The Ten Thousand Island area of southwest Florida has been colonized and in part stabilized by a combination of red mangroves and an oyster, *Crassostrea virginica*. Once firmly established, a mangrove

swamp provides an excellent habitat for wildlife. Lizards and birds make a living in the canopy, and below, the forest of mangrove roots is settled by sea squirts, mollusks—particularly oysters and their kin—and a host of crustaceans. At high tide, the sea brings with it fish to hunt over the humus-rich mud.

Rafts of floating vegetation are not uncommon at sea. These tend to be launched in the tropics during the monsoon, when swollen rivers undercut their banks and wash out chunks of land, each held together by a tangled mass of roots. Sometimes the rafts can be of considerable proportions and travel a long way. One of three quarters of an acre of forest growth with trees 30 feet high was seen off the coast of North America in 1892. Between 8 August and 19 September it was tracked for 1075 miles as it drifted along with the currents into mid-Atlantic. Floating "prairies" cruise down the Mississippi into the Gulf of Mexico; uprooted palms are swept into the Gulf of Guinea by the swollen Congo; and sailors often meet with mats of vegetation moving slowly out into the Pacific from the west coast of South America. Should these be beached on an island, there is a small chance that some of the vegetation, or a few of the seeds that it carries, may become established. We know that African material borne along on the main Equatorial Current drifts across the Atlantic and is stranded on the Brazilian coast or in the West Indies. At the longest, such a voyage would take no more than 12 weeks.

Some of the rafts carry animal passengers. The wood may contain adult insects or their larvae. Lizards or snakes, or perhaps tortoises, may still be lurking in the undergrowth. Some rafts even carry mammals. The skipper of a ship plying between Singapore and Saigon in 1939 observed a drifting island with trees and grasses, over 50 feet long, and standing up to 20 feet above water level. Marooned on it was either a squirrel or a monkey that was "jumping about in a most lively manner." Even large creatures may find themselves in this predicament, doomed to drowning in all but perhaps one in a million cases. A Negro who must have fallen asleep on the banks of the Congo River was luckier. He found himself adrift on a mat of vegetation more than 300 feet long and many miles out in the Atlantic Ocean before he was rescued by a passing boat.

Rafting has probably been very important in the dispersal of animals to islands. Scientists believe that Madagascar has never been joined to the African coast, so that the ancestors of all its nonflying animals except hippos may have come across the Mozambique Channel on drifters. Hippos could have made the journey by

swimming. The reptiles of the Galápagos Islands may all be derived from the passengers of rafting invasions from the South American continent 600 miles to the east over the course of 1 million years or so. Lizards now live on many Polynesian islands, and upon New Caledonia; it is inconceivable that their ancestors could have swum or merely floated unaided to such places. The only feasible explanation is that the ancestral lizards or their eggs arrived on rafts. An analysis of the kinds of insects found most frequently on remote islands supports the view that many arrived on floating vegetation. About 80 out of the 482 kinds of beetles found on the island of Madeira are weevils, the larvae of which live in wood. St. Helena is even more isolated, and 31 of its 60 beetles are weevils; on Kerguelen

Some tropical plants yield seeds that can float for thousands of miles, then sprout on some island shore. Such plants include the screw pine and coconut palm. Above: screw-pine fruit. Left: coconut palm growing on Praslin Island in the Seychelles. Because it leans, the tree drops its coconuts into the water, helping their seaborne dispersal. Below: young coconut palm.

Island, weevils account for no less than five out of the nine kinds of beetle. Land snails are also good candidates for beached rafts. On the Galápagos Islands, there is a land snail whose ancestors must have come from the *west*, because it belongs to a group of Polynesian mollusks unknown in South America. These ancestors appear to have floated from islands at least 3000 miles away, probably on a raft of buoyant plant material.

Some animals may have survived sea journeys preserved on ice! Iceland's native land mammals may have arrived at her shores on icebergs. It is otherwise difficult to see how field mice and Arctic foxes could have colonized an island that had been completely covered by glaciers at the height of the last ice age. Polar bears still occasionally reach Iceland by riding on ice floes.

Our own species must rate as the most successful colonizer, groups of settlers reaching islands by means of purpose-built rafts or boats. Sometimes even quite modest boats can travel great distances. There is evidence that Eskimos, perhaps from Greenland, have turned up on the northern shores of the British Isles. At the beginning of the 18th century, a kayak—an Eskimo canoe—was taken at sea with "an Indian" passenger. Alas, he could give no intelligible account of himself when brought ashore at Aberdeen, and died soon after. However, his kayak is still preserved in the museum of Marischal College as a testament to the Eskimo's Atlantic journey. There are other such records, but no Eskimo appears to have settled in Scotland. The story of long-distance voyaging by native vessels is quite different in the Pacific.

The Dutchman Jacob Roggeveen is given the credit for discovering a small Pacific island about 27 degrees south of the equator and about 109 degrees west of Greenwich. Because he first saw the place on Easter Sunday 1722, he named it Easter Island. He was, however, more than 1000 years too late to claim the real honor of discovery. That belonged to the ancestors of the thriving community of 3000 to 4000 people whom Roggeveen found already living on Easter Island, which they called *Te Pito o Te Henua* ("The Navel of the World"). The island's inhabitants understandably believed that they stood at the center of things because from the top of Maunga Terevaka, the island's tallest volcanic peak, all they could see was ocean. Chile is 2300 miles to the east, and Pitcairn Island, the nearest inhabited place, lies 1400 miles to the west. But, although they could not be expected to know it, the islanders lived far from the center of the world. In fact, they stood at one corner of the so-called great Pacific Triangle, a figure formed by drawing lines between Easter Island in the southeast, New Zealand in the southwest, and Hawaii in the north. This enormous triangle encloses Polynesia, a far-flung "continent" of islands colonized (long before Roggeveen arrived) by brave sea-going, Stone Age peoples. These pioneers sailed big and speedy ocean-going canoes across the Pacific and found habitable islands dotted around an area four times the size of the USA. Reaching remote Easter Island had been their crowning achievement.

The doorway to the Pacific was through Southeast Asia. From here, archipelagoes form stepping stones that continue down through the Solomon Islands, the New Hebrides, Fiji, and the Tonga Islands. This was the route by which fair-skinned peoples from Asia burst out into the uninhabited Pacific to become the Polynesians of the present day. In many a move, perhaps only one or two canoes of Polynesians were involved, sometimes storm-driven and lost, perhaps at other times purposefully seeking virgin islands.

Buoyant tissue helps floating mangrove seeds to colonize island shores throughout the tropics. Above: black mangrove seedlings taking root in shallow water on a sandy seabed. Right: red mangroves with stiltlike prop roots make up most of this swamp forest on Culebra, an island to the east of Puerto Rico.

Rafts of floating vegetation broken free in the rainy season drift down the Guayas River at Guayaquil in Ecuador. The plants and any animals riding on them float out into the Pacific. Some land species may have thus colonized the Galápagos Islands.

One can only guess at the miserable fate of the majority, no matter how skilled they were in surviving at sea. One by one, however, the larger islands were settled by a few pioneers who increased their numbers until overpopulation forced some of the more enterprising individuals to take to their boats in search of new lands. Tonga and Samoa were settled 3000 years ago, and from these centers the Polynesians thrust east toward the rising sun, reaching the Marquesas Islands some 2000 years ago, about the time that Julius Caesar's Roman soldiers were raiding Britain. By A.D. 500 Roman rule in western Europe had collapsed, but the Polynesians were still pointing the prows of their canoes to the horizons of the Pacific and finding more islands to settle. Already some of the Marquesans had landed on Hawaii, and others had evidently come upon Pitcairn and Easter Island. When the soldiers of William of Normandy were sharpening their arrows in preparation for conquering the Anglo-Saxons, Raiatéa in the Society Islands not far from Tahiti was the chief cultural and religious center. From here, high-ranking sailor adventurers voyaged far and wide to establish their rule in the Hawaiian, Cook, and Tubuai islands, and the Tuamotu Archipelago.

Although New Zealand was first occupied perhaps more than 1000 years ago, most of its living Maoris trace their ancestry back no more than 20 or so generations, to immigrants from the Society Islands who manned a great fleet of double-keeled canoes with names such as *Te Arawa* ("Shark"), *Tokomaru* ("South Shadow"), *Kuruhaupo* ("Storm Cloud"), and *Mata-atua* ("Face of a God"). Their homeland was rife with warfare and cannibalism, and they were escaping to *Ao-tea-roa* ("the land of the long white cloud") 2000 miles away, discovered four centuries previously by a Polynesian sailor-explorer Kupe and his wife, according to the legend. The settlers supposedly reached New Zealand in their well-victualed boats about 1350.

Of course, penetration of the Pacific would have been impossible without the development of fine craft capable of surviving long and possibly rough journeys, because, despite its name, the Pacific is often far from peaceful. Polynesian canoes can be traced back to simple dugouts used for fishing. Hollowed-out tree trunks gave way to deeper hulls built of carefully fitted planks. Stabilizing devices known as *outriggers* originated as a log resting on the water parallel to the

canoe, to which it was joined by two poles. Simple outriggers eventually became replaced by a second hull and the intervening space was decked over to produce a seaworthy catamaran, with thatched quarters for sheltering women and children. Local plants provided the necessary materials for boat building. People rolled coconut-husk fibers into string that they then braided into tough cord. This served for lashing the hull planks together, and the fibers themselves served for caulking. Sails evolved from plaited palm leaves. Shipbuilding became a skillful art, marked by religious ceremonies, prayers, and feasts. Tahitian craftsmen even put their adzes to sleep in sacred places, asking Tane, the God of the Land, to endow them with power; next morning, when work resumed, they "awakened" the adzes by dipping them in the sea.

Although products of Stone Age culture, some of the canoes were impressive in size and per-

Land snails at Algedo Crater on Albemarle (Isabela) Island in the Galápagos. The snails' ancestors probably rafted in, one kind coming at least 3000 miles from Polynesia in the west.

formance. An English buccaneer named William Dampier observed these hand-hewn boats lashed together with coconut fibers performing in 1686 and commented that "they sail the best of any boats in the world." Captain Cook saw a Tahitian war canoe that measured 108 feet long, almost as long as his own ship *Resolution*. One of his crewmen also noted that the Tongan boats could sail "about three miles to our two." Fijian "dreadnoughts" designed for battle were 80 feet long, carried 200 warriors, and under full sail would cream along at 15 knots. If the wind slackened, the crew could paddle them. Deep-water voyages of exploration in search of new islands were made in such double-hulled canoes, each vessel transporting 60 passengers with provisions of plants and animals for several weeks. According to tradition, the first immigrants to Easter Island disembarked from such a canoe.

The spread of mankind into the Pacific was taking place long before Columbus set course westward across the Atlantic, his men half in fear of sailing off the edge of the world. In contrast, Polynesians faced the Pacific with confidence. They had no sextants, maps, or compasses to help them. The Pacific navigator trusted his gods and the orderly universe, in which sun, stars, and moon rose and set in a predictable way. His compass consisted of 150 stars. Latitude could be judged by the position of key zenith stars. For example, Arcturus passes over the Hawaiian Islands along the Tropic of Cancer. Thus when this star stood directly overhead, a Polynesian navigator seeking the islands knew that his boat must be in the correct latitude. Sirius passes overhead in the latitude of Raiatéa near Tahiti. The flights of seabirds returning to their nesting colonies, and distant clouds forming over land, were two additional signposts that the skilled Polynesian navigator could use. Even the slap of waves on the hull of the canoe could provide clues as to where he was. Ocean swells bounced back from different islands to produce complicated patterns far beyond the islands' horizons. Once his senses became attuned to the swell patterns, which change from place to place, the oceanic navigator could tell where he was perhaps simply by lying on his back, listening to the rhythm of waves battering the canoe's hull, and feeling the movement as the canoe was tossed around. The islanders can still make long-distance journeys without modern navigation aids. In May 1974, two Satawal canoes from the

Carolines in Micronesia set sail on a 1100 mile trip north to Saipan in the Marianas Islands and back, and experienced no difficulty. Similar voyages can be accomplished even by Western man, providing he can read the signs. Dr. David Lewis, a veteran solo transatlantic sailor, set course from Tahiti to New Zealand in 1965. He made landfall with an error of only 26 miles.

Of course the Polynesians had to make a living on their islands. This they did by fishing and gardening. The seas around many islands abounded in edible life, and a great deal of cunning and enterprise went into developing techniques to catch fish. Hooks, nooses, traps, weirs, spears, nets, dredges, rakes, and even poisons were developed to harvest the sea. Hooks could be fashioned out of sharp shells, and the pearly insides formed lures for the big, predatory bonitos. In Hawaii, octopus lures were made from cowrie shells. Seafood proved particularly important on low coral atolls where the soil was poor and sweet water especially scarce, but higher volcanic islands with rich soil and plenty of fresh water were ideal for farming. The immigrants brought with them a whole variety of useful plants, such as taro (a tuberous vegetable), yams, and breadfruit. Coconuts, too, were cultivated. Sago, a starch, was made from the pith of palm trees, and on poor coral islets the *Pandanus* palm was a staff of life, but on the more luxuriant islands, it was famine food only. Settlers introduced pigs, chickens, dogs, and the harmless Polynesian rat, the latter being fattened for food. Whether or not the islands were "spoiled" is beside the point. Biologically, some were certainly enriched by Polynesian man and his domesticated flora and fauna rafting from the west—and perhaps now and then from the east. On Easter Island, the natives grew the sweet potato and the bottle gourd, both of which are South American in origin. Could the Marquesans have made an incredible 4000 mile trip to Chile and back to Easter Island, bringing with them these two South American plants? Whether the Amerindians ever set sail into the sunset and penetrated the Pacific has always been a controversial subject with anthropologists. Thor Heyerdahl tried to show that it would have been

Polar bear on ice floes that have buckled and fused where the edges met. In summer, melting separates many floes and bears on these drifting slabs of ice may journey hundreds of miles with ocean currents. Some even reached Iceland in this fashion.

possible for them to make the journey.

Heyerdahl was a zoologist who fled the civilized life of Oslo for the Pacific islands. After a period on Tahiti, he and his wife arrived in 1936 on Fatu Hiva in the Marquesas, where they learned of legends that the natives had come from a country to the east under command of a divine king called Tiki. There is a Peruvian legend about a pre-Inca ruler called Kon-Tiki, who dominated an area in the vicinity of Lake Titicaca, high in the Andes. Kon-Tiki, the story goes, was defeated in battle, built a raft, and, with an assemblage of loyal friends and followers, sailed into the Pacific sunset. Thor Heyerdahl was impressed with the idea that Kon-Tiki was the person who also features in the Marquesan myths. To see just how practical the theory was, Heyerdahl and four companions arrived in Ecuador at the close of World War II, and constructed a square-sailed raft made of balsa-wood logs cut from the native forests. He named the vessel *Kon-Tiki* and on 28 April 1947 set sail from Callao in Peru. Aided by the prevailing southeasterly winds and the westward drift of the Humboldt and South Equatorial currents, the raft floated thousands of miles to the west, and, after 101 days, foundered on a coral reef off Raroia in the Tuamotu Archipelago.

The voyage of the *Kon-Tiki* showed that a journey from South America to Polynesia may have been possible for the Amerindians, but there is no proof that they ever penetrated the Pacific Triangle. They did, however, make the 600-mile voyage to the Galápagos Islands in prehistoric times, as excavations by Heyerdahl and two archaeologists demonstrated.

The first men to set foot on remote islands such as the Galápagos Islands and others scattered around the Pacific were probably thankful to be alive, to feel solid land underfoot, and to see plants and animals that could form the basis of an acceptable menu. It was not until a century and a half ago that scientists started to wonder about the strangeness of the life forms that inhabit some islands.

Above: Kon-Tiki, *a square-sailed balsa raft with which Thor Heyerdahl set out to prove that Polynesia had been peopled from South America. Named for a pre-Inca king supposedly figuring in Polynesian myth, and launched off Peru in 1947, the vessel drifted 4300 miles in 101 days before it ran aground on Raroia, halfway across the Pacific. Even so, scientists believe that Polynesians came from Asia, not America.*

Satawal canoes in the Caroline Islands of the western Pacific. Left: canoes fishing out at sea. Below: manhandling a canoe to its boathouse. Fragile vessels like these completed a 1100-mile trip north to Saipan in the Marianas Islands and back in 1974. Such voyages show how Stone Age men from Southeast Asia must have probed the Pacific, until some of them had colonized the far-flung islands comprising Polynesia.

Workshops of Evolution

Those who believe that magical things happen on islands could well be forgiven. On a few of the Sunda Islands in Indonesia, there lives a nine-foot-long species of lizard that can kill goats. On many Indo-Pacific island paradises, great crabs behave like monkeys, climbing palms to get the coconuts. In the Hawaiian and Galápagos archipelagoes, relatives of the daisies and sunflowers grow as big as trees. If we were able to turn the clock back a few centuries we should have even more justification for thinking that a magician had a hand in making island life. Ugly dodos strutted on Mauritius. These flightless, turkey-sized relatives of the pigeons were aptly chosen for the topsy-turvy world of *Alice in Wonderland*. New Zealand and Madagascar were once the respective homes of moas and elephant birds, the largest of which would have made ostriches seem small. Strange things have happened on islands on a much smaller scale, too. The larvae of damselflies are voracious predators that terrorize small fish and shrimps in ponds and streams, and yet on Hawaii some have left the water and evolved larvae that scamper over the ground for their food. But it is the mix-up of traditional occupations that strikes visitors to some islands most forcibly. In the Galápagos Islands, giant tortoises live like goats, and a finch takes on the job of a woodpecker. On Madagascar a lemur, the aye-aye, makes a wood-peckerlike living, extracting grubs from the dead wood, but doing so in its own special way by clever finger work. Aye-ayes have uniquely long fingers, especially the middle one of each hand. Such a digit appears as slim and bony as a twig, and it is vital for the aye-aye's way of life because it serves as a prospecting hammer, tapping branches so that its owner can locate grubs by the hollow sound of the wood. When the tone sounds promising, the aye-aye's teeth chisel away to reveal the grubs' galleries, and a slender probing finger tweaks out the wriggling tidbits.

Naturalists have discovered that many oceanic islands possess unusual animals and plants, but for sheer strangeness of its wildlife no group compares with the Galápagos Islands—often referred to as the "Enchanted Isles." There seems

Komodo dragons devouring the carcass of a goat. Largest of all lizards, these giant, nine-foot-long monitors live only on Komodo and a few other Indonesian islands. Free from the competition of big predatory mammals, they survive to fill the role elsewhere occupied by lions and tigers. On a number of remote oceanic islands there are equally strange beasts that evolved in the absence of competitors.

Scenes illustrating the volcanic origins of the Galápagos Islands. Right: a view from a cinder slope on Bartolomé Island. Below: rope lava on nearby James (San Salvador) Island. When the Galápagos Islands boiled up out of the Pacific, they were without land plants and animals. Over many thousands of years a few species arrived—almost all from South America. From these unpromising ingredients emerged the extraordinary forms that convinced Darwin that life is not created, but evolves.

little excuse for calling the Galápagos Islands enchanted in any complimentary sense. From the moment they became known to the Western world, it was made quite clear that they were no Garden of Eden. In 1535, Tomás de Berlanga, bishop of Panama, came to the islands and had a terrible time. Searching in vain for water, he survived by chewing cacti. He noted that it looked as though God had caused it to rain stones. In a sense he was right, because the archipelago was made by volcanoes spouting lava and pumice so porous that rainwater tends to soak straight through rather than running over the surface in refreshing streams. Time and

time again, travelers and visiting scientists have found all of the 14 main islands drab and depressing. Dr. David Lack, a British ornithologist on an expedition to the Galápagos Islands in 1938, found his keen interest in the wildlife offset by the "monstrous scenery, dense thorn scrub, cactus spines, loose sharp lava, food deficiencies, water shortage, black rats, fleas, jiggers, ants, mosquitoes, scorpions, Ecuadorean Indians of doubtful honesty, and dejected, disillusioned European settlers." Just over a century beforehand, Charles Darwin had been unimpressed with the archipelago at first, and likened it to slag heaps around the iron foundries of Staf-

fordshire. But what is the real Galápagos scene?

The archipelago straddles the equator about 600 miles from Ecuador. To the west there is no land for about 3000 miles. Albemarle (officially called Isabela) is the largest of the islands, about 80 miles long and rising 5600 feet above sea level. Several of the others are between 10 and 20 miles across, with peaks of between 2000 and 3000 feet. The islands vary in age. Chatham (San Cristóbal) is the oldest, and its jagged volcanic profile has long been eroded to leave nicely rounded contours. Narborough (Fernandina) and some of the other younger islands are still volcanically active. Narborough is today the last unspoiled

Rugged rocks decorated by basking sea lions and resting boobies are among the first sights to greet seaborne visitors to the Galápagos. The sea lions belong to a southern species of eared seal, which reaches its northern limit in these islands.

island in the Galápagos group and is especially valued as a biological Shangri La. And yet, like all volcanic islands, the survival of its plants and animals is dependent upon the capricious nature of the fire in its belly. The volcano exploded as recently as 11 June 1968, destroying much of the life in the crater lake and around the rim. Many of the unique pintail ducks and land iguanas must have perished.

Low cliffs of black lava, ornamented with bright scarlet crabs that scuttle in and out of the waves and crevices, greet visitors to the Galápagos Islands. Hundreds of incredible dragonlike lizards can also be seen lazing around on the rocks. They are amphibious in their habits, and

eat seaweed, which they reach by diving. There is nothing like them in the rest of the world. Sandy beaches are inhabited by sea lions and marine turtles. On Punta Espinosa, which is today the richest colony of sea-oriented life in the archipelago, there are Galápagos penguins, the most northerly members of the penguin family. These cold-adapted seabirds can live happily here on the equator because the islands are bathed by the cool waters of the Humboldt Current, which sweeps up from the south close to the South American coast, before being deflected past the Galápagos Islands and farther out into the Pacific. Offshore, brown pelicans and boobies dive onto schools of fish. Strange, flightless cormorants have ragged, tiny wings that look ridiculous on such large birds.

Behind the teeming shore life, cactus deserts shimmer in the heat haze. The most prominent plants on the arid lowlands are tall tree cacti, appropriately called torch thistles by the buccaneers who used to visit the islands to replenish their ships' larders. Two kinds of tree cactus abound in these barren wastelands. One has long, branched, fluted cylinders and is called *Cereus*; the other is more familiar to world travelers as the shrub-sized prickly pear *Opuntia*, but on the Galápagos Islands its spiny pads rise to about 30 feet. Sometimes the cacti combine with a matrix of unpleasantly poisonous or spiny shrubs such as *Acacia* to form an impenetrable barrier. Underfoot, volcanic glass grit can wear out a pair of boots in a very short time, and make falling a painful, if not a downright dangerous, experience.

Inland, at higher elevations, the scenery changes, because here more moisture is available. Rain generally falls from December through March. Outside these months, however, the highlands also receive moisture from mists that cloak the tops of the islands when the Southeast Trade Winds blow. The forests on the upper slopes are in places luxuriant. The air is humid, the soil is black with humus, and the trees are covered with orchids and draped with mosses and lichens. One of the most characteristic trees is a member of the daisy family, which elsewhere in the world tends to comprise low-growing herbs. Its dande-

Two kinds of large herbivorous lizard adapted to the Spartan conditions of the Galápagos Islands. Left: marine iguana swimming. Unlike any other lizards on earth, these three-foot-long amphibious reptiles browse underwater on seaweed. Right: land iguana munching the fruit of a prickly pear. Land iguanas are bigger than their marine kin, and forage from sea level to slopes a mile high.

lionlike flowers set in rosettes of leaves are carried as high as a double-story house on trunks a few inches thick. Among these trees grow clumps of grasses higher than a man, and groves of tree ferns. On the way through the rich growth of trees festooned with ferns, one sees giant turtles that weigh 500 pounds, and big land iguanas either sunning themselves or lumbering noisily into their warrens. Beyond the forest, the trees give way to open grassland, with ferns, liverworts, mosses, and club mosses; and this kind of vegetation continues to the rims of the craters.

The islands are odd as much for what is absent as for the strange animals and plants that live there. Compared with the mainland of South America there are obvious omissions. A botanist will look in vain for conifers, palms, arums, and lilies. A number of dominant South American plant families are poorly represented, for example the loosestrife and myrtle families. Herbivorous mammals are not found in the Galápagos Islands, but their niche is filled by turtles and

Two kinds of seabird that live only in the Galápagos Islands. Above: Galápagos cormorant. With no enemies, and thus no need for flight, the species has wings reduced to stubs that serve as balancers. Below: Galápagos penguin—a coldwater species kept cool here on the equator by the chilly Humboldt Current.

lizards. Very few kinds of land snails munch down the green Galápagos vegetation compared with the incredible numbers found in South America; but one, *Nesiotus*, has produced a diversity of forms. The bird watcher will waste time looking for a colorful array of terrestrial species. All he will find is a cuckoo, a hawk, a flycatcher, some mockingbirds, and a few finches. The first person to comment on the bird life was Captain Colnett, who surveyed the islands in 1793. The captain declared that he found "no great number or variety of land birds, and those I saw were not remarkable for their novelty or beauty." As it happened, he was rather rash in his condemnation of the little brown and black "sparrows" that scratched around the Galápagos Islands, because it was Darwin's study of these birds that made plain the process of evolution.

It was lucky that Darwin ever had a chance of seeing for himself the weird wildlife of the Galápagos Islands and their dreary little finches, because he had been destined for the Church, not

Brown pelican flying (above) and blue-footed booby displaying its beautiful feet in a dance (below). Like the Galápagos cormorants and penguins, these pelicans and boobies feed in the fish-rich seas off the Galápagos; but not only here. Both of these species also nest on South America's western seaboard.

for the life of a professional naturalist. The Darwins were upper-class Whigs, and prosperous members of the medical profession. Charles's grandfather, Erasmus, was a famous practitioner and well-known for his verses on scientific and evolutionist themes. Charles's father, Robert, aspired to no great heights of scholarship, but was nevertheless a successful country doctor who managed to send his son to Edinburgh University to study medicine. This proved an utter failure, however, because Charles could not stand the sight of blood! From Edinburgh he went to Cambridge to read classics, which he loathed, and mathematics, which he could not understand. Nevertheless he obtained a degree, then devoted himself to natural history and partridge shooting, intending at this stage to become a clergyman. Charles's plans changed in 1831, when a friendly botany professor secured him the post of naturalist on H.M.S. *Beagle*, a ship the British Admiralty was sending around the world to chart the South American coast and to obtain improved deter-

Above: A stand of the cactus Brachycereus *near the northern shore of Narborough (Fernandina) Island in the Galápagos. Taking root in lava fields that retain no moisture, this species of cactus thrives where few other kinds of plant cling to life. Some Galápagos cacti even grow tall enough to resemble trees.*

Galápagos cacti that grow like trees include the prickly pear (right), which takes this form on islands where tortoises eat prickly-pear pads. Tall cactus trunks lift pads out of reach, and spines and thick bark protect the trunks. Below: prickly pear flower provides a moist meal for a Galápagos mockingbird.

minations of longitude. The notion of Charles's going to sea appeared quite preposterous to most of the Darwin family, and the credit for encouraging him must go to his uncle, Josiah Wedgwood of pottery fame.

Robert Fitzroy, the *Beagle*'s captain, was a deeply religious man who interpreted the Bible literally and hoped that Darwin's discoveries would confirm the teachings of the Book of Genesis about early life on earth. Genesis proclaimed that God had created all life forms in three days, later destroying most living things in a great flood with which God punished sinful man. (Fossils discovered in rocks were widely held to be victims of this divinely engineered disaster.) As a budding clergyman, Darwin must have found a great measure of agreement with Fitzroy. Nevertheless, he must have been partly influenced by the outrageously heretical views of his grandfather, who was completely skeptical of the orthodox Judeo-Christian view of the divine creation and destruction of life forms. Darwin knew, too, that most people firmly believed that, in one sense at least, creation had not yet stopped. Individuals of some kinds of animal were believed to appear spontaneously instead of being born or hatched. Did not the sun breed crocodiles from the mud of the Nile, and mice mysteriously form in heaps of old clothes? Similarly, bad meat bred bluebottles, and maggots were created deep inside apples. Such things did not need parents, it seemed. The prospective clergyman was to knock that idea firmly on the head, and to call into question the credibility of the Bible itself.

In 1835 the *Beagle* put South America 600 miles astern, and dropped anchor in the Galápagos Islands—a routine stop of no great importance in her itinerary. She did not stay for long, but Darwin managed to linger a little on James, Chatham, and Floreana, observing and collecting all manner of wildlife, including birds. He was puzzled by the uniqueness of the wildlife, and at first failed to understand how it was that the Galápagos Islands should have animals and plants unlike those of all other island groups and of South America. He became aware of the fact that even individual islands within the archipelago have unique selections of species. This is true particularly of the mockingbirds; these birds differ so much from island to island that the forms on Chatham, Hood, and Charles islands rank as separate species. This puzzled Darwin because

Above: part of a forest of so-called sunflower trees (Scalesia pedunculata) *growing on the damp upper slopes of Indefatigable (Santa Cruz) Island. Below: giant tortoise on the forest floor. About 1000 of these tanklike reptiles roam a reserve of several thousand acres established on Indefatigable.*

Above: giant tortoises wallow in rain-water pools on the island of Albemarle (Isabela) where mist and periodic rain help to keep the upper slopes damp and lush. Left: giant tortoise feeding on Hood (Española) Island, an arid place. Contrasts between vegetation cover on different Galápagos islands help to explain differences in the shell shapes of their tortoises. On islands where nourishing plants are low growing, the shells are dome shaped. But on islands where most of the edible vegetation is well above the ground, tortoises evolved saddle-shaped shells that allow the reptiles to crane their necks upward to reach food. Yet in spite of adaptation to local conditions, tortoises are now numerous on only 2 of at least 10 islands colonized by their ancestors and fewer than 10 Hood tortoises survive.

Below: the unique, tool-making and tool-using woodpecker finch of the Galápagos in action. This small bird lacks the beak of a true woodpecker, but makes up for this disadvantage by using its bill to snap off a twig or cactus spine. It pokes this tool into a hole in a tree trunk and levers out the wood-boring grub that lurks inside.

these islands are less than 60 miles apart, almost within sight of one another. There seemed to be no obvious reason why each island should have its own kind of mockingbird rather than all sharing one species.

Then Darwin's awareness was sharpened by something said about the giant tortoises by Mr. Lawson, the acting vice-governor. Lawson remarked that he could tell which island a tortoise came from merely by looking at the shape of the shell. Captain Porter of the U.S. frigate *Essex* had also noticed the geographical varieties back in 1812, when he put his sailors ashore to raid different islands for tortoises with which to feed his crew. Both men were right. Tortoises of the southern islands have saddle-shaped shells, whereas those from the north of the archipelago have dome-shaped shells, but shell shapes also differ in detail from island to island. As with the mockingbirds, there seemed no obvious explana-

tion for such variations. However, they fitted a hypothesis that was beginning to form in Darwin's mind. This was that species are changing, not immutably fixed, and that the tortoises and mockingbirds on any one island had been changing independently of those on the others, and thus biologically growing apart. Slight differences in shell shape do not necessarily add up to much, but in the end an accumulation of small differences will result in such profound modifications in design that members of a single species of tortoise stranded on two islands will give rise to two dissimilar species. The Galápagos tortoises were in fact all deemed to belong to the same species, but some of the mockingbirds had diverged much more sharply. Armed with such observations, Darwin turned to a study of the Galápagos finches with renewed enthusiasm when he returned home.

In all, 13 kinds of Darwin's finches (as we now

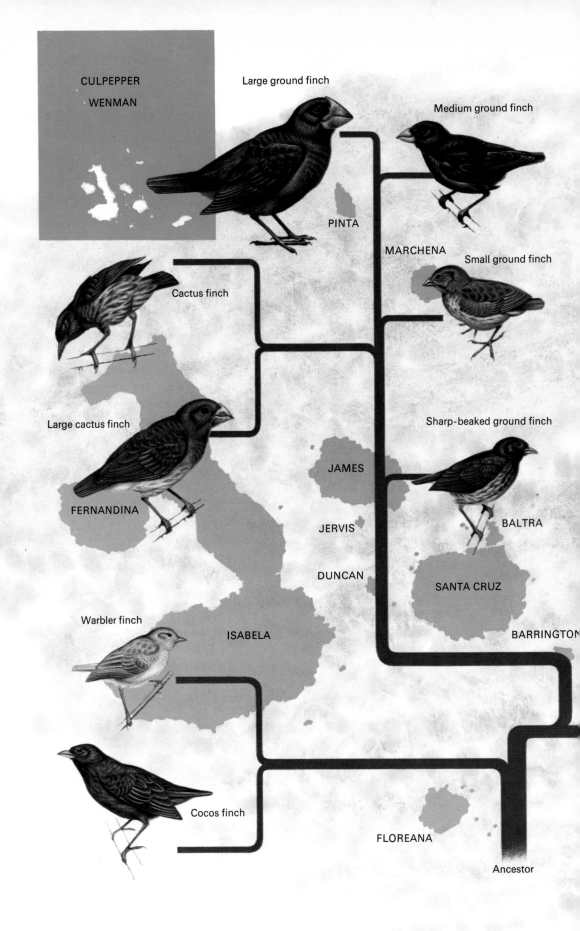

CULPEPPER

WENMAN

Large ground finch

Medium ground finch

PINTA

MARCHENA

Small ground finch

Cactus finch

Sharp-beaked ground finch

Large cactus finch

JAMES

FERNANDINA

JERVIS

DUNCAN

BALTRA

SANTA CRUZ

Warbler finch

ISABELA

BARRINGTON

Cocos finch

FLOREANA

Ancestor

Darwin's Finches - The Galápagos Islands

Woodpecker finch

Mangrove finch

TOWER

Large tree finch

Medium tree finch

SAN CRISTÓBAL

Small tree finch

Vegetarian finch

HOOD

The thirteen species of finch found on the Galápagos Islands were all derived from a common ancestor, as was the 14th member of the group shown here, the Cocos finch, which lives on the island of Cocos 600 miles northeast of the Galápagos Islands. Over the years the descendants of this common ancestor have sought out new feeding grounds and then exploited them. Because of the lack of competition from many mainland bird species—such as woodpeckers, parrots, and warblers—the finches have evolved to take the roles of these birds. Each of the species depicted on this diagram has evolved its own beak size and shape to cope with a different diet. Some of the finches are seed-eaters, such as the large ground finch, which has evolved a large hard beak that can cope with the hardest of seeds. Other finches have become insectivores, and their beaks have also become modified to suit their feeding habits. The phenomenon of adaptive radiation, by which different species evolve from a common ancestor, is therefore well shown by this fascinating group of birds.

Hawaiian honeycreeper with a long, curved beak able to probe flowers for insects and nectar. Several million years ago the honeycreepers' American ancestor probably had an all-purpose bill, but gave rise to more than 20 species with beaks specialized as probes, seed crushers—even as monkey wrenches.

call them) are found on the Galápagos Islands, and another species lives on Cocos Island, 600 miles to the northeast. As a group they share many characteristics. All are monogamous and build roofed nests in which they lay white eggs spotted with pink. Most of the finches are grayish brown, and in some kinds the males have a greater or lesser amount of black feathering. It was the *differences* between the species, however, that impressed Charles Darwin. In 1839, when describing "the most singular group of finches," he noted the perfect gradation in beak size between species, from birds with enormous nutcrackers to birds with slim bills suitable only for tweaking insects. He went on to conclude: "Seeing this gradation and diversity of structure in one small, intimately related group of birds, one might really fancy that from an original paucity of birds in this archipelago, one species had been taken and modified for different ends." It is amazing to what ends the little creatures are modified.

Darwin's finches can be divided into three categories, each designed for earning a living in a special way. Firstly, six species are grounddwellers adapted for feeding on seeds and the fleshy fruit of cacti, but each species has a beak of a special size. The larger the beak, the harder and the larger the seeds it can deal with. The big ground finch sports by far the heaviest-duty seed crushers and can live comfortably on nourishing kernels too hard for its less powerful-billed relatives. Finches with the slimmest beaks in this group take insects in addition to seeds. Because each of these ground-dwelling birds is equipped to deal with a different range of food, the six species can live together in the same habitat without competing with each other. In fact, four of the six kinds coexist on many of the islands, which shows that they are ecologically separated, and perhaps prevented from poaching on each other's food supplies by their different feeding tools. The two other species live on outlying islands, and have comparatively long medium-duty beaks adapted to a mixed diet of insects and seeds. But the species that appropriately enough inhabits Wolf Island has become more ferocious in its feeding habits. Here one of Darwin's finches has developed a taste for booby blood and become an avian vampire. While the seabirds are on their nests, a finch will sidle up to a sitting booby and peck the bird at the base of its wing feathers until blood has been drawn.

The second category of Darwin's finches consists of six species that feed in the trees and have beaks adapted for catching insects, except for one that has a thick beak recalling a parrot's. Like a true parrot, this tree finch is a vegetarian thriving on a diet of buds and fruit. On the other hand, the mangrove finch is fully insectivorous, and confined to the mangrove forests that line the shores of some of the islands. The sixth tree finch is one of the most remarkable little birds in the world. It has the habits of a woodpecker, searching and probing cracks and crevices for insects and grubs. It is at a disadvantage, however, because it lacks a woodpecker's long, sharp, chisellike bill and so cannot bore into wood to expose wood-mining larvae, and furthermore has no long tongue to spear grubs and winkle them out of deep recesses. The woodpecker finch has developed a useful trick to make up for drawbacks in its equipment: it uses cactus spines as tools for probing likely crannies to bring reluctant grubs and adult insects to the surface. What makes the woodpecker finch even more remarkable is that the bird fashions its tool to the right length and nips off any unwanted sections that would be likely to interfere with the spine's function as a deep probe. The third category consists of the warbler finch. Like true warblers, it has a slim, pointed beak suitable for catching small insects as it flits through the foliage. Even the uniform of this species is very warblerlike; although the color varies from island to island, these birds tend toward olive-brown upper parts and yellow-olive below.

Darwin was right in supposing that all of these birds were derived from a common ancestor whose descendants underwent modification in all sorts of directions, and gave rise to different species. This is a widespread phenomenon called *adaptive radiation*. It is particularly marked on islands where first-wave colonists have their new homes almost to themselves; the field is clear of competition and there are plenty of opportunities to exploit novel ways of making a living. For example, the Galápagos Islands are beyond the range of woodpeckers, small parrots, and most insectivorous warblers, and the original seed-eating finches have gradually evolved to take over the roles of those birds. On the mainland such developments are held firmly in check by severe competition from real woodpeckers, parrots, and warblers, which are much more efficient than finches in the early stages of de-

The Laysan finch feeds on insects, seeds, roots, the flesh of dead seabirds, and terns' eggs, which it cracks open with its beak. Adaptation to a varied diet enabled this small land bird to survive as a species on tiny, two-and-a-half square-mile Laysan Island, in the west of the Hawaiian Archipelago.

White-eye feeding young. Named for the ring of white feathers around each eye, these birds comprise more than 80 species of Old World nectar-eaters. New species emerged on certain islands from successive invasions by the same parent stock. By the time the second wave arrived, the first had given rise to white-eyes that were sufficiently different to keep the two from interbreeding.

viation from the finch norm. In the cut and thrust of the crowded mainland, any offspring that differ markedly from the parent finches are usually weeded out by natural selection. However, on the Galápagos Islands, a strange deviation in feeding behavior or feeding tools may be an *asset* rather than a liability. The finch with a tweaking beak and a taste for insects may find that it can suddenly live well on a source of food untapped by competing warblers and flycatchers. If it breeds and leaves more youngsters with the same characteristics, then the path is set toward the evolution of a species of insectivorous bird with seed-eating ancestors.

Remote islands are like holiday resorts, where rules of the life game are relaxed, at least initially. Animals and plants can try novel designs and ways of making a living. The original raw material may be limited but it evolves fast in the initial period when competition is reduced. Darwin's finches are not the only clear-cut example of adaptive radiation. Had Darwin studied the fauna and flora of the Hawaiian Islands, he would have found plenty of examples to set him thinking; in particular there is one family of birds on Hawaii as good as, if not better than, the finches for illustrating adaptive radiation.

A long time ago, a few warblerlike or tanager-like birds were blown across the Pacific and made landfall on the Hawaiian Archipelago. Here, they had the islands very much to themselves and rapidly evolved into a unique and extraordinary family called the Hawaiian honeycreepers. Many have been given colorful but tongue-defying native names, such as *ou, iiwi,* and *akiapolaau.* The Hawaiian chieftains admired their plumage and liked to have the feathers woven into cloaks and helmets. Unlike the somber-plumaged Darwin's finches, many of the honeycreepers are gay little birds decorated in strong poster colors, and thus ideal for ceremonial regalia. The plumage of the iiwi and apapane provided marvelous shades of red, and the mamo was prized for its yellow feathers, as was the Hawaiian oo, a spectacular, dark, forest bird with brilliant yellow feathers at the sides of its breast. Unfortunately the honeycreepers have proved very sensitive to civilization; several, including the mamo and the oo, have become extinct, and several of the 12 surviving species are in danger.

Fundamentally, honeycreepers show considerable uniformity, which underlines their close relationship. As with Darwin's finches, the differences that have evolved are related to divergent sources of food and the tools and techniques for exploiting these; again, shapes and sizes are especially significant. As the family name suggests, some honeycreepers—the iiwi, for example—have highly specialized equipment for extracting nectar from deep inside blooms. These nectar-sippers tend to be fairly small birds, in red or yellowish plumage and armed with a long, slender, decurved beak, with a matching tongue fringed at the tip for lapping up the sugar fluid from the tubular lobelia flowers in which Hawaii is especially rich. Then there is a wide array of insectivorous honeycreepers, each with its own method of intercepting prey. Several kinds have conventionally shaped, slender beaks for seizing their food. But the akepa has the tips of its mandibles crossed, like the more familiar crossbill finches of North America and Eurasia. This helps the bird to force open tree buds and seize the bugs that often hide inside them. Akepas can even pry open buds of the koa tree when these are fastened together by caterpillars' or spiders' webs. Four honeycreeper species evolved upper mandibles much longer than their lower ones. The bill of the extinct akiapolaau was the most extraordinary of all, because each mandible had a different part to play in bringing insects out into the light of day. The lower mandible was not only short, but also very stout, and upcurved to such an extent that when the bird closed its beak the edges of the two mandibles failed to meet. Akiapolaaus used their lower mandibles to chisel away tree bark to expose galleries in the wood, from which insects could be winkled by the long and decurved upper mandible. The pseudonestor has a different way of exposing grubs hiding in wood. It has a massive beak like a monkey wrench, with a huge upper mandible a good deal longer than the lower mandible and hooked downward beyond it. It uses this bill to break open dead twigs, particularly those of the kola tree, in order to reveal the larvae of the longhorn beetles that munch their way through the decaying wood. Dead, dry wood is often harder than living wood, and the pseudonestor's strong beak and powerful muscles are adapted to supply the great force needed. In some ways, these birds make a living in the manner of small parrots, many of which thrive on a diet of wood-boring grubs, which they find by chewing and shredding wood. There are even honeycreepers, such as the palila, that live like seed-eating finches. The palila survives precariously in the Hawaiian mountain forests, where it uses its short stout beak to crack the seeds of the mamani trees.

By no means all Hawaiian birds are such specialized feeders as the honeycreepers. The Laysan finch, with a stout conical bill similar to that of the grosbeaks, has a wide diet that includes insects, grass seeds, roots, and flesh from dead birds. This finch has even developed a taste for terns' eggs, which it cracks with a few deft blows of its beak.

Just how effective islands are as species factories can be judged by the results of stock-taking on Hawaii. More than 90 per cent of the 1729 kinds of flowering plants recorded there are found nowhere else in the world. Taxonomists have looked carefully at those unique to Hawaii and have worked out that they all evolved from about 270 original colonists. Some 250 kinds of ancestral insects have generated 3722 species unique to the islands. Browsing on tree-top leaves, there are 215 species of land snails, all of them descended from one species. The 77 unique kinds of native birds can all be traced back to 14 ancestral species. Repeated elsewhere in the oceans, the evolutionary process that produced distinctively Hawaiian species explains why well over one half of the world's 8700 species of birds are islanders.

Sometimes several species can result from multiple invasions of an island by the same parent stock; by the time the second or third wave of invaders arrives, the initial immigrants have evolved sufficiently to keep them from interbreeding with the newcomers. Such may be the case of the blue chaffinch, which now shares the Azores with the European chaffinch; the former

Hawaiian rain forest (right), featuring tree ferns and other tropical vegetation, still harbors distinctively Hawaiian birds and insects. Of special interest in evolutionary studies are kipukas, patches of forest isolated by old lava flows. Below: lava flows flanking a kipuka. The black lava comes from a flow of 1935; the reddish-brown lava dates from 1843. Such flows cut off one forest fruit-fly population from its neighbors, and in time its individuals evolve special features that distinguish them from other fruit flies.

is a much older inhabitant than the latter, which is obviously a recent arrival because it is not much different from the mainland form. Several kinds of fruit pigeons that live on Fiji may have developed from three separate waves of colonists. So, too, may the white-eyes of Norfolk Island, 800 miles east of Australia. There are three kinds, differing in color and beak size, on the 20-square-mile island. Norfolk Island is so small that it is inconceivable that these three species separated out from a single invasion. Each is probably derived from a separate colonization from either Australia or Lord Howe Island.

To transform one species into multiple species

on one island it seems necessary to fragment the original invasion force as much as possible, and as often as possible. This can happen locally on a single island in the case of plants and invertebrates, which may become split up by topographical features such as valleys. No less than 31 kinds of weevil live on the solitary island of St. Helena, stuck 1200 miles from West Africa in the Atlantic. One invasion of land snails may have produced about a dozen species, and trees of the daisy family have adaptively radiated also.

Island clusters are better than single lumps of land as species factories for flying animals such as birds and insects. It is no accident that the

Galápagos and Hawaiian islands can boast some of the best examples of adaptive radiation, because the volcanic islands have been appearing and disappearing for millions of years, each producing its own brand of life from the limited raw material of the original invaders. Each island may become a base from which its own kinds of birds or plants may invade other islands in the group; it may in turn receive wildlife colonists that evolved on neighboring islands. In this way the Hawaiian lobelias have multiplied to produce 146 species and varieties from a very limited number of original colonists. However, nothing compares with the fantastic divergence

among fruit flies in the Hawaiian archipelago. They illustrate with great clarity that the speed at which species are evolved depends upon the extent to which the populations can be divided, and upon how easy the living is.

You need a good magnifying glass to get a clear view of these tiny flies, scientifically known as *Drosophila*, which means "dew loving," because they feed on fermenting fruit juices and sap. In Hawaii there are about 700 species, most of which have evolved within the last 700,000 years. It is the best example of evolution at breakneck speed in the world.

The natural features of Hawaii have helped in this respect. The island has a diversity of habitats where the flies can live, from moist cloud forests high up on the mountain slopes, one of the wettest places in the world, to semidesert in the rain shadow of the trade winds. Every few years volcanic activity destroys swathes of forest, replacing them with areas of solid lava; in time, plants colonize the lava in patches that spread until they knit together to form a continuous blanket of green. Meanwhile, each patch of green can be colonized by a population of flies. Lava flows have a further effect. Often, they stream through the forests and cut off groves of vegetation that, with their fly inhabitants, escape being either burned or buried. Such forest islands are so much part of the Hawaiian scenery that they are given a name—*kipukas*. To tiny drosophilas, a kipuka a few hundred yards from other parts of the forest is a whole world in itself. Providing it is surrounded by a stretch of country hostile enough to deter immigration or emigration, its fruit flies will thus evolve independently from their neighboring relatives, and change into unique forms. This could not happen with birds, because they could easily fly from one kipuka to another. Even a gully, however, can be a prison for snails. On the Hawaiian island of Oahu, there are five deep valleys that run southward into the sea, parallel to each other. The mountainous ridges separating them have also split up the snail population, enabling five distinct species of *Achatinella* to develop in the valleys, each with its own unique shell markings. But to come back to drosophila, the production of a chain of islands one after another has led to the proliferation of populations of fruit flies on a wide scale. This in turn has generated species by the hundred.

Kauai is the oldest island of the archipelago, and the others have emerged at intervals to the southeast. From the point of view of flies that once lived on the old islands, new lands have appeared successively across the sea on the horizon and so have encouraged island-hopping. The arrival of a pregnant fly on a new island allowed its descendants to diversify into a multitude of different forms, members of any one of which may be whisked away on the winds to begin a dynasty of drosophilas on another volcanic spoil heap. Diversity is encouraged right from the beginning.

The original colonist itself may not be a good average representative of its kind, because individuals vary tremendously. For example, the average height of a human female is five and a half feet, but we all know of some women who are six feet and others who barely reach five. If a pregnant woman were picked at random to start her own race on an island, the chances of choosing Mrs. Average would be slim. Pure chance might result in a clan of relative giants bred from a genetically tall woman, or in a clan of dwarfs if a very small female happened to be the castaway. From the start, such island populations would differ markedly from the parent population, not because they were better adapted to the island conditions but because of the random nature of the way the original colonist was picked. This phenomenon, called the "Founder Effect," holds true for all animal castaways. Size and coat color, for instance, are variable within species, and colonists are not necessarily average in other respects either. Genetic bias in castaways therefore encourages diversification. So does freedom from biological competition. It is no accident that nettles have lost their stings on Hawaii!

The first fruit fly to reach a Hawaiian island must have found it empty of tiresome enemies and competitors, but with plentiful food supplies. The mortality would be low, and all kinds of freaks could survive. Then came the day of reckoning, when the flies outran their food resources. Perhaps a population crash reduced the flies to scattered groups. These would include some strange new forms adapted somehow or other to survive, providing they did not inter-

Nesomicromus vagus
A normal winged species

breed and so lose their identities. Populations that have been kept apart by stretches of water, lava, or inhospitable country tend to accumulate small non-adaptive genetic differences that, in the end, turn the populations into separate species, and these can live side by side should they come to share the same area. Natural selection will then favor the development of biological devices that prevent mixed matings. These devices keep the species independent and at the same time reduce the risks of infertility that go with mixed mating. The Hawaiian fruit flies exhibit some wonderful barriers to breeding infertile offspring. The male of some species impresses his mate by displaying his patterned wings in front of her. If the pattern is right for her species, the female will consent to mate; several species share the same technique, but the wing patterns are different. Other species are wooed by wing music, by perfumes, or by the male's style of dancing. Some breeding barriers or "isolating mechanisms" are purely mechanical. Mating insects literally grapple with each other, using their genitalia; the male's grappling tools must mesh with the female's for successful copulation, and each species has its own design, which is more or less incompatible with those of other species. Complex courtships and mating mechanisms are necessary only when there is some real danger of interbreeding with related species. This is not always the case on islands. Dabbling ducks are a case in point.

The drakes of many surface-feeding ducks have

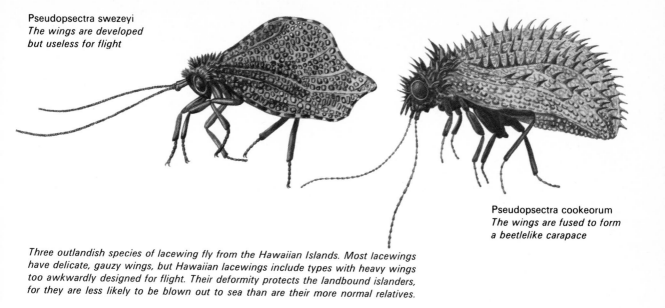

Pseudopsectra swezeyi
*The wings are developed
but useless for flight*

Pseudopsectra cookeorum
*The wings are fused to form
a beetlelike carapace*

*Three outlandish species of lacewing fly from the Hawaiian Islands. Most lacewings
have delicate, gauzy wings, but Hawaiian lacewings include types with heavy wings
too awkwardly designed for flight. Their deformity protects the landbound islanders,
for they are less likely to be blown out to sea than are their more normal relatives.*

bright plumage: for example, the male mallard has an iridescent green head, a white collar, a reddish-brown chest, and a metallic blue patch on each wing. In contrast, his mate is a mottled brown, camouflaged for her job of incubating the eggs. We know that the distinctive dress of the drake helps the duck to make the right choice, and to mate with a male of her own species. Likewise, the female's speculum (wing patch) is like a national flag, and the drake will tend to court only ducks that show a matching flash of color. Color identification is especially important on mainland areas, where pairing often takes place in the autumn when wetlands are full of mixed flocks of closely related ducks such as pintail, gadwall, and black duck—all capable of intermating with mallard. On remote islands, there may only be one kind, as there is for instance, on Hawaii and on Laysan. In appearance, the drakes are very different from the bright birds of the mainland, because they have lost their gaudy colors and look like females. On Laysan and Hawaii the ducks have no confusing choice to make because they are confronted with only the drakes of their own kind. The selection pressure for maintaining colorful plumage is lifted, and camouflaged drakes are at no disadvantage when it comes to mating, so the bright breeding plumages have been lost. The same is true of many other species. Gadwall have reached Fanning Island, south of Hawaii; pintail have colonized Kerguelen and Crozet islands in the southern Indian Ocean; and chestnut-

breasted teal have settled on Auckland Island, south of New Zealand. In becoming islanders, all the drakes have become duck-colored. This phenomenon is fairly widespread among island birds. Ducks also show some changes that survival on their island havens has favored.

Most island ducks are much smaller than their mainland ancestors. This is hardly coincidence, and must mean that reduced weight is a product of natural selection. Remote islands are often poor in the foods that mainland ducks eat, and such conditions favor the duck that can keep its options open, and cope best with transitory shortages. This means being small, and unspecialized in feeding habits. Although most of the oceanic island ducks are derived from freshwater dabblers, many seek food in salt water as well, and take more insects and other invertebrates than their ancestors did. Thus, the fact that the Kerguelen pintail has a much shorter beak than the northern pintail from mainland North America may be linked with the Kerguelen bird's crustacean-based diet. By far the most highly modified species is the mallard-derived Laysan duck, which feeds on insects, taking them largely from the land. Proportionately, it is much longer in the leg than the mallard, and so has a good stride. So, too, has the néné or Hawaiian goose, which inhabits the volcanic slopes of Hawaii. It has lanky legs, long toes, and much reduced webs because these are of no use to a walking goose. A different trend occurs in the chestnut-breasted teal. Teal from Australia can

101

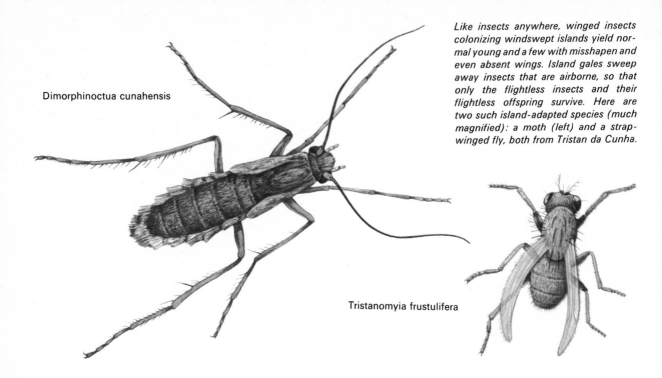

Dimorphinoctua cunahensis

Tristanomyia frustulifera

Like insects anywhere, winged insects colonizing windswept islands yield normal young and a few with misshapen and even absent wings. Island gales sweep away insects that are airborne, so that only the flightless insects and their flightless offspring survive. Here are two such island-adapted species (much magnified): a moth (left) and a strapwinged fly, both from Tristan da Cunha.

fly strongly, the New Zealand form less so, but the birds from Auckland Island have small wings, and are grounded.

Some of these characteristics shown by island ducks are worth examining in more detail, because they are shared by many other animals as well. Take small size, for instance.

On many islands there is a shortage of space. Large animals, particularly carnivores, need more room than small ones, so if there is a premium on space, then a species that needs a relatively small amount of elbow room for its living requirements will be at an advantage. On the Balearic Islands, off eastern Spain, the mammals are limited to mice, weasels, hedgehogs, and bats. Bears, wolves, and big deer have never been able to flourish there. In an earlier chapter we noted that jaguars have never thrived in Trinidad, although the smaller ocelot has, and Bali appears to be the smallest island to have supported a viable population of tigers.

Perhaps these facts help to explain why many islands support dwarf species. Cuba has its own kind of small deer. Celebes used to have its own pygmy brand of Asian elephant, about half the size of those on the mainland, but it is now extinct. A range of small cattle has been luckier. About 100 tamarau survive on the rugged Philippine island of Mindoro. Although small, tamaraus are not to be tampered with when they

have calves in attendance, because the parents have a reputation for being dangerously aggressive, and their size makes them nimble and highly maneuverable into the bargain. Tamaraus have cause to be defensive because they have been virtually wiped out by trigger-happy Filipinos. By far the smallest island buffalo lives on Celebes; indeed, the anoa is the smallest species of wild cattle in the world, the bulls standing only three feet high at the shoulder. By comparison, mainland Asia's domesticated water buffalo and the banteng, a big wild ox, are double the anoa's height at the withers. All of the dwarf island species need less land than their normal-sized relatives, and so the trend toward smallness may be an adaptation to reduced land space. This explanation is not so easy to swallow uncritically, however, in the case of such islands as Celebes. Although not the largest of islands, Celebes is a sizable landmass and largely covered with lush jungle. But other advantages go hand in hand with dwarfism. Small means more; in other words, many more anoas or tamaraus than big buffalo could fit into the respective island homes of the dwarf cattle. This has tremendous advantages for a species cut off on a relatively small landmass. Small populations that are confined to limited areas live in constant danger of being wiped out overnight by disease or by a temporary but disastrous food shortage. There is also the menace of too much breeding between closely related individuals. Variation is generated chiefly by outbreeding, and variety is the fodder of evolution. A population of highly inbred beasts all genetically similar has reduced its potential for change, and that is an invitation to extinction if conditions alter—a fact that holds true for wild and domestic animals. Admittedly, we know that the pharaohs practiced inbreeding with success, producing a whole line of very talented and beautiful people; but as a long-term strategy for survival, breeding within the family tends to give rise to such disadvantages as reduced fertility and lack of vigor. These dangers are magnified in island communities, and can best be guarded against by developments that favor large numbers of individuals, if necessary at the expense of individual bulk. Thus on Celebes many herds of small anoa will perhaps survive better than a few herds of big oxen.

Nothing seems more absurd than a bird with wings too tiny for flight, yet flightlessness is part of many birds' and insects' total commitment to island life. We might usefully start to explore this strange fact by asking why animals should fly at all; after all, active flight is a very energy-consuming activity. Although flying may be fun to us, creatures do not career through the air simply for pleasure. Winging away from trouble, particularly from earthbound enemies, has been a major use for flying. Many animal aeronauts also catch their food in the air, or need to fly to their food, which may be located on fragile branches on the outermost tips of tall trees. But there are often very good reasons for island-based birds and insects abandoning flight.

On islands, flying creatures may be at a positive disadvantage. Some islands are windswept all the year, and being caught up in gale-force winds is a serious business if your land base is a small speck in the middle of an inhospitable ocean. A moth and a fly that have both lost their wings live on Kerguelen Island, which has a very fresh climate, to say the least. Having colonized Kerguelen—itself a chance in a million—the species' winged ancestors found their best hope for survival with those individuals that took to the air only reluctantly. Natural selection eventually weeded out all but totally flightless flies and moths. As their name suggests, the insects called lacewings have large and diaphanous wings, but on Hawaii there are species with heavy, almost grotesque, wings that

A lack of natural enemies on its island home helps to explain why the kagu has almost lost the power of flight. This long-legged relative of the cranes and rails lives in the mountain forests of New Caledonia, situated to the east of Australia.

Guam rail, a species from Guam Island in the western Pacific. Rails are usually reluctant fliers, and many weak-winged members of their family lost the ability to fly after colonizing predator-free islands where flight was no longer needed.

are useless for flight. This deformity is a subtle form of protection because it means that the wind that ferried their forebears in, cannot whisk these lacewings away to almost certain death in the depths of the Pacific. On Tristan da Cunha and Gough Island there is a strap-winged fly that flies no more, and another species on Campbell Island, south of New Zealand, has no wings at all. On the Galápagos Islands there lives a grasshopper that only hops, although its progenitor probably flew in on functional wings a long time ago. Selection pressures favoring flightlessness must be quite severe in places, because the loss of wings can occur very rapidly. It took a group of pearly underwing moths a mere 450 years to become landbound. This winged species was introduced to Gough Island that long ago, and today its descendants are small and wingless, hardly looking like moths at all, and are classified as a separate species.

Small land birds that readily take wing are also in danger of being blown out to sea, but their island homes may be free of enemies, so that a major force driving them into the air is removed. Many island birds are weak fliers, Darwin's finches, for example. Cranes are strong fliers, but the kagu, a relative of the cranes that lives on New Caledonia, is scarcely airworthy. Some of the Mascarene Islands, east of Madagascar, had herons that could merely flap their wings when flustered. The Gough Island rail can just get off the ground by fluttering, although it is descended from the American purple gallinule, which is a good aeronaut. On New Zealand, a couple of water hens have forsaken flight. The better-known of the two is the takahe or *Notornis*, once thought to be extinct. A population of these chicken-sized birds lives in the South Island, among tussocky wetlands high up on the Murchison Range above Lake Te Anau. The other water hen is the weka, a nocturnal bird that lives in densely forested country. Island-living rails show all the stages between those that can fly and those that have evolved small, obsolescent wings. For example, the Aldabra land rail can just fly if hard pressed, whereas rails from Inaccessible Island in the Tristan da Cunha group have to run for their lives. Of course, under natural circumstances in their predator-free island they would not have to do that, which is precisely why they had no need of flight. The St. Stephen's Island wrens of New Zealand gave up flight too soon, and did not bargain for a lighthouse being built

in the middle of their predator-free patch. When one of the lighthouse keepers decided to keep a cat, the pet grew fat on the defenseless little green birds, which became extinct almost overnight. Dodos took a little longer.

The dodos, from the Mascarene Islands of Mauritius, Réunion, and Rodriguez, now represent all that is degenerate, defunct, and stupid. This must have been the impression of the Portuguese navigator Pedro de Mascarenhas, who gave his name to the island group that he reached in 1513. His crew conceivably saw hundreds of these incredible, ugly birds, which had pathetically small wings, and curly tufts for tails, and were tame beyond belief. The Portuguese used the word *doudo* ("simpleton") to christen these doomed avian morons. Less than 200 years later, dodos were extinct. There are skeletons in New York City and Washington, D.C., the British Museum possesses a foot, a head is in Copenhagen, and a small fragment in Prague—sad trophies of our mindless destruction of the largest and most interesting of the dodos.

Yet the dodos and their solitaire cousin illustrate another interesting effect of what happens when evolution goes unchecked by the struggle of competition. Dodos were nothing more than great, fat, flightless pigeons that found temporary peace in the Mascarenes. Without enemies, they had become earthbound and they enjoyed rich food resources untapped by native mammals. Over the course of time, the birds became large enough to occupy the ecological niches that would normally have been taken up by some kind of herbivorous mammal.

On lusciously vegetated oceanic islands, there are many vacant ecological niches. Terrestrial mammals are poorly represented in such places because of their difficulty in crossing large stretches of sea, and so their role in the community is often taken by other kinds of animals. Herbivorous giant tortoises on the Galápagos Islands, Aldabra, and Madagascar made a grand living because of the absence of native mammals. In some Indonesian islands Komodo dragons (giant monitor lizards) take over the role normally occupied by big cats. Birds have sometimes taken over the role of grazing and browsing mammals. There were a number of such birds in Madagascar, where hippos and forest hogs were the only big herbivorous mammals somehow to make the sea crossing from Africa. Some of these

The takahe is a big, flightless water hen that lives in narrow mountain valleys on New Zealand's South Island. Its brilliant green-blue plumage and red frontal shield make the takahe a handsome, if ungainly, bird. But what is most remarkable is the survival of this landbound species in spite of predatory stoats and weasels, and its rediscovery in 1948, just 50 years after its supposed extinction.

Madagascan birds grew very tall indeed.

The Europeans' first inkling of big birds in faraway places came from the famous Arabic collection of Eastern tales called *The Thousand and One Nights*. In one of the stories, Es-Sindibad of the Sea, more commonly called Sindbad the Sailor, told of a gigantic white bird called the ruhk, which lived "on a beautiful island abounding with trees bearing ripe fruits, where flowers diffused their fragrance, with birds warbling and pure rivers." He mistook an egg of this bird for a great white dome and looked vainly for a door leading inside. Unfortunately the egg got broken, and the pair of parent ruhks took revenge by dropping stones on Sindbad's ship and sinking it. This they easily accomplished because, from the accounts of Sindbad, and, later, of the Venetian explorer Marco Polo, ruhks were designed for feeding on elephants, which they killed efficiently by raising them aloft and smashing them onto the ground. Marco Polo was branded a liar, only good for tall stories. There the tale rested until France claimed Madagascar in the 17th century and French colonists began reporting tales of colossal birds' eggs used by the natives as water casks. It seemed increasingly likely that the eggs were laid by "ruhks" and that Madagascar was Sindbad's "beautiful

Birds colonizing New Zealand adapted to fill roles elsewhere taken by other birds or by mammals. The kakapo (above), a big, flightless parrot, plays the part of a deer by chewing ferns. The kea (below) evolved a cruelly hooked beak and became the parrot's carrion-eating answer to ravens, kites, and vultures.

island." However, fancy must have embroidered the facts of the legendary ruhk. The "fearsome" birds that had spawned the fable and laid the outsize eggs did not eat elephants, but gorged themselves on grass; they could not fly; and they had been wiped out by immigrant hunting men several hundred years ago. When alive, they had been none the less impressive.

Three kinds of elephant birds, to give them their modern popular name, are known from bones and eggs found on Madagascar. They must have looked rather like giant emus, although they were totally unrelated to them, being placed in their own family, the Aepyornithidae ("high birds"). The largest may have stood 10 feet tall, weighing nearly 1000 pounds. Flocks of these heavily built birds must once have wandered across the open areas of Madagascar, cropping the rich grass like so many avian cattle. They were the culmination of a trend for increasing size that so often happens where food abounds and competition and predation are excluded. There are in fact fairly precise upper limits to the size of muscle-powered flying creatures, so if

A kiwi with its egg (one quarter of the hen bird's size, and comparatively the largest egg laid by any bird). Three species of these primitive, flightless birds as large as chickens inhabit New Zealand. Kiwis are the sole living relatives of the extinct giant moas, which stood twice as tall as a man.

natural selection favors the retention of flight for some reason or other, then birds rarely get beyond the weight of swans. Once this restriction has been lifted, species can go on growing to exploit the advantages of bulk, providing the island is large enough to support them, as Madagascar certainly was. Large animals are more efficient at utilizing food than small ones, taking in comparatively less for their bulk; a big bird may also have the advantage over smaller rivals when it comes to fighting over food or mates. And if, suddenly, predators should appear on the scene, big birds may be able to run faster than smaller individuals, and keep ahead of the danger. The strategy seems to have worked for ostriches and a handful of big flightless birds that have survived in South America and Australasia, but it failed miserably on the arrival of mankind on Madagascar and also in New Zealand, where an astonishing array of giant birds likewise evolved in the absence of dangerous enemies and stiff competition from mammals.

New Zealand is, in some ways, very similar to Madagascar. It has been a world apart for 190 million years. Separating from the nearest continent long before mammals evolved, New Zealand became a place dominated by a dynasty of birds. The forests acquired a host of unique wattle birds, of which the lately extinct huia was an incredible example, cock and hen possessing complementary beaks for getting the grubs of longicorn beetles out of trees. Pigeons and doves reached New Zealand, with a couple of owls, two diurnal birds of prey, and a few warblers, flycatchers, wrens, and honeyeaters. Parrots also took up residence and produced some strange kinds indeed. The kea developed a cruel beak like a meat hook, took to the mountains, and became the parrot's answer to the carrion-eating raven. Another parrot became large, flightless, and nocturnal, and made a living chewing ferns; the kakapo, as it is called, occupies an ecological niche suspiciously like that of a small deer or rabbit. Several species of skulking, secretive rails also evolved in New Zealand. There were also a jumbo-sized swan and goose, both incapable of taking to the air. Most magnificent of all, however, were the moas.

These birds were probably on the decline long before the first Polynesians set foot in New Zealand, disturbing the peace and reducing most of the moas to piles of bones. It is chiefly from the remains of kitchen middens and natural graveyards in caves and swamps that zoologists have pieced together what moas must have looked like. All were specialized for keeping their feet firmly planted on the ground, and had lost their wings. Between 20 and 30 species of moas have so far been described from subfossil remains, and some were very big indeed. *Dinornis maximus* ("greatest of the terrible birds") was the giant of them all, with legs like those of a cart horse, a cow's appetite for grass, and a small head carried 10 to 13 feet off the ground. This species weighed only half as much as Madagascar's bird titan but was still three times as heavy as a man. There is evidence that a few of these big birds were alive at the turn of the 16th century; the remains of some are so fresh and well preserved that the gizzard contents can

be identified. Not only berries, seeds, and grass were eaten, but the gizzard also held up to $5\frac{1}{2}$ pounds of stones, probably as millstones for grinding the seeds. In ecological terms these moas were New Zealand's big game, which browsed and grazed the steppes and forests.

It is a shame that no giant moa remained by 1769 when the naturalist Joseph Banks began to sail along the New Zealand coast in Cook's ship *Endeavour*. People love to dream of finding lost worlds inhabited by prehistoric monsters, however, and there was no shortage of moa-seeking expeditions in the 19th century. The explorers, looking for 10-foot-tall birds, failed to find even any turkey-sized species, at least one of which undoubtedly still lived. This was the South Island's bush moa, and it survived until about the year 1880. Mrs. Alice McKenzie did not miss the individual that appeared then, when she was sitting on some sand dunes around Martin's Bay. She was surprised to see a large bird standing close to her, but not too surprised to note that it was $3\frac{1}{2}$ feet tall, and had dark bluish plumage, big bulging eyes, and broad beak, and powerful scaly legs as thick as her wrist. Perhaps it was the last of the bush moas. None has been seen since. There is, however, one surviving relative—the kiwi—that gives us a glimpse, though a poor one, of the great moas. The kiwi escaped the fate of its larger cousins because it made itself scarce by day, coming out only at night to probe in the forest litter for worms, using its long beak, sensitive to taste at the tip. The kiwi also has the distinction of laying an egg one quarter the size of its body, comparatively the largest for any bird. After laying her egg, the hen leaves the business of brooding it to her mate, while she recovers and replenishes her resources.

We turn now to a very different group of flightless birds. Without the safety of islands, it is doubtful whether a family of oceanic aeronauts resembling the shearwaters would have lost their long slim wings 60 million years ago to produce penguins. Penguins have traded the power of flying in air for skill in "flying" underwater. If they needed their wings to escape the gnashing teeth of mammals such as foxes, coyotes, or bears, then the evolution of water wings would have been impossible, because the engineering demands of flight and swimming are to some extent incompatible. Small auks manage to use their wings for both purposes, but Brünnich's murre, 18 inches in length, seems to have reached the size limit for wing-propelled seabirds that can also fly. Beyond this size, wings for flying must be so large and flexible that they cannot operate efficiently under water. Only one auk species passed the size barrier, and that was the great auk (the "penguin" of the auk family), utterly incapable of flight, but undoubtedly an excellent underwater mover. The Galápagos cormorant is also a large, underwater fisherman with atrophied wings; but this species, like its airborne cousins, paddles itself along with webbed feet. Penguins, in size, take over where the auks leave off. The smallest of these birds of the Southern Hemisphere is the Australasian little blue penguin, which reaches 16 inches, whereas the Antarctic emperor penguin, the largest living species, reaches 48 inches. Penguin flippers are adapted for providing powerful thrust in dense water; they are rigid, supported by broad flat wrists and finger bones, and, when skulled up and down, can propel penguins through the water at up to 20 knots to intercept fish and the shrimplike creatures called krill. During the breeding season, penguins base themselves on islands, often in rookeries containing millions of birds.

Such wildlife cities can exist only in areas free from fierce predators. For this reason, a globe-trotting traveler will find that many oceanic island sanctuaries are much sought after as breeding sites and nurseries. He will see beaches that have been turned into seal slums or turtle hatcheries, cliffs converted into auk high-rise tenements, soil honeycombed into shearwater ghettos, and flat spaces so densely covered in squatting seabirds that it is impossible to put a foot down between their lunging beaks. Laysan Island holds great attractions for 10 million seabirds of 23 different species. At times a selection of terns, tropic birds, boobies, and shearwaters is nesting at an unbelievable density of 8200 birds per acre, to make Laysan one of the most spectacular nesting colonies in the world.

On the continents, healthy competition from a host of land-based insects and vertebrate predators has kept crabs firmly in the sea. But on islands, chiefly in the Indian and Pacific oceans, these crustaceans have adapted to life on land, where they could exploit food resources that normally would have been commandeered by

Little blue penguin, a member of the world's smallest penguin species, off Philip Island east of Australia. Penguins are flightless but survive by their superb swimming ability and by nesting upon island sites free from terrestrial predators.

other animals. That crabs should live on land is amazing enough in itself, but that a monstrous hermit crab should climb trees like a monkey is a marvelous testament to the fact that, in the long run, evolutionary processes can accomplish almost anything. This so-called robber crab is the most romanticized of all crustaceans, on account of its habit of climbing up coconut palms. Whether or not robber crabs actually pick the fruit remains a point for debate. There is no doubt about their liking for coconut meat, and their ability to gain access to the pulp. A fully grown robber crab measures one yard across and possesses incredible strength. Tin crates, wired down for added security, or boxes of 1¼-inch-thick timbers are not strong enough to keep a robber crab imprisoned, and not surprisingly, because this beachcomber needs strength to appease its appetite for nuts. Robber crabs are powerfully built, with muscular pincers that operate as both wrenches and hammers. Like most shore crabs, this species is a carrion feeder but will take almost anything edible, especially the coconuts that abound on the beaches and beneath the palms. A crab opens a coconut by first removing the fibrous husk fiber by fiber, then hammering the region around the "eyes" until it has made a hole large enough to admit a slender claw to scoop out the white meat. It is hard work, and by all accounts robber crabs favor an easy living, feeding on softer fruits or coconuts that have already been gnawed open by rats or split by falling. Sometimes the crabs give the coconuts a little encouragement to break open by carrying them aloft and dropping them. One robber was seen to repeat the process 10 times before its coconut cracked on a stone.

Both land crabs and robbers have become extensively modified both in their structure and in their life-support systems to enable them to survive out of the sea. The ancestors of robber crabs were conventional hermit crabs, which have an advantage over normal crabs insofar as they shelter inside the shells of sea snails, a fact that helps to keep them moist out of water. Robber crabs retrace their evolutionary footsteps during the course of their lives, because, when they first emerge from the sea, the young protect the vulnerable soft rear parts of their bodies by tucking them inside snail shells. These they discard as they grow large and tough-skinned. The adult robber crab's armor is not only stout enough to withstand a fall from the top of a tree, but also

Frigate birds nesting on Laysan Island, a Hawaiian haven where 10 million seabirds annually raise their young. Safe from landbound predators, fish-catching seabirds teem on favored islands. Their success in turn has favored the evolution of the frigate birds— aerial pirates that not only catch their own fish but force other seabirds to disgorge their prey and then snatch it up in mid-air.

helps to seal moisture inside the body, because drying out is one of the dangers always facing a crustacean on land. Their habit of spending the hot days in burrows, coming out only at night, helps the robber crabs to conserve water. Even so, most terrestrial crustaceans tend to lose moisture fast, but they have evolved a high tolerance to desiccation, some being able to lose 79 per cent of their body weight by evaporation and live. By drinking, they can rapidly replace what they have lost. Each night robber crabs visit the sandbars for a drink of sea water to top up their body fluids. Their "kidneys" or green glands, which open at the base of the antennae, have become adapted for concentrating "urine" in the interests of water economy. By day their gills are no longer bathed in water, however, and this has posed something of a problem for land-living crustaceans. The ghost crabs that scamper across tropical beaches and the colorful fiddler crabs have gill chambers that are built like tanks and can thus hold supplies of sea water. The fluid prevents the gill leaflets from congealing, and air is constantly bubbled through the chambers, so keeping the respiratory system functioning on land. Robber crabs have become even more highly modified for breathing air; the upper part of each

The monstrous land crabs of tropical islands are proof that evolution can produce almost anything in the absence of normal competition for survival. Left: colossal robber crab shinning up a coconut palm on a Fijian island. Above: robber crab on Aldabra proving that its kind can actually carry coconuts.

gill chamber has been converted into a lung, but the lower part of the chamber still retains small gills.

The changes in design have left robber crabs high and dry, however, because their gills are now so small that they are unable to take up enough oxygen from the sea. If immersed for too long, robbers drown!

The sense organs, too, have become adapted to operating in air; the antennae—organs of touch, which are so important in the sea—assume less importance in land species, which rely much more upon their eyes. Land crabs are also much swifter and more purposeful than their marine relatives, and doubtless possess a more sophisticated nervous system for controlling locomotion. In one important respect, however, land crabs are still tied to the sea, because the females must cast their eggs into the waves. In the sea, the eggs hatch almost immediately into tiny planktonic larvae (also called *zooae*), which spend a month or more drifting and feeding in the ocean currents. This explains the widespread distribution of land crustaceans such as robber crabs throughout the remote corners of the Indo-Pacific.

Seclusion is the gift of islands. The remoteness that gave the crabs a chance to become land-lubbers, and the seabirds of Laysan improved odds of rearing their chicks, is also responsible for allowing the tiny fruit fly that originally drifted in on the wind to generate its own unique populations. On islands cloistered from the rough and tumble of the outside world, evolution is given its head, and richness is created from the few individuals that manage to reach the remote shores. Darwin noticed this on the Galápagos Islands, tussled with his conscience for nearly 20 years, and finally published his theory of the way in which life had developed on our planet. Suddenly, man's ideas of his place in the universe and of his relationship to all other living things were turned upside down. This change gave, and still gives, mankind much food for thought. Visitors to islands have on the whole been less thoughtful than Darwin, however, and more concerned with their own survival. To them, islands were crowded with creatures that "God made . . . for the sustenance of man." Islands were supermarkets placed on the ocean highways, where the food was free. There was no shortage of takers, ready to plunder and exploit the oceanic paradises.

Islands Exploited

It is no use looking for Elugelab Island any more. This was one of the Marshall group, midway between the Hawaiian archipelago and the Philippines. Elugelab was formed slowly out of the affair between coral polyps and their algal partners, but its death was quick and dramatic, because the island was chosen by the United States Government to experience a mere spark of the kind of power that drives the sun. On 1 November 1952 the peace of the western Pacific was shattered, and Elugelab was smashed, cremated, and scattered high into the stratosphere by the incandescent inferno of the first hydrogen bomb. When the fireball dispersed, the dust settled, and the sea rolled in to fill the crater, an island had been obliterated from the face of the world. This violent destruction must be the ultimate in man's exploitation of islands. Luckily, our treatment of these places has not always been so vicious. Nevertheless, our relationship with islands has all too often been scarred by greed and desecration in which near-paradises have been turned into graveyards.

Despite the destruction we shall later describe, people who actually settled on islands, particularly small islands, occasionally came to terms with the wildlife communities, and exploited them in a sensible way so as to promote the long-term survival of hunted and hunters.

Such an arrangement worked well on the St. Kilda group, off northwest Scotland. The islands scattered around the coast of Scotland are not the easiest of places to thrive on. Although the summer days are long, the sun is never high in the sky and always sparing with its warmth. Vegetation grows for only a short period each year, and so the pasture will not stand intensive cropping by sheep and cattle. Depression after depression, sweeping in from the Atlantic, sheds plenty of mist and rain onto the peaty islands, and the wind stunts and twists the trees that manage to take root. The only

A Faeroe Islands fowler leaving a rocky coast, birdcatcher's net borne upon his shoulder and puffins slung from his waist. Islanders who hunt for subsistence take only what they need from nature's larder. But visiting hunters killing purely for profit have slaughtered entire populations of island animals.

resources that make life tolerable in many of these grim places are fish and seabirds. The island group of St. Kilda was one such place. Today it is uninhabited except for a small military radar tracking post. More than 100 people used to live on Hirta, the main island. Hirta is difficult to reach by sea, because of great cliffs that plummet into the Atlantic, and storms that frequently make a beach landing dangerous, if not impossible. Such places have to be self-contained, and the populations have to come into balance with the resources their island homes have to offer. The St. Kildans had a diet of fish, mutton, milk, and seabirds and their eggs. Seabird colonies can provide free, abundant, and nourishing food providing the harvest is a calculated one, leaving enough healthy adults and young to make up for old birds that will die before the next breeding season. By trial and error, people who depend upon seabird resources have found that they can take all of the first crop of murre (guillemot) eggs, because the birds quickly lay replacements. They can also wring the necks of up to half of the fat young birds without jeopardizing the size of the colonies.

The St. Kildans were a hardy race of fowlers until 1930, when they were resettled on the Scottish mainland. Each person ate on average one bird a day every day of the year, mostly fulmars, gannets, and puffins. Between 1829 and 1929, when there were up to 130 people on Hirta, an average of 115 fulmars per person per year was taken, mostly fat, young birds sitting on the breeding ledges during early August. Bird-catchers probably harvested about one half of the reproductive output of the St. Kilda fulmar population. The stacks to the north of St. Kilda are the breeding sites of about 17,000 pairs of gannets, and about 5000 young were taken for the pot, well within the breeding potential of the colony. Puffins, like penguins, are popular favorites among seabirds, but that did not stop the St. Kildan fowlers killing more of them than any other species. They were often captured in vast numbers by women, for their flesh and feathers. In 1894, more than two tons of feathers came from a catch of close to 90,000 birds. These were dragged from their nests, snared by horse-hair nooses strung out on their favorite roosting grounds, or skillfully knocked out of the air by long stout poles.

Although the bird-based St. Kildan economy has now ceased, fowling is still a vital operation in Iceland and the Faeroes. The puffin is still the most important bird to the Faeroese, who deftly scoop up flying puffins on *fleygastongs*, which look like elongated lacrosse nets. Working quickly by a busy flight line close to a cliff face, a man can sometimes catch as many as 900 puffins a day, although one quarter of that would be a creditable number. Braised with thick gravy, served with boiled potatoes, and sweetened with sugar and jam sauce, the puffin makes a handsome dish. The common murre is less satisfactory, and yet the Faeroese fowlers kill about 100,000 a year, and take several hundred thousand eggs, which they preserve for the winter in water glass. Once out of the nest, the young birds are still not safe. While swimming away from the cliff face, they are lured onto rafts and snared in nooses. Such are the methods by which ingenious hunters reduce the odds against catching their prey. But these hunters have restrained their greed. There is little doubt that they could take a greater toll of life, but there is next year to think about, and the year after that, and the long-term welfare of the fowlers' children to consider.

The real damage to island bird stocks is usually done by people with the mentality of frontiersmen, who plunder today, knowing—or hoping—that there will be new riches somewhere else to cash in on tomorrow. They have no need to stay, settle, and work out a strategy for survival. The great auk was an island casualty of marine-frontiersmen.

Great auks resembled razor-billed auks, and reached up to a man's thigh when standing upright. From the days of the Vikings, ships seeking provisions sought these creatures, which they found conveniently flightless, absurdly confiding, and massed in vast breeding colonies around Iceland and Newfoundland. One such auk city stood on Funk Island, 40 miles east of Newfoundland. It is a grim, gray, granite rock a quarter of a mile long, half a mile wide, and as tall as a house. Yet it was a welcome sight to mariners for centuries, because of the millions of great auks and other seabirds that made it their breeding quarters. So significant was Funk Island that it was one of the first places to be named in the New World, being boldly marked as *Y-dos-aves* on the 1505 Pedro Reinel map. During the great age of exploration Funk Island started to receive some quite distinguished European visitors. Sir Walter Raleigh's half brother, Sir Humphrey Gilbert, landed there. So did Jacques Cartier, credited with the discovery of Canada. Cartier noted: "This island is so exceedingly full of birds that all the ships of France might load a cargo of them without one perceiving that they had been removed." And that is virtually what happened, because the great auks of Funk Island victualed the fishing fleets of Spain, France, and England stationed in the vicinity of the Newfoundland Banks during the 16th and 17th centuries. Writing about the importance of the auks in 1622, Richard Whitbourne commented: "God made the innocencie of so poor a creature . . . such an admirable instrument for the sustentation of man." In this, the great auks were so obliging that the stately birds could be driven aboard boats by means of planks until so many were loaded that the sea was lapping the gunwales. By the 18th century, however, the slaughter had become a systematic massacre as the Newfoundland merchants got into the act. By 1785 there were still millions of great auks on Funk Island, but the end was only 15 years away. Several crews of men were living all summer in the stinking seabird colonies for the sole purpose of killing for feathers. The great auks were headed into stone compounds, and later thrown into cauldrons of boiling water to loosen their downy breast plumage. As there was no wood on the island, the great auks' fat bodies were used as fuel to keep the fires aflame. Meanwhile, salted great-auk flesh was being sold in Newfoundland as a substitute for cheap pork, and some was used to tempt the cod to bite on fishermen's hooks. By 1800, only moldering bones and rotting feathers were left. The goose had been killed along with its golden eggs.

Why worry, however, if other great-auk rookeries still offered rich pickings? Some did, for a few more years, but breeding colonies on the Orkneys, Shetlands, Faeroes, and St. Kilda had been exterminated by the turn of the century, and the hunters turned to where the last great auks lived on a couple of islands off Iceland. Fate was not on the auks' side, because their most inaccessible, and thus safest, stronghold sank beneath the waves in a series of volcanic explosions in the 1830s, leaving only Eldey—another unpromising place, because Eldey means Fire Island. Here, though, it was not the fire that the auks had to worry about, but the Icelandic fishermen, who pursued the last few with undiminished fervor for the high rewards offered by collectors. The numbers taken speak for

Only the plinth it stands on betrays the fact that this lifelike great auk is actually dead and stuffed. In 1844—when two great auks were killed on Iceland's Eldey Island—this specimen became one of the 80 preserved skins that alone survived as reminders of an island species exterminated by man's greed. Before European hunters had begun their centuries-long massacre, these plump, flightless seabirds—"penguins of the north"—abounded on secluded North Atlantic islands. Their meaty bodies and flammable oil proved their undoing. Sailors killed most; hunters after collectors' rewards took the rest.

themselves: 24 were killed in 1830; 13 in 1833; 9 in 1834; and 3 in 1840. The end came four years later, when three men jumped ashore, spotted a pair, cornered them, throttled them, and smashed their single egg. The killers were well pleased, because they sold the two birds for about $18— a remarkably cheap price for the last of the great auks. Today, the few remaining skins change hands for thousands of dollars.

Profit has always been a powerful motive for those who have exploited islands, and this is best illustrated by the thorough way in which men pillaged the wildlife of the subantarctic. The discovery of the southern oceans and their islands was a reversal of the normal story of exploration, because those who sailed south went in search of a place clearly marked on their maps. Shown as an enormous continent covering the southern end of the world, and christened *Terra Australis Incognita* ("the Unknown Southern Land"), this suppositious landmass was a legacy of Greek armchair geographers. Voyage after voyage of unrewarded exploration drove the shores of this legendary continent farther and farther back toward the South Pole, and the wealth revealed by these journeys was not gold and silver, but skins, blubber, and meat.

The Portuguese were the first to round the southern tip of Africa and to get a hint of the wild wealth of the Southern Hemisphere. Bartholomeu Dias reached the Cape Coast in 1488, followed nine years later by his fellow-countryman Vasco da Gama. Both must have stumbled upon places such as Dassen Island, strategically placed to the south of Africa and teeming with strange birds that could not fly, but swam like fish and brayed like asses. They were jackass penguins, and the Portuguese must have been the first Europeans to set eyes upon such flightless seabirds, unique to the Southern Hemisphere. Doubtless the early explorers used Dassen and other Cape bird islands for victualing their ships. After their long, hot journeys through the equatorial doldrums, the sailors were probably tired, perhaps suffering from scurvy, and certainly scared·of what lay beyond. Here at least, on Dassen's scorching sandy back, they could

Magellanic penguins crowding a beach at Punta Tombo, southeast Argentina, recall scenes witnessed by early navigators rounding South America. Hungry explorers saw penguin islands as providential foodstores. Because penguins proved helpless on land, each ship's crew easily killed them by the thousand.

replenish their stores with fat jackass squabs (nestlings). We know that mariners who edged their ships around the storm-prone southern tip of South America stocked up with penguins. In 1520 Ferdinand Magellan discovered a winding channel (the Strait of Magellan) between the Atlantic and Pacific oceans. He saw not only the glow of Amerindian fires on the shores of Tierra del Fuego ("Land of Fire"), but also penguins closely related to the African jackass, and now named in his honor. In 1578 Magellanic penguins provided food for Francis Drake, who had sailed south in search of trade and plunder along coasts that the Spaniards and Portuguese claimed as their exclusive properties. He entered the Strait of Magellan and noted "such plentie of birds, as is scant credible to report." The words have a familiar ring, for Cartier had written similarly of great auks on Funk Island. Drake landed on a penguin island, since renamed Santa Magdalena,

and recorded that he found a "great store of strange birds which could not flie at all, nor yet runne so fast as that they could escape us with their lives; . . . and such was the infinite resort of these birds to these islands, that in the space of one day we killed no lesse than 3000."

The 16th century saw a great increase in traffic round the capes, and the penguin rookeries continued to sustain the seamen. In fact, without these conveniently placed seabird islands, many a voyage of exploration might have proved impossible. Mariners such as Sir Thomas Cavendish, who victualed his ship in 1587 on "three tunnes of penguins" from Santa Magdalena, clearly regarded the island wildlife as a sort of heaven-sent chandlery store. "These birds and seals seem to have been bestowed in quantity on those desolate shores, as resources in extremity to distressed voyagers."

In 1599 a storm blew Dirk Gerritsz, the captain of a Dutch boat, more than 300 miles south of Cape Horn, and he probably saw the snowy peaks of the South Shetland Islands, well south of the 60th parallel. By 1771 explorers had discovered Australia and New Zealand and learned that these were islands and not parts of the southern continent. As ships penetrated the cooler regions at the southern end of the earth, the shores of Terra Australis receded, but a host of islands was placed on the map. In 1772 the Frenchmen Marion Dufresne and Jacques Kerguelen-Trémarec discovered Marion Island and the Crozet Islands, and then came upon a green land that they hailed as the southern continent. Joyfully they called the place South France, and a year later returned with settlers and cattle, only to find that, far from flowing with milk and honey, "South France" was merely a desolate island set in a gray, cold ocean. Disgusted, they departed, saying they would rather live in Iceland. South France became Kerguelen Island.

It was Captain Cook of the British Navy who swept the southern continent beyond the 70th parallel and indirectly paved the way for the hunters who did the real damage to the wildlife communities of the subantarctic. James Cook was a solid, unpretentious man, the son of a Yorkshire laborer, who got his sea legs as a mate in Whitby colliers (ships transporting coal). He joined the Navy at the age of 27 as an able seaman, but rose in the ranks for his merit as a leader of men and his ability as a navigator. His charting of Newfoundland convinced the Admiralty of his potential, and at the age of 40 he was promoted to lead a series of ventures that were to make him one of the greatest explorers and navigators of all time. On his second ex-

Hunters clubbing fur seals to death on Lobos Island off Uruguay. Controlled killing keeps Lobos Island's fur seal population one of the largest in the Southern Hemisphere. But in the 19th century, unbridled slaughter for pelts and oil decimated far larger seal rookeries on some subantarctic islands.

pedition, begun in 1772, Cook must have felt particularly at home, because he sailed south to the edge of the Antarctic pack ice in a converted Whitby collier called *Drake*, but renamed H.M.S. *Resolution* so as not to upset the Spanish in the southern seas; it was no larger than a modern tug. Zigzagging across the Southern Ocean, he was moved by the grandeur of the scenery and the size of the icebergs, gorgeously translucent and shot with delicate shades of blue and green. He discovered the New Hebrides, New Caledonia, Norfolk Island, and icy South Georgia, "a savage and horrible country, not a tree to be seen, no shrub even big enough to make a toothpick." He nevertheless claimed it for Britain. Driven along by the Westerlies, he charted what we now call the South Sandwich Islands— a series of snow-covered peaks looming out of the Antarctic seas. The fact that Cook and his crew were the first to set eyes on land so far south meant little to him; he dismissed the grim place as the most horrible coastline in the world.

Other things captured Cook's attention, because the seas and the islands he visited seethed with wildlife. All the time, Cook's ship was surrounded by seals, and the oily vapor from whales' blowholes left a stench in the air. Seabirds of all kinds could be seen from the decks; petrels pattered across the waves, picking morsels from the surface, and great albatrosses weaved across the boat's wake. Where the men landed, they found elephant seals and southern fur seals ("sea bears") gathered in such masses that there was scarcely room to put a foot between the creatures. Penguins, or "jumping jacks," also jammed the beaches. The descriptions are familiar. The accounts are littered with such words as "incredible." On Staten Island, south of Cape Horn, *Resolution*'s crew put the seabirds and seals to good use, to make oil for the ship. This was a taste of things to come.

At the end of July 1775 *Resolution* dropped anchor in Plymouth Sound, having been away for three years and 18 days and having sailed the equivalent of three times around the world. Cook brought safely back with him all but four of his crew, and accounts of fabulous wildlife, something unexpected of those cold southern latitudes. Just as important for those who could see profit in penguins and seals, however, he also brought back accurate charts to make finding the creatures' island homes an easy business.

News of the magnificent new hunting grounds came at the right moment for the northern sealers, whose overhunted Arctic and subarctic sealing grounds were showing signs of running dry. During the late 1770s whaling and sealing fleets put out from Le Havre in France, Hull in England, and New Bedford and Nantucket in America, and raced to cash in on the Antarctic bonanza of skins and oil. South Georgia was one of the chief destinations because its beaches were a rendezvous for vast numbers of fur seals and elephant seals. There was a buoyant market for fur-seal pelts in Europe and China and the hunters began beating the pathetically tame fur seals to death with heavy clubs studded with nails. Small boats would lie offshore until sufficient seals had mustered on the beach, then the sailors would move in to cut off the seals' retreat, before rounding up the beasts for massacre. Those that did not succumb to one or two blows on the head were killed by the flensing knife. After a day's work the beach would be littered with evidence of the carnage: bodies, bones, entrails, and a mess of congealed blood. And one day's work saw a lot of action and a great toll of wildlife. The crew of a single ship in the South Shetland Islands would expect to kill 9000 seals in three weeks. There is a record of 60 men from two ships slaughtering no less than 45,000 seals during one season. As each pelt was worth a golden guinea back home, there can be little wonder that men caused the Antarctic Seas to run red. By 1791 no fewer than 102 vessels were collecting skins and oil from the Southern Ocean. No one knows how many seals they took. In less than 50 years, 1,200,000 fur-seal pelts reached the London market alone.

Once the fur seals had been exterminated, the sealers moved on to the sea lions, elephant seals, and penguins, boiling down their bodies for oil. On island after island, hunters exterminated rookery after rookery, killing almost every creature that was marketable. Moving south from New Zealand, the slaughterers had exploited the Antipodes, and Auckland, Campbell, and Macquarie islands by 1810. From South Georgia, sailors caused carnage on the exposed South Sandwich Islands and Bouvet Island. The South

The Resolution *and* Adventure *at Matavai Bay, Tahiti, painted by the landscape artist William Hodges in 1773 during James Cook's second visit to the island. Cook's favorable accounts of lush Tahiti attracted other Western visitors. By the 1800s Tahitians were suffering from imported alcohol, disease, and missionaries' attacks upon the sins of easygoing island life.*

Shetlands were rediscovered in February 1819, and soon after that, gangs from nearly 100 ships cleared the beaches. In four years, the South Shetland Islands had yielded 320,000 fur-seal skins and nearly 1000 tons of oil. By 1825 the islands were hardly worth another visit, such was the efficiency of the hunters. Indeed, by that time new hunting grounds were desperately needed, and some of the sailors—James Weddell and John Biscoe, for example—turned to explor-

ing and searched farther south. They discovered some new islands, but it soon became clear that no new riches lay beyond the known frontiers. The sealing bonanza was all over within a few decades of Cook's memorable voyages. Oiling gangs still worked intermittently throughout the 19th century on islands including Macquarie, Kerguelen, and Heard. When all-but-exterminated fur-seal populations started to recover, the hunters resumed the annihilation until

falling demand and other factors caused them to desist. But at least none of the cropped species followed the great auk into oblivion.

When Europeans opened up the oceans, wildlife was not the only sufferer. Island peoples also felt the impact of intruders from the north. In particular, Cook's accounts of what he had found in the Pacific played their part as a catalyst in the degradation of Polynesia.

On 13 April 1769 the *Endeavour* dropped anchor in Matavai Bay, and James Cook and his 100 seamen caught sight of what many of them must have viewed as paradise. They found a lush island, with bright green vegetation aflame here and there with frangipani blossoms and red hibiscus blooms, and highlighted by the little white blossoms of tiara Tahitis. Sparkling waterfalls provided fresh water, and everywhere groves of tall palms were laden with coconuts, and breadfruit trees displayed their wares like green Chinese lanterns. About 40,000 beautiful brown-skinned people lived there in Arcadian bliss. They had developed a life style and culture that promoted their long-term survival and had come to terms with the resources that their island had to offer. Unlike the Nantucket hunters who could afford to wipe out every seal on an island and move on, these islanders had nowhere else to go, and dared not overexploit their small world. The Tahitians and their food plants and animals had come into balance, and people here had evolved a cheerful society based upon primitive gardening and fishing. Tahitians cultivated coconuts, breadfruit, and bananas; they kept chickens, and had a taste for dogs and Polynesian rats; and they excelled in catching fish off the reefs.

To Cook's men it seemed an idyllic life, and yet there was more to it than lounging beneath the frangipanis. Overpopulation is always a danger where resources are limited, and the white intruders soon learned that drastic measures were taken to bring births into balance with deaths. Instead of preventing surplus babies arriving, Tahitians literally murdered a proportion of the newborn. And this was not the only way in which they helped to contain the population. Tribal wars—perhaps themselves a result of tension caused by a build-up of too many people—led to vicious killing, to which women and children fell victim along with the defeated warriors. Ritualistic sacrifices and cannibalism were also not unknown on overcrowded Polynesian islands. In those days, many a mariner's nightmare was being shipwrecked in New Zealand and served up well cooked at a Maori feast. On Easter Island there is clear evidence that internal conflict, the development of war games, and cannibalism were

Monolithic stone heads on remote Easter Island in the southern Pacific Ocean. The unique island culture that gave rise to these giant figures died out in the 1800s and early 1900s—a victim of its contact with "civilized" Western peoples who introduced slave raids, epidemic smallpox, and missionizing.

all related to the mounting pressure of a rising population upon a limited food supply. On that island, mammalian meat was in short supply, and so the people prized human flesh when it became available. In the Fiji Islands, however, population control was at least partly attempted through family planning. No self-respecting couple would have a baby each year; after the birth of a child, husband and wife kept apart for three or four years to avoid producing a number of children in quick succession.

Arrival of the first Europeans meant that the islanders had been touched by a dominant and domineering culture and were about to have their life style brutally changed, not necessarily for the better. Cook could see what was coming. He wrote in his journal: "It would have been far better for these poor people never to have known our superiority in the accommodations and arts that make life comfortable. . . ." The steady succession of European ships that followed Cook's brought all manner of undeniably useful goods, including guns and iron tools. But they also introduced potentially harmful products such as alcohol.

Soon Tahiti was a regular port of call for the Nantucket sailors and whalers plying their way between the markets in the north and the hunting grounds in the south. Almost overnight the islands became the haunt of an international bunch of tough seamen, brawling and lording it over the locals. In the 19th century, any thug with a couple of pistols could set himself up on a small island as a despot; and many did just that. Meanwhile, sickness spread by Europeans claimed scores of victims. Tuberculosis grew rife along with dysentery, smallpox, and venereal diseases; and the even, pearly teeth of the Tahitians were becoming black with decay caused by introduced European foods.

The Pacific islands and their peoples became the prized objects in a scramble. Politicians wanted the islands as colonies for their expanding empires; merchants valued them for trade; and, encouraged by stories of human sacrifices and sexual depravity, missionaries wished to claim the pagan souls of the natives for Christianity.

In 1795 the London Missionary Society was formed, and the members at once turned their evangelical zeal toward the Pacific. In March 1797 the *Duff* reached Matavai Bay after a nonstop voyage of 14,000 miles. Out stepped 39 people, including clergymen, butchers, weavers, and three wives with their children. The newcomers hated nudity, dancing, and sex—except for making babies—and came determined to clean up the island and to spread the gospel among the Tahitians. It was not a difficult task, because the islanders wished to become as much like their white visitors as possible, aping their manners and adopting their beliefs. The missionaries were clever enough to convert the ruling classes first; the rest then followed. By 1820, when the Russian explorer Thaddeus Bellingshausen landed, the Tahiti that Captain Cook had described was almost unrecognizable. Sacrificial murder and infanticide had gone for good. So had nudity; all who could afford it wore European-style clothes, and men and women had cut short their glossy black hair, which in the case of girls used to grow down to their waists. It was more sanitary when short, or so they were encouraged to believe. Likewise the missionaries discouraged tattooing, banned alcohol, condemned free love, and generally saw that Christian guilt supplanted lack of shame. Thus, in a mere decade or two, Pacific island cultures were being destroyed no less effectively than the animal communities way to the south. The parallels between the fates of man and beast were even closer on Easter Island, where the islanders' first encounter with white men was far from happy.

When the Dutch ship under Captain Jacob Roggeveen hove to on Easter Sunday of 1722, the goodwill befitting Christians on that festive day was hardly in the forefront of the minds of the crew. A well-aimed musket shot felled an inquisitive islander who had canoed out to meet the strange ship. Later, as the captain and some of his men were visiting, the edgy and trigger-happy Dutchmen fired into the watching crowd, wounding and killing more islanders. During the next 150 years the Easter islanders were to receive more lessons in how little their new visitors regarded life. In 1805 a North American schooner out of Connecticut arrived to take slaves for sea-lion hunting. After a bloody battle, 10 men and women were bound and taken aboard the *Nancy*. Between 1850 and 1862 Peruvian ships carried out such abductions on a grand scale. The islanders were lured onto the beach with flashy trinkets, and when a crowd had gathered, the Peruvians seized as many as possible and shot those who resisted. Their captors transported at least 1000 prisoners to

Peru's offshore Chincha Islands, where they were forced to mine guano—another island resource, and, as we saw earlier, one that seabird colonies abound in. Most of the kidnap victims died of disease or overwork, or simply pined to death. With free labor pressed into service from places such as Easter Island, it is little wonder that the enormous profits from guano financed Peru's whole national budget between 1849 and 1884. In time, other countries learned that Peru was using slave labor to scrape away the nitrogen-rich dung of the tens of millions of guanay cormorants, piqueros, and brown pelicans. But by then the Peruvian Government could afford to be generous. Under diplomatic pressure from France, about 100 survivors were shipped back to Easter Island, but too late for most of them, who died on the return voyage. Moreover, some of those who lived brought smallpox with them; a few years later the disease reached epidemic proportions and reduced the once-healthy Easter Island population of 4000 to a few hundred.

As a species, man is a meddler, altering island landscapes to suit his needs, redistributing animals and plants by choice, and transporting by accident a whole host of hangers-on such as house mice and sparrows that steal man's food supplies, shelter in his dwellings, and die out when he departs. No islands in the world show the impact of man's meddling more clearly than the islands of New Zealand.

When Captain Cook traveled to New Zealand, he put ashore chickens, geese, sheep, goats, and "Captain Cookers" (pigs). He was acting from the best of motives, thinking that the livestock would benefit not only the Maoris but also future generations of settlers. Unwittingly he was helping to destroy much of New Zealand's unique flora and fauna over the next century and a half. But the Maoris themselves had already started that process. These Polynesian hunters had exterminated the mightiest moas, and brought with them rats that had probably stowed away on their canoes. These rats belonged to the small and gentle species that had hitchhiked along with the human colonizers of the South Sea islands. When the *kiore*, or Polynesian rat, reached New Zealand, it was the island's first four-legged terrestrial mammal, and quickly spread. Despite the fact that the Maoris hunted the kiore for food, it grew common throughout the main islands. Being small, it probably did little harm to the tame, ground-dwelling birds.

But the same could not be said of its larger European cousins, the black and brown rats.

The black rat was undoubtedly the second of the three rats to get ashore in New Zealand, because, by the turn of the 18th century, this species infested trading ships. Some time later, big, aggressive brown rats traveled on boats bound for the South Seas, and, wherever they landed, found abundant food on which they prospered and multiplied. Crops, ground-nesting birds, and the small, docile, Polynesian rats all fell prey to these greedy rodents, which promptly replaced their Polynesian relatives throughout the mainland of New Zealand. Wherever brown rats reached seabird colonies, they plundered eggs and ate chickens alive in their nests, and their scavenging was devastating.

Meanwhile, European settlers were unleashing new animal horrors. Australian immigrants realized that the grassy Canterbury Plains on South Island's east coast could support huge numbers of sheep. The consequence of rearing merinos by the million proved disastrous for the ecology of the island. Sheep need pastures, and the easiest way of making succulent grass is to burn the countryside. Sheep farmers set aflame not only the tussocky plains, but also New Zealand's unique forests. Some of the fires raged so furiously that by night you could read fine print a mile away from the inferno. With the trees and shrubs, the feeble-winged quail and other grounded birds went up in flames. Baring the land produced soil erosion, followed by flooding during periods of rainfall, because once the bogs and humus-rich forest soils had been destroyed, the rainwater that these would have soaked up and held back poured into gullies and rivers. By 1871, about 10 million merinos were nibbling their way across the newly created grasslands. So were rabbits.

Settlers had been introducing rabbits into Australia for sport, and it was not long before people let some loose in game-deficient New Zealand. No one realized what a curse they would prove. During the 1860s, several importations from New South Wales took place, and in a decade or so, rabbits had got a grip on the land. With no effective competition and no major enemies, they multiplied far beyond the requirements of sport. In the Canterbury pastures, they poisoned the land with their urine and droppings, cropped the grass down to the roots, and riddled the dry hills with their warrens. As fast as shepherds created new pastures, rabbits overran them, leaving only dust and unpalatable weeds. Sheep farmers were angry. A Rabbit Nuisance Act was passed in 1876, but its provisions did little to reduce the rabbit population. "Import stoats, weasels, and ferrets to deal with the menace," the government was implored. It agreed.

Unfortunately, the consignments of ferrets and stoats that arrived found easier game than rabbits, and began wiping out the absurdly tame native birds, including tomtits and fantails. Only later did they turn to the rabbits, and then had no real effect on their numbers. But although rabbits could not be eliminated, at least dealers were able to cash in on the skins and meat. Even as recently as 1945, New Zealand exported nearly 18 million rabbit pelts. But the end was in sight, because a concerted effort at control by shooting, poisoning, and fumigation of warrens has so reduced the rabbit population that it does not threaten farming at present.

The rabbit provided a painful example of what can happen when man lets loose on an island a prolific species unrestrained by competitors and predators. The people who formed acclimatization societies cannot be blamed, however, because they could not have known of such ecological subtleties. Largely in order to make the place more like home, acclimatization societies tried introducing all manner of British and other birds and beasts into the New Zealand countryside from the middle 1800s. Not that there

Man's meddling has altered New Zealand wildlife out of all recognition. Before people arrived, bats were the islands' only mammals. Now many mammal species imported from around the world roam the land and devastate its vegetation. Below: sheep grazing on a New Zealand farm. To enlarge the pasture available to these invaluable food animals, farmers burned forests, thereby exposing soil to erosion. Below right: red deer on the South Island's west coast. Imported to provide sport, the red deer nibbled tree seedlings, thus preventing the regrowth of healthy forest. Right: opossum eating apple blossoms. New Zealanders shipped in opossums from Australia with a view to harvesting their pelts. As these marsupials multiplied, their favorite food plants got scarce.

2

3

4

8

7

3

9

4

4

5

6

1

2

6

9

5

3

7

8

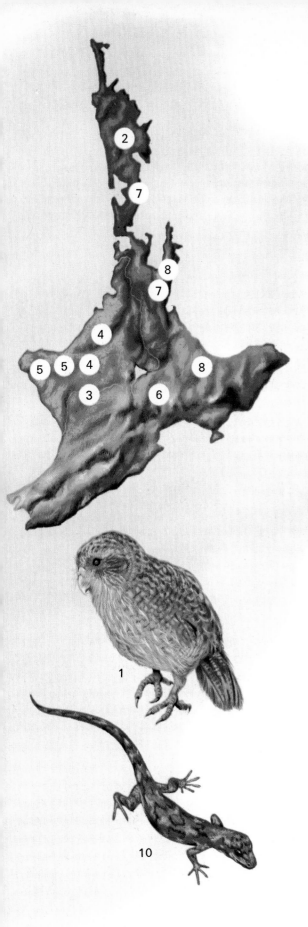

The Distribution of Endemic Animal Species on New Zealand

1	Kakapo	6	Skink
2	Kokako	7	Leiopelma
3	Mystacina	8	Tuatara
4	Kiwi	9	Kea
5	Wren	10	Gecko

Over the past 200 years the native creatures of New Zealand have been threatened by man's introduction of alien species. This diagram shows the present distribution of some of the native species. The gecko is found throughout New Zealand.

was much shortage of such imports anyway. Besides the mammal pests just described, wild cats, too, were busily destroying much of the native wildlife; and goats—some dating from the days of Cook—greedily ate their way across the uplands, reducing forest remnants to meadows of tussock grass. Undeterred by the ravages wrought by such animals, the acclimatizers began to import deer. In 1851 red deer arrived on South Island. They did not seem to increase in the forests as much as hunters would have liked, so for 50 years the acclimatization societies moved breeding stock in all directions, in the hope that fine heads would materialize in the gunsights. By the turn of the century they achieved their object, but already it was clear that by nibbling seedlings the red deer were preventing the regrowth of healthy forest. This was bad enough. But the societies had not stopped at red deer: fallow deer had followed in 1864, sambar in 1875, and sika deer a decade later. Moose, Virginian deer, wapiti, and Javan Sunda sambar deer all set foot upon New Zealand, although none established itself as well as the red deer. In 1907, men released chamois to graze (and erode) the high mountain slopes.

Deer place a great deal of grazing and browsing pressure on relatively low-growing forest vegetation. Brush-tailed opossums take their leafy meals from the tops of the trees. In Australia, these cat-sized marsupials do little damage, feeding chiefly on blue-gum foliage, and providing food for carnivores. In 1858 the New Zealanders thought that releasing these opossums into their "empty" forests and bushlands offered the promise of a rich crop of furs. But fortunes were never made on opossum furs in New Zealand. Under protection, the opossums spread and consolidated their position, until they became noxious pests by the middle of the 20th century. Opossums have their own likes and dislikes in foliage, and, where predators are missing, their selective feeding tends to eliminate plant species in order of palatability. These marsupials will attack orchards, and in one night a hungry family can gobble its way through a garden of prize vegetables and flowers. Apart from helping to ravage the New Zealand forests, brush-tailed opossums developed the annoying habit of climbing power-line posts and getting electrocuted by short-circuiting the supplies.

Originally New Zealand had no native mammals apart from bats, but by 1950 there were 29 kinds of mammals, all introduced from Asia, Europe, or America. The acclimatization societies also "enhanced" the variety of birds.

The birds that sang in the New Zealand spring were not to the liking of the early British colonists. They preferred the trilling of skylarks and the warbling of thrushes, to which their European ears were attuned. Before long it would have been hard to realize from the dawn chorus in the parks and woodlands around Christchurch that you were not indeed somewhere in southern England. Song thrushes, European blackbirds, hedge sparrows, skylarks, and various finches, along with rooks, starlings, pheasants, mallards, and little owls, were all released in a series of introductions from about 1864. Mynas, peafowl, doves, and chukor partridges were brought in from Asia. Canada geese and a couple of species of quail were imported from North America. Australian aliens were represented by kookaburras, black swans, two kinds of magpie, brown quails, and two parrot species—the eastern rosella and the white cockatoo. The sudden decline of native birds such as the brown teal, the red-crowned parrakeet, and the weka was perhaps due to the aliens' introduction of diseases to which the native birds were not immune.

Over the past 200 years, New Zealand has become an ecological mess. Much of its own flora and fauna has survived only in small pockets, or on some of the many offshore islands. The marvel is that so few species have been lost. During this period the huia was possibly the only forest species to become extinct. Stitchbirds and saddlebacks thrive on a few islands, although they no longer live on the mainland. The kakapo—a flightless parrot—is dangerously close to extinction. Shipwrecked sailors may have eaten the last of the Auckland mergansers, a

species not seen since 1905. Rats and cats still threaten colonies of mainland nesting seabirds such as the rare Westland petrel.

The havoc wrought upon New Zealand's wildlife by aggressive aliens is part of a worldwide pattern, as the following unpleasant instances all help to show. Although President Theodore Roosevelt declared Laysan Island in Hawaii a bird sanctuary in the early 1900s, someone deliberately introduced rabbits there, perhaps to profit from their skins. Unfortunately they virtually destroyed the vegetation and all but exterminated the unique Laysan finchbill and teal. By 1938 only about 1000 finchbills remained, at which point conservationists launched a campaign to rid the island of rabbits. Although the finchbill and the teal have recovered, action came too late for the Laysan reed warbler and Laysan rail. Luckily a few of the rails had been taken to neighboring Midway Island to give the species a chance. They certainly outlived their ancestors on Laysan, but became the victims of introduced rats about the end of World War II.

Meanwhile, at the end of World War I, a ship was wrecked off Lord Howe Island, east of Australia. Not all the rats on board drowned, and the descendants of those that swam ashore exterminated the Lord Howe white-eye, a fantail, a mountain starling, a thrush, and a flycatcher, all unique to the island. On Kusaie Island, in the western Pacific, more species disappeared. Two-pronged attacks by rats and cats have taken a great toll of flightless island birds such as rails. Tahiti has lost its red-billed rail. In various parts of the Pacific, the Chatham Island rail, the Chatham Island banded rail, the Samoan wood rail, and the Iwo Jima rail are all now defunct, as is also the flightless rail of Tristan da Cunha in the South Atlantic. Pigs and rats quickly eliminated the Tahiti sandpiper. The Bonin wood pigeon, collected on Nakondo Shima Island (south of Japan) in 1889 but never observed again, probably fell victim to feral cats. So did the crested Choiseul pigeon from an island in the Solomon group. Cats accounted for the Macquarie Island parrakeet, and for a unique shrew and two local rats on Christmas Island in the Indian Ocean.

Mongooses have a great reputation for clearing areas of unwanted vermin, and men have therefore released these fierce little hunters on a number of islands to clear them of rats and snakes. But the mongooses also took a high toll of harmless native birds, including the Hawaiian rail and

Rare island survivors of the depredations of man and his introduced animals. Right: subspecies of saddleback, a weak-winged forest bird that persists only on some of New Zealand's offshore islands. Saddlebacks hop and flit through the trees, seeking fruit, nectar, and insects. They belong to the wattlebirds and seem to have evolved from the primitive, crowlike stock that also gave rise to Australia's birds of paradise. Below: Laysan teal, one of the world's rarest species of ducks, photographed on its only home—tiny Laysan Island in the western Hawaiian Islands. This duck survived only thanks to the extermination of introduced rabbits that had destroyed much of Laysan's vegetation.

the bar-winged rail of Fiji. In the West Indies mongooses have exterminated burrowing owls and wrens from Antigua and Guadeloupe, the Jamaican pauraque (a night hawk), and a handful of strange shrews. Biological control is a subtle business that can often backfire.

No matter where you look, islands have been so messed around that it is hard to realize what they were like before man started interfering with them. When the first European explorers reached the Seychelles two centuries ago, they found hardwood forests teeming with strange birds and giant turtles; streams that harbored a freshwater crocodile of a kind never seen before; and shallow seas rich in the strange mammals called sea cows or dugongs. Nothing of that now remains on or

around Mahé, the largest island in the group.

Most of the Hawaiian Islands are now unrecognizable because of the impact of introduced species. Much of the flora you can see on the main island has been introduced in order to "improve" the local landscape. The native plants and some of the native animals now live only in high mountainous areas or on outlying islands. But some species, less sensitive to civilization, have actually profited from man's interference. A few of the native honeycreepers have exploited man-made habitats and are probably more numerous now than they were before man arrived in

African giant snails emerging in rain. More than a century ago, such snails found their way by boat to India. Some later invaded Formosa and Polynesian islands far out in the Pacific.

Hawaii. But other honeycreepers have had their niches usurped by alien birds or have been decimated by diseases spread by mosquitoes such as *Culex fatigans*—a night-biting mosquito thought to have arrived from a ship as early as 1826. To the honeycreepers, the tangle of influences means that only about one third of the species and island subspecies stand a chance of long-term survival.

The speed and extent of modern travel makes the problem of accidental introductions much more of a headache to conservationists. Small creatures that might never have endured a slow sailing-boat journey now whisk across oceans unharmed in the holds of jet aircraft, or travel comfortably in speedy ships. The Argentine ant is one such example that finally reached Hawaii. This particularly fierce and implacable invader arrived in New Orleans, Louisiana, in 1891, in ships bringing coffee from Brazil. From the deep South, the ants marched across the United States with a little help from trains and trucks, invading houses and orchards, raiding stores of food, robbing bees of honey, waging wars of annihilation on local ants, and generally being a nuisance. From California it was not long before Argentine ants were infesting quarantined cargoes being sent to Hawaii, and in spite of efforts to block them, some had arrived on Oahu by 1940. The ant situation was already confused enough on that particular island, where an aggressive, introduced leaf-cutter was displacing a previously introduced alien. Between them, these voracious ants ate their way through much of the native insect life up to the lower part of the damp mountain forests. Leaf-cutting ants had also already reached the Canary Islands and Madeira, but there, too, the Argentine species finally landed and slaughtered the leaf-cutters.

A similar story could be told for the giant snail *Achatina fulica*, a bulky species with an eight-inch shell and an appetite to match. In this case, however, the durable migrant set out in the slow boats that were crossing the Indian Ocean more than a century ago. Originally confined to tropical African forests, this mollusk had reached Madagascar, Mauritius, the Seychelles, and the Comoro Islands by the middle of the 19th century. In 1847 individuals were released in Calcutta, and from there the snails and their descendants began to slither their way across Asia. It was not long before big snails hitching rides in ships had started to eat the crops on islands in Micronesia and Polynesia. In Guam, especially, the species

became a plague. In 1936, two individuals were taken from Formosa to Oahu, and despite attempts to stop them, giant snails were soon invading Hawaiian farmlands.

Occasionally, disrupted island communities can be restored. On Laysan, for example, conservationists have killed the rabbits and reseeded the coral rock and sand with native plants. Yet the island's future will never be secure; one pregnant rat from a ship could jeopardize the safety of the entire ecosystem, because, as we have seen, once predators have gained a foothold on an island, they are uncommonly difficult to dislodge. All over the world, conservationists are trying to undo some of the damage inflicted upon vulnerable lumps of sea-girt land by centuries of neglect, plunder, and the thoughtless introduction of pests and pets. On Ascension Island, where big, ferocious, tabby cats have played nighttime havoc in the sooty tern colonies, every attempt is being made to trap and kill these wild descendants of domestic cats, doubtless brought in to cure the rat menace. In 1960 the Department of Agriculture in the Seychelles killed 80 cats on Frigate Island to make life easier for the magpie robin. Goats and rabbits are a problem on Raile Island, one of the Mauritius group. Poisoning was the method chosen for removing these immigrants that, by cropping the plant cover, began threatening the survival of some unique reptiles, petrels, and a species of rare palm reduced to about 50 individuals. But the plans of conservationists do not always run smoothly, and the poisoning project met opposition from an influential animal-welfare group whose members felt that even pests should have the right to reasonable justice.

On the whole, though, most of us feel that mankind must do its utmost to preserve the best of island wildlife. For instance, it is unthinkable that anyone should let the unique wildlife of the Galápagos Islands succumb to alien animals.

Saving life on islands poses two closely connected problems. The first is how to protect individual kinds of plants and animals that are especially at risk. Island populations of some species are very small and therefore easily wiped out. For example, the Mauritius kestrel is down to a handful of wild birds, and the species' future may depend upon successfully breeding captive birds. On Cousin Island, in the Seychelles, a privileged visitor may be lucky enough to hear a fluting song drifting from the fluffy casuarina trees. It comes from the brush warbler, one of the rarest birds in the world, because all the dozen or so individuals live on this 60-acre desert island. Not far away, on the beautiful island of Frigate, about a dozen pairs of magpie robins survive precariously from year to year. Two or three acres of tall vegetation is the last stand of the Mangareva Island parrakeet: someone with an ax could exterminate the species in a day or two. Drainage of the Zapata Swamp on Cuba would exterminate the dwarf hutia (a rodent) and a wren. If our descendants are to have the chance of glimpsing these and many other islanders, we must take special measures now to keep the creatures' populations above danger level.

Because no organism can live in isolation, this task of saving individual species is bound up with the second problem—saving entire interrelated island plant and animal communities, or at least the most precious ones. Some such island ecosystems do remain relatively unspoiled. Examples come readily to mind. Of the 75 islands of the Seychelles, Aride and Cousin are wonderfully unspoiled treasure houses. Green turtles nest on their beaches, and frigate birds, noddy terns, and shearwaters nest everywhere. The International Council for the Protection of Birds has taken over Cousin Island as a sanctuary. To the north lies the raised reef of Aldabra and its virgin community, which includes unique species of kestrel, flightless rail, pigeon, and giant turtle. Aldabra's ecosystem was reprieved when Britain scrapped a plan to build an air base there. Danger Island, another raised reef in the Indian Ocean, is a unique jewel of the Chagos Archipelago. It has its own special subspecies of booby—a new species in the making—besides spectacular seabird cities unplundered by rats.

Most of us feel that it is no use having treasure around unless we can enjoy it in some way. Accordingly Aldabra has become a mecca for scientists visiting under the auspices of the British Royal Society. Many Antarctic and subantarctic islands—Macquarie for instance—are also haunts of wildlife scientists. Since the 1950s, tourism in faraway places has been a burgeoning business, and even Aldabra used to be a port of call for a luxury wildlife tour boat bringing a mixed bunch of serious naturalists and vacationers seeking offbeat enjoyment. From Mahé you can take a light aircraft to Bird Island and its million pairs of nesting sooty terns.

Some of these beautiful places are administered by governments too poor to care for unique ecosystems, and tempted to replace an economically barren wilderness with profitable plantations. The government of the Cook Islands, in the central South Pacific, has shown one way of dealing with the conservation problem by presenting to the world one of its pristine coral atolls. The future of Manaue as a world marine park has thus become a world responsibility.

The story of islands typifies what man has done to the world as a whole. All too often he has made a mess of things: mixing up animals and plants never designed for living together, destroying nicely balanced communities, and in their place making semideserts or farmlands where a variety of life forms gives way to monotonous fields of corn or cattle.

Islands therefore teach the unhappy lesson of man's power to blight. Yet the island story can give those with a philosophical bent a tremendous charge of optimism for the future. No matter how we desecrate our planet, and whittle down the number of species on earth, nature has monumental powers for creativity—powers nowhere more dramatically revealed than on some islands. What could be more marvelous than the native wildlife of the Hawaiian archipelago—a tiny string of beads on the world map, thousands of miles from the nearest continent? In spite of their remoteness, over the course of a few million years the islands' stark volcanic rocks acquired a coat of luxuriant green. What is more, from a few animal castaways a wealth of variation was slowly created; a single invasion of tanagers probably generated the Hawaiian honeycreepers in all their different forms. The miraculous evolutionary processes did the same for plants and insects. No matter how limited the colors in the palette, it seems that the evolutionary brush can stir and blend them to paint a gay, bright picture. What can happen on islands, can also happen elsewhere. That is the *happy* lesson I believe we can learn from islands.

The thousands of sooty terns at this nesting ground suggest that some tropical islands are still wildlife paradises. Sooty terns breed so prolifically (nesting every nine months) that even if islanders take many eggs for food, the birds can keep up their numbers. But one pregnant rat shipwrecked on this island could wipe out its vast bird city. Fending off such dangers poses a colossal problem of conservation.

The life and death of islands today rests in man's hands. He can deliberately anni-
hilate their very bedrock in proving the destructive capability of weapons like the
thermonuclear device seen here (above) exploding somewhere in the Pacific Ocean.
More insidiously, man can destroy unique island plants and animals by introducing
crops, food animals, factories, and the pets and pests that tend to accompany his
travels. But man also has the power to protect. Conservation can save wildlife sanctuaries like this fulmar-haunted stub of rock (right). Unless we spare the islands,
we stand to lose many of the most unusual and exciting of all earth's living things.

Index

141

Picture Credits

Cover: Aspect
Title Page-9 Heather Angel
11 Audrey Ross/Van Cleve Photography
12 Eddie van der Veen/Colorific
14(L) Ed Mullis/Aspect
15 Patrick Thurston
16 T. la Tona/ZEFA
17(R) A. Winspear Cundall/Natural Science Photos
18 Anthony Howarth/Susan Griggs Agency
21 S. Jonasson/Frank W. Lane
22 David Moore/Colorific
24 Terence Spencer/Colorific
26 The Mansell Collection
28 NASA from Colorific
29 Camera Press Ltd.
30 B. Crader/ZEFA
32 I. Polunin/NHPA
33(R) Douglas Dickins/NHPA
35 W. Stoy/ZEFA
36(T) Isobel Bennett/Natural Science Photos
36(B) Valeria Taylor/Ardea London
37(R) Peter Johnson/NHPA
39(B) Nicholas de Vore/Bruce Coleman Ltd.
41 R. Halin/ZEFA
42(L) Adam Woolfitt/Susan Griggs Agency
43 Carl Purcell/Colorific
44 E. Hummel/ZEFA
45(R) Heydemann/Müller/ZEFA
47 Bruce Coleman Ltd.
48 Tanaka Kojo, Animals Animals © 1975
49(R) Werner Zepf/NHPA
50(L) Frederic/Jacana
51(BL) Douglas Dickins/NHPA
51(T) A. Eddy/Natural Science Photos
51(BR) L. Robinson/Frank W. Lane
52 Frank W. Lane
54(T) John Markham/Bruce Coleman Ltd.
54(B) Bert/Jacana
55 S. C. Bisserot/Bruce Coleman Ltd.
56-7 Gerald Cubitt

58(T) Fritz/Jacana
58(B) Gerald Cubitt
59 Peter Johnson/NHPA
61 Adrian Warren/Ardea London
62(L) Renaud/Jacana
62(R) W. T. Miller/Frank W. Lane
63 Heather Angel
64 Frank W. Lane
65 W. H. Müller/ZEFA
66 Frederic/Jacana
67(R) Kenneth W. Fink/Ardea London
68 J. Gerbec/ZEFA
69(TR) I. Polunin/NHPA
69(BR) J. L. Mason/Ardea London
70-1 Bill Rainey/Tom Stack & Associates
72-3 Heather Angel
75 Tanaka Kojo, Animals Animals © 1975
76 Nicholas de Vore/Bruce Coleman Ltd.
77(TR) George Allen & Unwin Ltd., London, and Hafner Publishing Company Inc., New York
77(B) Nicholas de Vore/Bruce Coleman Ltd.
79 Peter Arnold/Bruce Coleman Ltd.
80-1 Heather Angel
82 J. Bitsch/ZEFA
83(T) Hans Dossenbach / Natural Science Photos
83(BL) Philippa Scott/NHPA
83(BR)-85 Heather Angel
86(T) Adrian Warren/Ardea London
86(BL) Heather Angel
86(BR) Norman Tomalin/Bruce Coleman Ltd.
87(T) Heather Angel
87(B) Ardea London
88(T) Heather Angel
88(B) M. P. Harris/Bruce Coleman Ltd.
89(R) Alan Root/Bruce Coleman Ltd.
92 J. A. Hancock/Bruce Coleman Ltd.
93 P. Morris Photographics
94 R. M. Bloomfield/Bruce Coleman Inc.
96-7 Photos Andrew J. Berger

98 De Klemm/Jacana
100-2 Michael Tweedie, *Atlas of Insect* Aldus Books Limited, London 1974
103(T) Jack Fields/Photo Researcher Inc.
103(B) Kenneth W. Fink/Ardea London
105 G. R. Roberts, Nelson, New Zealand
106(T) M. F. Soper/Bruce Coleman Ltd.
106(B) Frank W. Lane
107 Photo Centre Ltd./NHPA
109 Francisco Erize/Bruce Coleman Ltd.
111 Photo Andrew J. Berger
112 Keith Gillett/Tom Stack & Associates
113 C. B. Frith/Bruce Coleman Ltd.
115 Adam Woolfitt/Susan Griggs Agency
117 Peter Green/Ardea London
119 George Holton/Photo Researchers Inc.
120 Diego Goldberg/Camera Press Ltd.
123 National Maritime Museum Greenwich/Michael Holford Library photo
124 George Holton/Photo Researchers Inc.
128, 129(T) Bill N. Kleeman/Tom Stack Associates
129(BR) G. R. Roberts, Nelson, New Zealand
133(T) M. F. Soper/Bruce Coleman Ltd.
133(B) George Laycock/Photo Researchers Inc.
134 Jane Burton/Bruce Coleman Ltd.
137 Valerie Taylor/Ardea London
138(L) Salmer/Bruce Coleman Ltd.
139 S. Jonasson/Frank W. Lane

Artist Credits

© Aldus Books: David Nockels 38-9, 90-130-1; Tony Swift 100-2

WORLDS APART

Part 2
Nature in the City

by John Andrew Burton

Owls for sale on a sidewalk in Katmandu in Nepal. Pets, pests, and animals independent of man live in the cities he builds.

Series Coordinator	Geoffrey Rogers
Series Art Director	Frank Fry
Design Consultant	Guenther Radtke
Editorial Consultants	Donald Berwick
	David Lambert
Series Consultant	Malcolm Ross-Macdonald
Art Editor	Susan Cook
Editors	Damian Grint
	Maureen Cartwright
Research	Enid Moore
	Peggy Jones

Contents: Part 2

Editorial Advisers

DAVID ATTENBOROUGH Naturalist and Broadcaster.

MICHAEL BOORER, B.SC. Author, Lecturer and Broadcaster.

Introduction

The majority of the people reading this book will be city-dwellers. And very many of those will also have a yearning for the countryside and its wildlife. Sadly, though, they will also often ignore the wildlife living on their own doorstep.

As the "developed" world becomes increasingly built-up, and the wilderness areas of the surrounding countryside become tamed and enclosed, more and more plants and animals are bound to disappear. Some will survive only in remote fastnesses, others will become extinct. These are the brutal facts that every wildlife conservationist has to face sooner or later.

But wildlife is also very resilient. After all, man himself is only another animal, and subject to the same laws of nature. However much he tampers with his environment, however hard he tries to dominate it, he will never completely control wildlife. As fast as he exterminates certain species, others move in and take over.

In the city habitat wildlife ebbs and flows. In a matter of a few years a whole range of plants and animals may come and go. Surprisingly, naturalists have largely ignored the cities, preferring to escape to the wilderness. Yet the cities are the homes of the dynamic and successful species—it is in them that evolution is most clearly evident. The Galápagos Islands are to a city what a museum is to a zoo.

Already naturalists have missed countless opportunities to study urban wildlife, but I hope this book will encourage us all to look around and study our immediate environment—it may also lead us to try to improve it!

The Living City

A barren desert or a living part of the natural world? When you stand in any city street in the rush hour as traffic hurtles by, it is hard to believe that wildlife can coexist in the midst of all the concrete, tarmac, glass, filth, and noise. But look up for a while and you may see a bird of prey flying across a gap between some buildings. Listen hard enough and you may hear the chirping of sparrows above the roar of traffic; if you take the sideroads, you may even hear several songbirds. As dusk falls and man begins the evening migration to the suburbs, the animals start to migrate too. Flying in tight formation, starlings pour onto the ledges of city buildings where they gather noisily on their roosts. Beneath the streets and along ventilators and roofs, rats scamper, cockroaches scuttle, and a host of lesser creatures become active. As the human beings disappear, giving you a chance to look more closely at the pavement, you will see bits of plant life pushing up through the cracks.

The exact species of plant and animal to be found in a particular city will vary, depending on the part of the world. But every city has nature in its midst. In some places, the wild creatures have to fight hard to survive; in others, the human inhabitants pamper and tend nature's last survivors; but nowhere is man alone.

What, then, distinguishes the city from such other terrestrial habitats as the desert, the grassland, the forest, or the mountain peak? On the surface, it would seem easy to define the habitat that forms the subject of this book. We are all aware of the many features that are common to cities and towns—the busy streets, the office buildings, the shops, the packed rows of apartment houses and other dwelling places, the occasional carefully preserved green spot. Man, the animal that created all these things, may think them very special, but to the nonhuman city dwellers they are simply one more environment. The windborne seed or nesting bird does not distinguish between the window ledges of an office building and the rocky ledges on a cliff. To man, the city's attractions are not only such fine buildings as the churches, museums, and shopping centers but also its parks; and it is amazing how many birds and other creatures find food and shelter in the city's gardens and parks, as well as in its streets and buildings.

For our purposes, we can perhaps agree to use the word "city" rather loosely to stand for any sort of urban habitat composed of a large number of dwellings collected together in one place.

Historians, writers, politicians, and economists all differ widely in their individual definitions of a city. In Denmark, a community of more than 250 people is officially urban, but in Korea the urban community has to contain more than 40,000 inhabitants. The nearest to a standard definition of an urban unit (= city) was propounded in the USA in 1956, in which an urban unit was defined as "containing a population of at least 100,000 people, being an area embracing a central city . . . and with 65 per cent or more of their economically active populations engaged in nonagricultural activities."

Obviously, there is considerable variation in the size and make-up of the world's cities and towns. Much depends on the environment within which they have been built, for people have congregated in an enormous variety of situations in vastly differing climates. Most big cities are in relatively low-lying areas close to sea level, but a few lie at great altitudes: Mexico City, for instance, is over 7500 feet above sea level, Nairobi nearly 6000. Cairo and Hong Kong both have roughly the same average monthly temperatures, but whereas Cairo has an average annual rainfall of little more than an inch, Hong Kong has around 85 inches. New York and Rome lie at about the same latitude, but New York's winters are considerably colder. Similarly, Moscow lies at nearly the same latitude as Edinburgh; yet, whereas the Russian capital has below-freezing temperatures throughout the winter, Edinburgh's winters tend to be mild.

If, then, we try to define the urban habitat by means of the criteria that we would normally apply to natural habitats, we can find little to use as a common denominator. The only features that we can pinpoint as universal are that all cities were built by man, and that they and the life within them are continuously changing. As for urban wildlife, the features that really determine what will survive in a given city are: its

distance from open country, the amount of open space within the city itself, and the attitude of the human inhabitants toward wild creatures (including, of course, such "pests" as rodents and cockroaches). To ease our way toward an understanding of the ecology of cities, let us look at some of the changes that our own cultural development has wrought in the way we live together.

Originally, man was a hunter-gatherer roaming the primeval world in search of animals and fruits, much as the Indians of South America, the Aborigines of Australia, and other survivors of Stone Age cultures do today. At the beginning of the Neolithic period our ancestors discovered agriculture, and this necessitated forming a settlement. At first they probably farmed in the way that Amazonian Indians and Papuans still do: slash and burn, followed by a few years of crops until the soil has been exhausted, then move on to clear another area. Gradually the natural tribal units of the hunter-gatherers settled down into village communities. These small settlements would have had very little impact on the indigenous wildlife of a given locale except for the intensively tilled fields that eventually surrounded them. Many wild creatures, deprived of their accustomed food and shelter, could no longer survive in the area.

In modern times the same thing has happened, only on a larger scale. In a city such as Peking, set in the midst of thousands of square miles of intensively farmed lands, you will see little of the original wildlife of the region. But in Brazilia, the brand-new capital of Brazil, the situation is very different. Brazilia is not, and never has been, agriculturally self-supporting. It was built right in the middle of a vast wooded plain—and wild animals from the surrounding area can be seen straying into almost all parts of the city. Neolithic man and his descendants through the ages have also built their Brazilias: Stonehenge, Karnak, Delos were all religious centers that may have had large settlements near them. Most towns arose for more practical reasons, however—because it was convenient to establish a communal dwelling place where everyday necessities were readily available from agricultural lands in the immediate vicinity.

Ornamental trees, shrubs, and water plants are here arranged to beautify a Tokyo public garden and its pool. But such man-made urban landscapes also incidentally afford food and shelter for sizable numbers of wild creatures, especially birds.

Metal and concrete make unlikely homes for at least some birds and plants. Above: European blackbird sitting on a nest it has built upon a gas meter in an outbuilding. Below: these plantains grew from seed that lodged in a crack in a sidewalk.

As agriculture, and later animal husbandry, developed, so did the need for craftsmen who neither tilled land nor herded animals. With increasing populations, pressure from neighboring groups also increased, and the enlarged villages became walled towns. Such technological advances as irrigation, metallurgy, the plow, and the wheel enabled man's development to make a series of great leaps forward. Towns provided protection for the new-found wealth, and prosperity bred bureaucrats and officials— the first real townspeople, tied to no basic production but relying on others for the provision of food and shelter. All this happened in a relatively short space of time between 7000 and 5000 years ago, in the "Cradle of Civilization," a region of the Middle East that has now largely become barren desert. Cities of a primitive type and size still exist, however, in that part of the world, and we can judge from them the effects they had on wildlife.

Because the early towns usually grew up in a landscape that had already been molded and altered by agriculture, urban wildlife would have mainly consisted, just as it does today, of species that man either tolerated or could not get rid of. In many a Middle Eastern town, then as now, kites, buzzards, and vultures circled overhead, swooping down on refuse or offal. Jackals and pariah dogs scavenged around city outskirts, cockroaches and geckos scuttled over the rafters of the buildings, and a host of lesser animals such as fleas, flies, and flukes, lived near, on, or even in the human body. If there were small birds they were generally destined for the pot.

One of the earliest known cities was Çatal Hüyük, which was built on the edge of the Fertile Crescent, in what is now the Anatolian part of modern Turkey. The remains of Çatal Hüyük that have been excavated date back more than 8000 years, and we know a good deal about life in the town from the artifacts, wall paintings, and bones that have been found there. At a time when most of the world's human populations were living in the open or, at best, in rudimentary shelters, Çatal Hüyük was a mighty metro-

Los Angeles, seen from the air. The city covers an extensive area of California with homes and the gardens and roads that serve them. This contrasts with many old cities of Europe and Asia, which evolved with tenement blocks, narrow lanes, and few gardens. Clearly, cities laid out on different plans in different climates offer wildlife a wide variety of urban habitats.

White-backed vultures, pariah dogs, and a crow pick clean the skeleton of a cow, somewhere in India. Tolerated by man, wild scavengers scour southern Asian towns for food just as their ancestors have done since man himself turned to urban living.

polis—a fully developed city of about 2000 people. These early citizens have left us an interesting record of the wild animals known to neolithic townspeople, among them wild cattle, deer, wild asses, wild boars, leopards, and wolves, all of which were no doubt hunted in the surrounding wilderness. Although these animals lived outside the city walls, the surrounding countryside was much closer to the city inhabitants than it is nearly everywhere today. A very early city such as Çatal Hüyük was like an ants' nest in a forest—a tiny center of organized activity in the midst of untamed wilderness.

It seems probable, then, that the earliest urban people had extremely close contact with what we think of today as "wild beasts." Although within the city itself, a few domestic animals would have been bred for food, and there would certainly have been plenty of rodents and insects, the wilderness was still nearly at their doorstep, and it played an important role in their lives. Apart from hunting and eating wild animals, man respected and in some cases revered them. One of the Çatal Hüyük deities is represented as a bird of prey, probably a vulture (a bird still seen circling over small towns in Anatolia).

By the time Çatal Hüyük had flowered and disappeared, really big cities had sprung up in and around the Fertile Crescent, changing the landscape considerably. The famous city of Ur, which has been dated to the third millennium B.C., had 250,000 inhabitants, and it has been estimated that the population of Babylon reached nearly 400,000 at its peak. We still know little, though, about the plant and animal life within

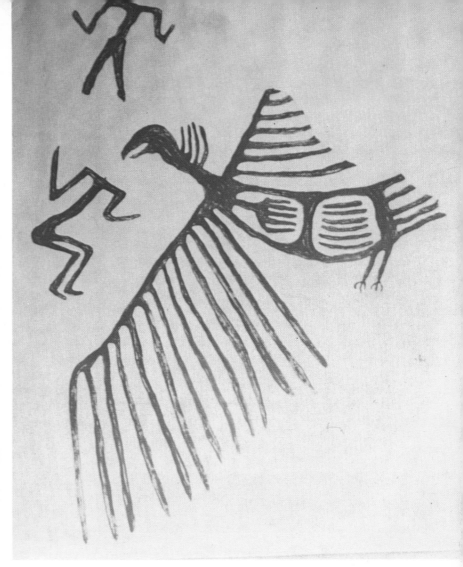

these great cities of the past, because the records they left particularly in tombs, emphasize the glamorous activities of their ruling classes. The rulers of Nineveh and Babylon, for example, are depicted hunting wild asses, lions, and many other animals—but not within the city walls.

One of the great blossomings of city life was, of course, in Ancient Egypt, although rather surprisingly, the Ancient Egyptians did not develop metropolitan "urban" centers. Theirs was a rather decentralized culture, very much based on agriculture, and the only really permanent buildings in their cities were tombs and temples.

The great number of scribes and officials left detailed records, many of which have survived the ravages of time, and, together with the many bones, mummified remains, murals, and sculptures carefully excavated by archaeologists, these can be pieced together to give a colorful picture of life centuries ago.

A vulture god or his priest in disguise attacking a headless human corpse—a wall painting roughly 8000 years old found in the ruined town of Çatal Hüyük in southern Turkey. Early urban man clearly had close contact with large wild animals.

In Ancient Egypt, man was still living close to the natural world—much more so than he does surrounded by the containerized, reinforced-concreted, plastic-coated artifacts of today. We get a picture of the Nile teeming with crocodile and wildfowl, and within a few miles of the cities large mammals such as giraffe, hippo, and various antelopes were still to be found. Tomb paintings depict the teeming variety of wildfowl that abounded in the marshes of the Nile. These paintings are so accurate that the species can easily be identified. The geese in the tomb of Het at Medum, dating back some 4500 years, are just like the illustrations in a modern field guide—accurate, simplified, but not stylized. It is quite

15

obvious that the artist had firsthand experience of the birds; in fact, he must have had specimens of red-breasted geese in front of him to work from.

Although the 20th-century visitor to Cairo and Alexandria will see a remarkable variety of birds, there are two notable birds of Ancient Egypt that he will not see: the sacred and the bald ibises. These birds were so familiar to the city dwellers of Ancient Egypt that they had their own hieroglyphs. But, like their relatives, the white storks of Europe, they were large and easy to kill, and relied on man's tolerance if they were to survive near his dwelling places.

The black-and-white sacred ibis was and is primarily a bird of papyrus swamps and marshy ground but, if its modern habits are anything to go on, the bald ibis, so-called from the bare neck below its scarlet beak and crown, may have actually nested in the towns. Like many city birds, it was a cliff-nester, breeding alongside

This tomb painting of a man evidently adoring a crowned heron reminds us that Egyptians once revered beasts as the homes of powerful spirits to be appeased by offering the creatures hospitality. Animals so favored probably abounded in the towns.

choughs, lesser kestrels, black kites, and jackdaws; the transition to nesting on temples and other buildings would have been an easy one.

One of the most important factors in the survival of city wildlife is man's degree of tolerance. His tolerance to animals living alongside him, even his active protection, has its roots in religion. A large number of animals were revered in Ancient Egypt for instance, as their mummified remains testify. The penalties for killing sacred animals were severe—usually death—and this religious protection was probably far more effective than present wildlife protection laws.

One of the most important animals in the Egyptian pantheon was the baboon-god, Thoth. Horapollo Nilous, writing in about the fifth century B.C., describes tame hamadryas baboons living in the Egyptian temples. These sacred animals led pampered lives and were embalmed when dead; in the Valley of the Kings at Thebes, a vast cemetry of ancient baboons has been excavated. The hamadryas baboon is, like so many of the animals of Ancient Egypt, extinct in that part of its range, yet at one time it was clearly a common denizen of the cities. The only ape now left in North Africa is the Barbary ape (*Macacca sylvana*). The Greek historian Diodorus Siculus writing during the Roman occupation of North Africa describes how apes were strictly protected and roamed freely in and out of the homes in many of the towns near Carthage; it is the descendants of some of these animals that roam Gibraltar's parks and gardens today.

Contemporary Buddhists revere apes, and in some Oriental cities monkeys are to be seen in the temples or wandering around the city without fear of man. From Japan to India, and south through Malaysia, various species of monkeys are worshiped. In India, as the embodiment of Rama, the hanuman or entellus monkey is second only to the cow as a sacred animal. The rhesus monkey also abounds in many places. But apes and monkeys are no respecters of property and have inflicted enormous amounts of damage in urban areas. This, and changing attitudes, and the demands of medical research, has led to a reduction in their numbers.

Because ancient religious taboos and totems gave protection to a wide variety of animals— crocodiles, vultures, falcons, cats, storks among many other species—it is likely that the towns, particularly the religious centers such as Karnak or Medum, abounded in animals.

Three artistic products of the ancient world illustrate the close connections between early civilizations and the world of nature. Near left: marble relief of about 668 B.C. depicts King Ashurbanipal of Assyria on horseback leading a lion hunt. Far left: a Roman-period cat mummy from Egypt. The Egyptians' reverence for certain animals lasted for thousands of years. Below: a vividly realistic tomb painting of about 1400 B.C. shows an Egyptian nobleman with a snake-shaped throwing stick hunting some of the game that abounded in the Nile marshes at the time. In visual records of this kind we can identify ducks, herons, egrets, ibises, perching birds, butterflies, fishes, cats, crocodiles, and even hippopotamuses.

17

Tolerance and the protection of animals are also of great benefit to man: many of the animals protected were scavengers and helped dispose of refuse—the vultures and kites, crows and storks, crocodiles and jackals functioned as nature's refuse collectors, just as they do today. Historians have gleaned what they can about ancient and medieval cities from the records and artists' impressions that have survived to this day, but to understand the living ecology of the past we have other evidence we can turn to. Many 20th-century cities in the underdeveloped areas of the world suffer from conditions very similar to those that must have existed hundreds

Held sacred in various countries of southern and eastern Asia, monkeys earn a special place in many towns and cities. Left: man and monkey join hands in a monkey temple at Varanasi, India. Below: rhesus monkeys—two with babies—perch nonchalantly on Swayambuth Temple in Katmandu, capital city of Nepal.

of years ago in the Western World—the same squalor, overcrowding, and inefficient social services, all leading to an abundance of organic waste on which scavengers can thrive.

By way of illustration, a recent study calculated that in Delhi (admittedly much larger than the ancient towns and cities and with a much greater refuse problem) there were about 3000 nesting pairs of birds of prey. Most of these were black kites, which formed over 80 per cent of the total. There were also about 400 pairs of *Gyps bengalensis* vultures and 100 pairs of the Egyptian vulture *Neophron percnopterus*. Significantly, the newer parts often had a density as low as one or two pairs of birds every square mile, whereas in the older areas the density could be 200 times as great. The average density in Old Delhi worked out at just over 120 pairs to every square mile; in New Delhi it was about 51 pairs, and in the newest quarters the figures work out

to round about nine pairs to every square mile.

A Russian scientist who studied Delhi's birds decided that there were three important reasons for the abundance: the enormous amount of food available (both other animals and garbage); the number of trees (nesting sites); and, most important, "the traditional goodwill of Indians to all living beings, including birds of prey."

At one time several of the scavengers (or their northern equivalents) found in Delhi abounded in Europe. In medieval London, for instance, kites and ravens were common, and protected by law. One of the best-documented accounts of London's kites dates from the visit to London in

Zebu cattle lounge unconcernedly upon the center reservation between two traffic lanes in New Delhi. Cattle roam the city streets at will in India because Hindus reverence the cow as Mother Earth's representative and the bull as a link with the god Shiva. Hindus refuse to kill cattle or to eat their meat.

Not a caricature of a morticians' convention but an assembly of marabou storks probing an urban refuse dump in Kenya. The birds' bare necks and heads are ugly but servicable—muckraking would clog neck feathers, creating an unsavory tangle.

1465 of the King of Bohemia's brother-in-law, Baron Leo von Rozmital. According to his secretary, there were vast numbers of the birds on London Bridge. He also commented on the large numbers of crows, ravens, and jackdaws, which, like the kites, were so tame that they would even snatch food from the hands of children.

Surprisingly, relatively few studies have been made of the scavengers in a city. Although such aspects of city life as rare birds, plants, or butterflies are well documented the basic ecology has, in most cases, yet to be examined in detail. Apart from the studies on the birds of Delhi described above, the only other similar scientific investigation appears to be one carried out in Kampala, the capital of Uganda.

Kampala is a fairly small town by Western standards, with about 331,000 inhabitants. The pattern of life in some ways closely resembles that of ancient and medieval towns and, as in Delhi, the inhabitants are tolerant toward wildlife. Again, a major similarity between this modern city and its historical counterparts is its garbage. Most of the waste on the town's two garbage dumps is organic—mainly plant remains (particularly bananas), fish, fowl, and mammal bones, with a few corpses of dogs and other animals. The proportion of inorganic waste—such as bottles, cans, and plastic—is very small compared with Western refuse. Pied crows and black kites (the same species as in Delhi) are

widespread throughout Kampala and on the garbage dumps marabou storks are also common scavengers. The dumps, and another major attraction for scavengers, the slaughterhouses, also attract large numbers of flies, which in turn provide the food for insectivorous birds and bats.

Another scavenger, mainly on the outskirts of Kampala, is the warthog—a direct parallel with the semiwild swine that often roamed city streets in medieval Europe. Then, swine could become very numerous and in London, for example, at the end of the 13th century men had to be appointed to kill them. In North America, also, bands of hogs wandered through the streets of towns and cities acting as garbage collectors as late as the mid-19th century. Even New York was described by an ex-mayor in 1832 as practically "one huge pigsty."

Most of these animals, however, have not totally adapted to life in the city. The birds still nest in trees and other "natural" sites, even within the towns. But as we shall see elsewhere in this book, drastic changes in habits are unusual: the animals and plants that colonize buildings and man-made structures are nearly always those that were originally cliff-dwellers, suited to an equivalent natural environment.

In spite of the rate at which modern urban de-

Pups unfamiliar with the inside of any human habitation hide from a camera in holes scratched in a Thai rubbish dump. Dogs that have reverted to the wild live like this on the fringes of many African and Asian cities. They are far less approachable and more aggressive than their household counterparts.

velopment has accelerated, displacing the traditional species of urban flora and fauna, wildlife still survives. Indeed, it shows a remarkable tenacity. In the period of rapid expansion of the urban centers of the world since the 19th century, man has endeavored to retain bits of the countryside within the city. In parks and gardens enclaves of countryside provide havens for a wealth of wildlife.

Some species, of course, have to go: like man himself, they find the modern city increasingly intolerable. Atmospheric pollution pushes out lichens; water pollution kills fish; the rooting out of old trees removes the habitats for beetles and hole-nesting birds. Other species disappear quite simply because they are not as well adapted to city life as the species competing with them.

Every time slums are cleared for development there is an opportunity to study the wildlife that is most aggressively colonizing the urban habitat. Few naturalists have examined this phenomenon closely, but what is known indicates that every situation is different. Even within a single city,

a species colonizing one year will have changed slightly by the next, and a decade later may be markedly different. Even though there is a trend toward a "cosmopolitan" wildlife due to a deliberate or accidental introduction of exotic species, proportions and dominance patterns constantly change.

The most successful of all invaders of the city are known variously as pests or vermin. The true naturalist does not overlook them; but these, the most abundant and the most successful forms of wildlife in the city—in fact, very often the only ones truly adapted to the city habitat—are usually completely ignored by the amateur naturalist. An interest in natural history—such as birdwatching—may well be escapism; many birdwatchers are city dwellers, and hence they spend most of their time seeking rarities, traveling away from the city to do so.

However, naturalists living in the industrialized world find it increasingly difficult to escape the urban environment and are thus beginning to turn their attention to the wildlife that has

Driving hogs to market, a common scene in country towns of the early 1900s. This photograph was taken in 1903 in the Midland English town of Deritend, since absorbed by the sprawling city of Birmingham. Not all urban hogs were always so closely controlled. For centuries, semiwild swine ranged freely through major European cities. At the end of the 13th century they were so numerous in London that men had to be appointed to kill them. In North America, too, bands of hogs wandered the streets of towns and cities, acting as garbage collectors. In 1832, an ex-mayor considered that New York itself virtually resembled one enormous pigsty.

Red deer still appear on the fringes of the forest that lies beyond the fields surrounding many a small town and large village in southern Germany. Population centers that remain small and contained may have a rich store of wild plants and animals just beyond their doorstep. But large wild species such as this deer have proved unable to adapt to spreading cities. For one thing, concrete and brick landscapes lack the large quantities of fodder that a deer needs. Also, automobiles and amateur hunters put the lives of large, conspicuous animals in jeopardy. In an urban setting, only man-made parks offer sufficient security for wild animals the size of deer.

been on their very doorstep, so to speak. Perhaps the future will produce studies by naturalists of pests and vermin that will help redress the present bias. We should not underestimate the significance of pests for I seriously think that science, technology, and politicians have lulled the city dweller into a false sense of security. The major epidemic diseases have been almost stamped out in most developed cities—but not quite. In the underdeveloped world, on the other hand, disease is barely controlled: plague, cholera, and typhoid are still endemic, kept at bay but always a very real threat. Rats and mice are only just contained by poisons, against which they rapidly develop immunity, so making necessary the development of still other poisons. The same is true of disease-carrying flies that become resistant to insecticides. A small collapse in a city's political and economic superstructure will be enough to unleash this reservoir of wildlife, which is ready to take back the cities from man.

While researching for this book, I have become increasingly aware of two facts. The first is how

little city man knows about his most important environment—and, apparently, how little he cares. Volume after volume has been published on the wildlife of rainforests, alpine meadows, deserts, taiga, steppe—practically every habitat except that of the city. Most naturalists, both amateur and professional, live in towns, yet they rarely appear aware of the fascinating changes that are taking place so close to them.

The second point is that man is not only just another animal, part of the urban ecosystem; he is also just as unstable as the other species in that system. Urban man is a very, very recent phenomenon dating back only some 10,000 years—a mere nothing in geological and evolutionary terms. Modern urban man—the megalopolis-dweller—is so recent that it is far too early to try to claim that the evolutionary experiment that created him is a success. If anything, the evidence of man's behavior as a city animal points to his failure in adapting to an alien environment, even though that environment is of his own making.

Wildlife Surviving

The wildlife that survives in a city is surprisingly rich and varied, and so we should be careful not to make generalizations about it. What survives in one urban area may disappear from another. No two are identical, and any of the numerous man-made changes that are continually occurring can alter finely balanced ecosystems.

As one form of support for the individual plant and animal species that survive, there is bound to be an important overall survivor from the past—bits of countryside, such as parks, green squares, suburban gardens, and even waste ground. In most instances, these are largely unnatural habitats, since they are man-made. A few of the larger parks in and around cities—for instance, Central Park in New York, the Bois de Boulogne in Paris, and Richmond Park in London—have a superficially natural appearance in certain areas, but everywhere man's influence is evident.

Parks have been features of city life for a long time. The ancient Romans relaxed in the gardens of Porticus Livia; the Imperial Parks were an essential part of ancient Chinese cities; and the Assyrians took their pleasure in the park at Khorsabad. Medieval European aristocracy set aside parks for hunting, and during and after the Renaissance public gardens were laid out in most cities. It was not until the Industrial Revolution, however, that parks assumed real significance for the general public. As cities grew, their inhabitants became further and further separated from the surrounding countryside. The wealthy could have town houses built in spacious squares overlooking wide lawns, or in tree-lined streets where there was plenty of room for gardens, whereas the laboring poor were likely to live in appalling conditions, rarely seeing a blade of grass. Eventually, though, the upper classes became conscience-stricken: one product of the Victorian zeal for reform was a determination to provide some open spaces for the recreation of the urban public.

Modern parks are among the world's richest

Canonbury Square in London. Here, trees and a patch of grass laid out by man produce an unnaturally rural habitat deep inside a city. Some wildlife, dispossessed by urban sprawl, takes refuge and survives upon such artificial islands of vegetation.

Edinburgh in the 19th century. Haphazard growth of industrial cities forced workers to live in places where they rarely saw a blade of grass until enlightened planners introduced parks.

The greatest variety of trees usually occur at the edges of forests, and a wide variety of shrubs, bushes, flowering plants, grasses, ferns, and other plants grow beneath them, taking advantage of the different degrees of available shelter and shade. These plants provide food and shelter for many different insects, which, in turn, are eaten by birds, mammals, reptiles, and amphibians. Forest wildlife and open-country wildlife, as well as the species that are solely forest-edge inhabitants, all occur alongside one another in natural forest-edge habitats, and this is also broadly the case in city parks.

It is quite possible that in the future the forest-edge habitat provided by urban parks and suburban gardens will play a vital role in saving rare species of plants, particularly trees. Already many city councils in various parts of the world have passed laws to control the felling of trees and the picking of flowers (though it must be granted, on the debit side, that too many city councils and private owners are only too willing to sacrifice a century or more of plant growth for the quick "development" of building sites).

The vegetation of cities and their suburbs is rarely, if ever, composed entirely of indigenous plants. Very often, most of the trees are exotic species, and most of the flowering plants are either similarly imported or have been under cultivation so long that they scarcely resemble their wild ancestors. The native plants that are not planted by man, but that survive in spite of him, are considered to be weeds, particularly if they compete with his chosen plants. By contrast, the insects and other animals that feed directly or indirectly on the plants are mainly natural survivors. Some, to be sure, will have been introduced into the environment along with the exotic plants, and some birds and mammals may also have been accidentally or deliberately introduced; but most are the natural survivors of the forest-edge habitat that existed before the city itself came into being.

Exotic trees have been a feature of cities for centuries. The maidenhair, or gingko, a primitive type of tree that has remained almost unchanged since Jurassic times, was once virtually restricted to Chinese parks but is now fairly common in parks and gardens in many other parts of the world. Long before Marco Polo visited Kublai Khan, oriental parks and palace gardens were well planted with trees, many of which were thoroughly domesticated. In Arabia, the

wildlife habitats, and they are unique in that they are hospitable to similar forms of wildlife in places as dissimilar as Tokyo, Bonn, Penang, and Caracas. They are also among the few habitats of today's world that are actually increasing in area. The main reason for the wealth of wildlife in cities is that parks and suburban gardens provide a "reservoir" of life for supplying built-up areas. This reservoir is an almost exact equivalent of a natural forest-edge habitat, and the edges of a forest always constitute an outstandingly diverse habitat.

Sycamores and poplars are among the hardy, decorative trees imported to enliven parks and streets in many a temperate-climate city. Left: bark of the London plane tree, an American-Oriental hybrid sycamore that sheds soot-laden bark in patches, enabling the tree to breathe. Right: the Lombardy poplar, a fast-growing, graceful variety of black poplar that probably originated in Iran.

sheiks cultivated palm groves; Samarkand, Bokhara, and other cities of central Asia were famed for their orchards and avenues of trees.

All over the world, people have planted trees for food, for beauty, and—particularly in urban areas—for shade. The famous cedar of Lebanon can no longer be found in more than a few isolated areas on the hillsides that were once thickly covered with it; instead, it is a common tree in city parks in Europe, North and South America, South Africa, and Australasia.

Two factors have always determined the kinds of tree that survive in towns: fashion and physical conditions. From the 16th to the 19th century travelers brought strange trees from the Orient, the Andes, and the Antipodes, back to Europe, and later to North America. Gradually, isolated examples of these found their way into gardens and parks throughout the world. By the 19th century the Western World was laying out public parks on a grand scale, and exotic trees that were particularly suitable for smoke-laden industrial cities now came into their own. Plane trees—most notably the so-called London plane,

The seemingly natural wooded landscape in London's Regent's Park dates from the early 1800s. From then on, this "English" style was to dominate urban park design in many countries, providing dwelling places for many native animal species.

which is a hybrid between the Oriental and American planes—were especially successful. An obvious characteristic of the London plane is the dappled appearance of the bark; this is caused when the soot-laden bark is shed in patches, to enable the tree to breathe. Its other adaptations to survival in the heart of a city are roots that can grow in the compacted soil of city streets and smooth, shiny leaves that are easily washed clean of pollution by rainfall. The first two hybrids were planted in London in about 1680, and those first trees are still alive today. Since then, London planes have been successfully planted in cities throughout the world.

As leader in the Industrial Revolution, Britain also led the way in the creation of urban parks. London's Hyde Park had been dedicated to the public by Charles I as early as 1635, but the great age of public parks really began in the early 19th century, when Regent's Park, originally designed by John Nash for private use, was opened to the London public. This "English" style of park was to dominate urban park design in much of the world for many years. Its main features were a combination of geometric formality in placement of buildings along with an apparently natural landscape of trees, shrubs, lawns, and lakes. In fact, most 19th century parks in Europe were anything but natural—the lakes were usually man-made, and most of the trees were imported exotics—but the artificiality mattered little to wildlife inhabitants. What mattered, and still does, is that the presence of trees and other vegetation made it possible for many native animal species to survive.

Population pressure in the cities of America came somewhat later than it did in Europe. Yet, by the end of the 18th century the idea of a park for New Yorkers had already been mooted. Nothing was done about it, however, until 1844, when William Bryant, the editor of the *Evening Post*, suggested setting aside the land on Manhattan Island that was eventually to become Central Park. In 1856, the area at last became available for public use, and two men who were to become leading figures in the creation of city parks in North America, Frederick Law

Olmsted and Calvert Vaux, were given the job of laying out Central Park. The plan that they produced and executed was a boon not only to people but to New York City's native wildlife, for it exploited the natural features of the land to full advantage and these provided a continuously hospitable environment for many species that might otherwise have been forced out of the city. The partnership of Vaux and Olmsted went on to create parks in Brooklyn, San Francisco, Detroit, Montreal, Boston, Philadelphia, and other cities in the United States and Canada.

The next major step forward in New York's parks came, surprisingly enough, during the Depression of the 1930s, when, under the direction of Robert Moses, some 80,000 workers unemployed by private industry were given work in an imaginative city-wide park-building project. In the early 1930s there were fewer than 15,000 acres of parks in New York's five boroughs; by the early 1970s the figure had leaped to nearly 40,000 acres. A recent addition to the city's park system is one of the most significant for the wildlife indigenous to the region—Jamaica Bay.

Jamaica Bay is very different from most people's concept of a city park. Until the 1960s this area, close to the center of one of the world's greatest cities, was an inhospitable wasteland heavily polluted with sewage and other outflows. Some 15,000 acres of entirely man-made wilderness have now allowed a wealth of wildlife to survive in the once-hideous region, or to return to it. In and among the ponds, dykes, saltings, and mudflats, vegetation has been planted and is flourishing. Other plants have colonized the park of their own accord. Birds and other animals have returned to the area, and now the main attraction of Jamaica Bay is undoubtedly its remarkably varied bird population. Pied-billed grebe, green heron, snowy and common egrets, and least bittern mingle with resident colonies of common terns and skimmers; and in autumn and spring Jamaica Bay is visited by hundreds of New York bird-watchers attracted by the large numbers of migrants that find refuge there. Wading birds such as phalaropes, avocets, dowitchers, godwits, golden plovers, Baird's and buff-breasted sandpipers all pause to feed in the mud and marshes of Jamaica Bay on their way to

Spring in New York City's Central Park. When its 19th-century designers took nature and embellished it with art, they incidentally created a sanctuary for the city's vanishing wildlife.

or from their breeding grounds in the far north. Many species of land birds also pass through, and in winter short-eared owls—a day-flying species—can be seen hunting over the marshes.

Jamaica Bay's success in helping native wildlife to survive is almost entirely due to the fact that, unlike all too many urban parks, it was conceived as a "natural" park, with emphasis on native types of vegetation rather than on spectacular exotics. A similar regard for natural conditions is largely responsible for the success of Bos Park in Amsterdam, Holland, which was built earlier in this century after a long period of extremely careful planning. Before construction began, a detailed study of the ecology of the flora and fauna associated with the area was undertaken, and the design of the park was ultimately based on the climax vegetation that could be expected to grow on land lying only three or four feet above the water table. The trees that now dominate Bos Park are oak, linden, ash, poplar, alder, willow, and beech, in

varying quantities, depending on the soil. Willows, hawthorn, dogwood, hazel, and yew were used to provide cover and protection during the early growth stages of the big trees. Of the 2200 parkland acres, nearly half are wooded; the rest consist of open water and meadows, and the only hill was formed from the excavation for drainage and lakes. Over the years since 1928 Bos Park has developed into a flourishing bit of woodland, important to the survival of many forms of wildlife, and yet it is less than four miles from the center of Amsterdam.

Naturalists obviously applaud the theory behind such big-city parks as Jamaica Bay and Bos. In cities where such sanctuaries do not exist, resident naturalists must eagerly await the day when their own native trees take pride of place in the parklands, and individual regional characteristics can once more be seen. Native trees are usually (although not always) better adapted to local conditions than exotics, and they are more readily colonized by other forms of native wildlife. Moreover, native wildlife rarely gives rise to the problems associated with exotic trees, flowers, or animals, which can become pests or, alternatively, require a lot of attention

Herring gulls and blackbacked gulls congregate on the partly frozen surface of West Pond, in New York City's Jamaica Bay wildlife refuge. Manhattan skyscrapers dominate the skyline.

to be lavished on them to assure their survival.

In most traditional city parks, the native wild plants that go on living among the planted exotics tend to be those species that are common in the surrounding countryside—species that are naturally colonists of wasteland and roadside verges. Because they flourish in freshly dug ground, gardeners regard them as weeds.

There is an old proverb, "One year's seed means seven years' weeding," and it has more than a modicum of truth in it. The poppies that flowered in devastated parts of Flanders during World War I are perhaps the best-known example of seemingly spontaneous flowering, but something similar happened in Dresden, Warsaw, London, and many other European and also Asian cities that were bombed during World War II: the rubble and ruins suddenly became a riot of color from an unanticipated growth of flowers. It has long been known that certain seeds can lie dormant for many years (the record is held by some Arctic lupine seeds from the Yukon that actually germinated after an interval of between 8–13,000 years). So, since a single plant can produce large numbers of seeds, it should not surprise us if, when a given piece of ground is disturbed—by bombing, say, or a building project—plants from a relatively distant past spring forth. Most of these "weeds" are likely to be alien invaders, but there is always the possibility of a dormant native rarity springing up.

There are several plant families that are outstandingly successful at surviving almost any vicissitude of city life. One of these, as every city dweller must know, is the family Compositae, which includes such species as chrysanthemums, goldenrods, daisies, asters, ragworts, sunflowers, thistles, and dandelions. The more adaptable species of this large family have not only survived in their native habitats but have spread all over the world, both as domesticated plants and as accidental colonists. Another group, the Cruciferae, includes several highly successful colonists of disturbed ground, as well as large numbers of such domestic garden species as cabbages, mustards, wallflowers, and candytufts. Many of these survive in the most unlikely situations, as do such members of the figwort family as toadflaxes, snapdragons, and foxgloves.

Among the animals, one might expect reptiles and amphibians to be perhaps the least likely wild creatures to be able to survive the rigors of

Several families of attractive flowering plants thrive in our cities in wild or cultivated form. Left: the asters that beautify this flowerbed belong to the daisy family (Compositae), which also includes the chrysanthemums, dandelions, goldenrods, and thistles. Right: self-sown Welsh poppies have sprouted between the paving stones to bloom outside this window.

Two of the numerous kinds of snake that prey upon rats and mice infesting cities of southern and southeastern Asia. Above: house snake, or common wolf snake, a plentiful species in Malaysia and Thailand, occurring even in the center of the Thai capital, Bangkok. Below: a cobra with neck inflated rising from the basket of a Bombay snake charmer. Cobras have killed many Asian city-dwellers.

city life. Yet they are often common in urban habitats of the tropics, and a few species occur elsewhere. True, the legendary alligators of New York City's sewers probably belong in the realm of mythology; although an occasional baby alligator or caiman may live for a few days or weeks in a cold climate, such creatures cannot breed there. But snakes do live in fairly large numbers in some temperate-zone cities.

In the crowded cities of India and Southeast Asia, of course—in Calcutta, Rangoon, or Kuala Lumpur—we find a wide variety of serpents, which feed on the rats and mice that infest those places. The Asian copperhead (*Elaphe radiata*), for example, is a rodent-eater that commonly lives in and around houses in Vietnamese cities, as does one of the largest urban species, the Indochinese rat snake; rat snakes more than six feet long have been found in the center of Saigon. Another species that lives in Saigon is the so-called flying snake *Chrysopelea ornata*, which flattens its body so as to launch itself off tree branches or the eaves of houses, making a short downward glide to another tree or roof.

Perhaps a rather more surprising reptile to come across in a city is the Indian cobra. This extremely dangerous creature is remarkably capable of thriving in the very heart of busy urban areas within tropical India and other parts of Asia, where it causes numerous fatalities among the human populations. Generally, however, city-dwelling snakes are less spectacular. They are rarely more than three or four feet long, and many are very small indeed. In African cities, for instance, little burrowing snakes are widespread. They are so self-effacing, though, that they often remain undetected except when an occasional specimen is dug up or found in a compost heap. And of the several small species that still inhabit many South American cities, only the brightly colored coral snake is likely to make its presence known. What matters, however, is that snakes *do* manage to survive in cities, even in North America, where the rather dull-looking, harmless Northern brown snake might almost be called the "city snake" because of the frequency with which it turns up in parks, cemeteries, and rubbish heaps. (In most European cities, very few snakes survive, but a legless lizard, the so-called "slowworm," often inhabits parks and waste ground.)

Frogs are a staple diet for some snakes, and there are several species of frog even in New York City, together with other amphibians such as salamanders, toads, and peepers (tree frogs). In tropical and subtropical areas, frogs, toads, and their relatives are likely to abound in parks and gardens, but because most species are fairly secretive, they may make their presence known only during the breeding season, when they are often extremely vocal.

Most parts of the world also have aquatic frogs, which bask on lily pads or on the banks of ponds ready to jump into the water with a noisy "plop" at the slightest provocation. In New York, the green frog is the most common species, while the massive bullfrog, with its "jug-o'-rum" call, is occasionally seen near pools of water. In Europe, two confusingly similar aquatic frogs may be found in city areas: the marsh frog and the edible frog; both can be seen in parks, lakes, drainage ditches, cisterns, and other damp habitats, mainly in and around such southern cities as Sofia, Athens, Naples, and Madrid. It is not only the French who eat frogs' legs: frogs have been widely eaten all over the world, and both marsh and edible frogs are bred for the table in many places. Even the bullfrog, a much larger species, is bred for eating in some American cities, and it has also been introduced into Europe. Not enough are eaten, however, to pose a threat to their survival.

The greatest threats to the survival of urban populations of frogs and toads are probably pollution, cars, and collectors. Runoff from roads, particularly of oil, can kill whole populations of tadpoles in the roadside ditches, and seepage of pesticides is an even greater menace. Thousands of adult frogs and toads are massacred by cars as they migrate to their traditional breeding ponds. Those that survive run the risk of being taken captive by small boys or of being picked up for use as specimens in biology classes.

Lizards, like frogs and snakes, are mainly tropical and Mediterranean in distribution; the number of species decreases rapidly as climates get cooler, and the few species that *do* withstand cold weather cannot successfully adapt to big-city life. In warmer climates, of course, they thrive. During the hot summer months, for instance, dozens of small, brightly colored wall lizards can be seen scampering among the ruins on Palatine Hill in the center of Rome or on the Acropolis of Athens. In the Middle East, Africa, and even some parts of southern Europe, agama lizards, which grow to a couple of feet in length,

Agile lizards thrive in tropical city homes and gardens. Left: the common or household agama occurs in much of rural and suburban Africa; this one was photographed in Nigeria. Right: a tokay gecko on a door jamb in a Thai city. Named for its nocturnal cry, this species makes its home in the dwellings of human beings. It scales walls easily and catches insects, mice, and small lizards.

sun themselves on suburban walls.

In Central and South America, the agamas' niche may be filled by the superficially similar iguanas. Waste ground and parks in practically any city in the warmer parts of the world offer sanctuary for lizards—but usually only if the ground has never been built over. Unlike birds and plants, most lizards cannot recolonize a site once they have been expelled from it. Because of their inability to travel long distances or cross wide roads, their survival is dependent on the continuity of their habitat.

One group of lizards that is spreading its range over many parts of the world—though still not into the cooler parts of the temperate zone—is the gecko family. Geckos do not just live *near* man in parks and on waste ground; they are among the few reptiles actually to have moved in with him. Many species have finger pads that enable them to climb smooth walls, and so they make their way into houses, where they usually hide in cracks and crevices among the rafters. Although they sometimes emerge to sunbathe by day, they are mostly nocturnal and have the big

eyes with a vertical pupil common to many nocturnal animals. Nor are these lizards all small, inconspicuous animals. One house-dwelling gecko—the great house gecko, or tokay, of the Far East—can be a foot or so long.

The reptiles and amphibians, then, are more successful at adapting to city life than many people realize. Still, their success is, as we have seen, rather limited in both number and geographical distribution of species. Throughout the world, in temperate and very cold regions as well as in the tropics, mammal wildlife is far more abundant in the cities. Most of the mammal species would be conspicuous if they wandered through city streets by daylight, but, because they are small and nocturnal, they generally escape our notice. Londoners, for instance, are usually astonished when told that quite a number of foxes live right in their midst. In fact, all you need in order to see wild urban foxes is to take a quiet drive through the suburbs at about 2 A.M. with your headlights on. If you look carefully, you are also likely to see hedgehogs, as well as bats, close to the city center.

New York City can boast not one, but two species of fox: the North American red fox and the gray fox, both of which manage to survive however, much more secretive than their London counterparts and can generally be glimpsed only in parks and tracts of wasteland. The red fox still survives in many other North American cities. And it even seems to be invading some places—Montreal, for example.

Among other North American mammals that are at least occasionally found even in big cities are opossums, moles, and bats. One of the most primitive of these is the Virginia opossum, which survives in many city areas where there are trees. In fact, opossums are doing rather better than merely surviving. Perhaps because they are omnivorous creatures always in search of new food sources, they are spreading to areas where they were previously unknown. It is easy to trace their spread, for they are common road casualties. As for moles, they tend to survive in subterranean tunnels beneath parks and golf courses, where they cause considerable annoyance to gardeners and groundsmen. And bats,

of course, can be seen hawking for insects over the foliage of practically every city park in the world. New York has at least four species, one of which—the big brown bat—used to hibernate, appropriately, in The American Museum of Natural History, near Central Park.

These are all among the nocturnal small fry; there are also larger urban mammals. On the outskirts of many an American city, the raccoon, looking like the caricature of a burglar with its black facial mask, carries out nocturnal raids on garbage cans. And any naturalist visitor to Philadelphia or Chicago should be well aware that the skunk is common, even though it is rarely seen alive: the crushed and highly "scented" corpse of a skunk can often be found on the roads that cross the parks, as well as in outer areas of the city. Raccoons and skunks

European red fox scrounging in an overturned trash can. Foxes that have learned to live off man like this abound in London suburbs. In New York City the North American red fox and the gray fox survive secretively on the fringes of the Bronx.

Aptly masked like the burglar it is, this raccoon cautiously climbs a porch fence at night to steal household scraps. These attractive mammals are notorious for their nocturnal assaults on garbage cans in the suburbs of many North American cities.

have similar feeding habits. Both animals are largely scavengers, but they occasionally do some damage in vegetable gardens.

The mammals that can be seen by day are fewer in number. In the parks of Budapest, Bucharest, and several other European cities, red squirrels (*Sciurus vulgaris*) are a common sight. In London, the antics of the gray squirrel delight visitors to parks—but this species is not a survivor; it is an import from America, where it abounds, tame and popular, in many a park and suburban garden. An American version of

the red squirrel (*Tamiascurus hudsonicus*), once common in New York, has now gone, like its British counterpart, from the city confines, perhaps driven out by the more adaptable gray species. (A black variety of this gray squirrel appears to thrive in Vancouver.)

The most attractive of New York's squirrels, though, is not a daytime creature; it is the nocturnal flying squirrel (*Glaucomys volans*), which cannot really fly, but merely extends its leaping distance by means of a web of skin that stretches between the fore and hind limbs on either side of the body. Although you are unlikely to get a clear view of one of these strictly nocturnal creatures, you might occasionally turn up a nest in an attic, or you might just catch a glimpse of a dark shape gliding through the trees. At one

time flying squirrels used to visit bird-feeders in the areas of Henry Hudson Parkway, where most of the people putting food out for birds were unaware that it was not early birds but flying squirrels that were taking all the nuts. These squirrels are less abundant in that traffic-ridden neighborhood today, however.

In many a North American urban area, muskrats, white-footed mice, meadow mice, voles, and meadow-jumping mice live in the rough grass and meadows. In outlying areas, cottontail rabbits sometimes manage to survive, and even whitetail deer wander very occasionally into the outskirts. Woodchucks and groundhogs are very rare, but chipmunks are still common in some places. So, considering the density of buildings and roadways, a remarkably long

A hedgehog's last glimpse is often of the automobile about to run it down. These prickly European mammals thrive in city suburbs, but each year thousands die as they cross the roads.

wildlife list of American city mammals can be compiled. It is a list that no European city could equal—though this could well be corrected if naturalists conducted more careful surveys.

Australian cities are more like those of Europe in that few native mammals seem able to survive in them. Black and brown rats and house mice do flourish, of course, in thickly populated places, but inner cities contain virtually no native mammals apart from bats, such as the gray-headed fruit bat and several insectivorous species. The open plan of Aus-

37

tralian city suburbs, however, is ideal for the survival of a wide variety of wildlife, and several mammals still maintain a foothold in suburban areas, in spite of attempts to oust them. Where there are large gardens, parks, and waste ground, such mammals—including marsupials—are quite common. Among them are the brush-tailed and ring-tailed possums and the long-nosed bandicoot; the tiger cat and spiny anteater may occur in some city suburbs; and there is even a small colony of koalas at Palm Beach near Sydney.

The European hedgehog is a fairly common sight in urban New Zealand (where it is not, however, indigenous). Hedgehogs are especially abundant, though, in the cities of Europe, as evidenced by the squashed remains on continental and British roads. Debate continues among zoologists as to whether or not urban and suburban hedgehogs still roll themselves up into balls at the approach of motor vehicles, or have learned to avoid death by escaping instead of lying still. I *have* seen urban hedgehogs running away in the headlights of an approaching car rather than freezing into a ball of spines, but I have also found rolled-up corpses on the same road. Still, even if the hedgehog is suffering an excessively high mortality from cars, it is certainly one of the most successful surviving mammals in towns and cities. Suburban gardens provide an ideal habitat for the spiny creatures, and the latter have the great advantage of being popular with gardeners because of the help they give in the constant battle against slugs and other invertebrate garden pests.

One form of wildlife that is very much at home in big cities—most of which are either coastal or have rivers running through them—is the water-dweller. New York City is an outstanding example of a great coastal city, and its neighboring waters teem with fish, including sharks. During the summer months, brown sharks are often sighted off the beaches of Coney Island or Rockaway. Dogfish, smaller relatives of the shark, are also commonly caught by New York anglers. On the bottom of the Atlantic are various flat fish, including three species of skate and sting ray, and so the anglers along New York's

Giant snails on a garden gatepost in Thailand. These mollusks grow up to six inches long, and ravage flowers and vegetables in the gardens of various tropical cities. Snails and other pests provide food for beasts more welcome to the gardener.

enormously long shore-front sometimes make spectacular catches—not only of dogfish or skate but hake, cod, tomcod, whiting, flounder, pollack, silverside, shad, striped bass, bluefish, mackerel, and even the mighty bluefin tuna, which weighs up to 1500 pounds. Nearly 250 species of marine fish have been recorded in the New York region, any of which could fall prey to local anglers.

Although the littoral fauna and flora of the New York city area have suffered heavily as a result of the vast human demands upon the environment, the mobility of fish enables them to survive outside the polluted inner waters. Recent attempts to clean up the Hudson River should not only allow the survivors to increase but should encourage an even wider variety to return and recolonize New York's coastal, estuarine, and riverine waters. Even now, New York can boast of an impressive array of freshwater as well as saltwater animals. Among the native freshwater fish is the pumpkinseed or sunfish, a popular aquarium fish the world over, which is sometimes found even in small pools and ditches. One of the most tenacious New York survivors is the tiny mud minnow—less than four inches long—which manages to keep alive even in very murky, muddy ditches.

One of the main problems a fish has to contend with in the usually polluted rivers and streams of an urban environment is lack of oxygen. Most polluted waters, particularly in warm climates, have very low levels of dissolved oxygen, and so the fish that thrive in such waters are the ones that have found ways to overcome the deficiency. Urban fish are often able to take in gulps of atmospheric oxygen, and that is the key to survival of mosquito fish and other species that live in ditches close to cities.

Perhaps the most interesting inhabitants of urban rivers are mammals: the dolphins, which are entirely air-breathing and are, in fact, small, toothed whales. Some marine species grow up to 20 or 30 feet long, but the river-dwelling forms are much smaller. One of the four species, the bouto of the Amazon, has not yet had much to do with urban man, but the other three all occur in rivers that pass through densely populated cities. The four-foot-long La Plata dolphins, which live in the estuary of the Río de la Plata adjacent to Buenos Aires and Montevideo, still survive in spite of the fact that fishermen kill a couple of thousand every year. In the Indus, Brahmaputra, and Ganges rivers lives another species, the susu dolphin, which survives in waters that flow through some of the most densely populated parts of the world, where the Ganges flows past Calcutta and through Bangladesh. Even though fishermen kill relatively few of the susu dolphins, it cannot be long now before their survival is seriously threatened. There are so few left that any increase in the kill, or pollution or other factors such as hydroelectric dams, could reduce numbers beyond recovery. The fourth species of river dolphin is the white-flag dolphin, which lives only in the Yangtse River system of China; a few of these creatures, which were not actually recognized as a species until the beginning of the 1900s, have been seen in and around Nanking and Shanghai.

Of all the forms of wildlife that survive in the world's urban areas, the most thoroughly studied are the birds. In city parks and private gardens, the bird fauna will usually reflect that of surrounding rural areas, but with significant differences. It is not always the rural rarities that are also rare in the city, nor are the common birds of the countryside always the commonest in city parks. The type of bird that is likely to find a home in a city park is the bird whose natural habitat is the edge of the forest—and there are many, many such species.

Recent studies in Moscow indicate that a wide variety of birds survive in that city, although most of the recorded species appear to be comparatively recent invaders. One noteworthy survivor is the rook, a species that is rapidly disappearing from most western European cities. Some years ago, when a big bridge was being built over Moscow's river, the Moskva, the construction drove through the middle of one of Moscow's largest rookeries in the Lenin Hills, forcing the birds that survived the destruction of their treeland habitat to move. In doing so, they established another rookery, unparalleled elsewhere, by nesting on platforms near the top of floodlight masts in Moscow University's sports complex, where they built between two and four nests on each mast. Interesting as this was to ornithologists, the electricians would not tolerate it, and so the nests were destroyed. Compelled to abandon their artificial forest, the rooks returned to the Lenin Hills to nest close to their former site, and the size of the colony has steadily increased since then. Like their few remaining counterparts in western Europe, the Moscow rooks have to fly more than a mile out of

Below: kestrel perching on a wire. Kestrels and certain other falcons nest on city-center buildings. They hunt over parks and wasteland, seeking mice, voles, birds, and insects.

town in order to find food. It is probably for this reason that the birds no longer nest in the very center of the city.

Despite the fact that they have moved away from the heart of Moscow, however, the overall rook population of the city has risen since the 1960s. In 1971 there was a flock of 1000 rooks there; by 1973 three large flocks and several smaller ones were nesting in Moscow and its environs. Unlike rural rooks, these city birds are increasingly becoming scavengers; one bizarre, and yet common, food of fledgling Moscow rooks seems to be ice-cream wrappers! In western Europe, by contrast, the only places where rooks are at all common as scavengers are along highways and on rubbish dumps.

In the hedges of the parks and gardens of Moscow, linnets were fairly common residents until quite recently. Their population has been drastically declining in many areas, but the reasons are now well known, and the decline may be halted if sensible countermeasures are taken. Until the 1960s some 100 pairs of linnets nested in the grounds of Moscow University, but by the late 1960s they were more or less extinct, driven

Left: black vultures alight on a roof in Belém, northern Brazil. These birds serve as street scavengers in much of tropical America. Below: cock house sparrow at its nest under the eaves. This adaptable Eurasian bird was introduced to Brooklyn in 1852 and now lives in cities around the world, devouring food scraps, seeds, and insects.

out by the cutting and trimming of hedges and the use of herbicides. The thick hedges had provided protection for linnet nests; when they were cut back, not only were many nests actually destroyed but those remaining were exposed to heavy predation from Moscow's large crow population. The herbicides were used mainly to keep university lawns free of dandelions—a deadly blow to the linnet population, because dandelion seed heads had provided an extremely important food supply, particularly for the fledglings. There is hope for the future, however. Linnets have proved to be remarkably adaptable to changing conditions. For instance, they have learned to use such man-made materials as cotton and string in building their nests. Indeed, one linnet nest, built near a hairdresser's, was lined entirely with human hair.

Many bird species, in fact, are remarkably capable of adapting to city life. A recent analysis of the numbers and types of birds living in an urban area of Ontario provides evidence of their adaptability. In the 25-acre area under study, there is a human population of 78,000, and 80 per cent of the land is given over to nonresidential

uses. Yet the study turned up nine species of birds, with a density of 800 birds per 100 acres. The most numerous are, not surprisingly, house sparrows, starlings, pigeons, and chimney swifts. The populations of the remaining five species are as follows: nighthawks (16 per 100 acres), robins (18 per 100 acres), common grackles (25 per 100 acres), goldfinches (8 per 100 acres), and chipping sparrows (8 per 100 acres).

Where human populations are less dense, bird species naturally proliferate. For example, the spacious suburbs typical of Australian cities attract a very wide variety, some of which come as a surprise to visitors. On lawns overlooked by the Australian seat of government in Canberra, it is possible to see flocks of cockatoos; and in suburban gardens the famous kookaburra, or laughing jackass, is quite common. Most Australian gardeners now grow large numbers of roses and other non-native plants, but wherever such nectar-rich native blossoms as banksias occur, they attract indigenous nectar-feeding birds of many kinds. Honey eaters, particularly the yellow-winged species, are frequently seen, as are willie wagtails, which look and behave like the unrelated pied wagtail of Europe. And on ledges of city buildings, the occasional Nankeen kestrel nests in much the same way as its American and European counterparts.

One of the most detailed surveys of city-dwelling kestrels was carried out in London in the late 1960s. It was found that the average density in the central area of the city may have been as high as one pair in just under six square miles. Kestrels have been recorded as breeding in London's central area ever since the 1930s, though they may well have nested fairly close in for many years before that. Since the 1960s the annual recorded density has dropped, but this is probably due to a lack of enthusiasm on the part of those who record breeding sites.

In New York, the sparrowhawk, or American kestrel (a more accurate name, since it is a small falcon), nests rather sparsely. And the Nankeen kestrel is a city dweller in parts of Southeast Asia as well as in Australia.

Starlings at a winter bird table. The millions of these adaptable, aggressive birds in North American cities all derive from 100 imports freed in New York's Central Park in the 1890s.

Most birds of prey are retreating from cities, and the days of most of those that survive are probably numbered. In Central and South America, "vultures" (South American vultures are not related to those of the Old World but to giant condors) still serve as refuse collectors in areas where they are free from persecution. The Brahminy kite of India (so called because it is sacred to the god Brahma) is often still abundant in the cities, particularly around harbors. Egyptian, black, and griffon vultures, and black kites of the old world are all, generally, retreating from urban areas. In fact, of the very few groups of birds of prey that can really be said to be holding their own, the most successful seem to be the falcons.

Starlings and mynahs are a particularly adaptable family. The common starling and common mynah are both extremely successful. In the Far East, there are several other species of mynah and starling that have also discovered the advantages of living in cities and suburbs. In Japan and South Korea, the gray starling (*Sturnus cineraceus*) often nests in built-up areas, under the roofs of buildings. However, in the

adjacent maritime territory of the USSR it apparently shuns human habitations. In this region, it is another starling, the Daurian small starling (*Sturnus sturninus*), that nests fairly densely in villages and in the suburbs of towns. In the Soviet city of Iman, on the Manchurian border, Daurian small starlings have taken to nest boxes as well as nesting in the crevices of buildings. Farther south in South Korea, the same species has been extending its range over the last few decades. But the greatest success in the family is the common starling. It has not only managed to survive in cities but has expanded into new territory, and with the help of man has become so successful as to be a pest.

The birds that survive in Asian cities are numerous and diverse. The birds of prey—mainly vultures and kites—have already been mentioned, but the most widespread and numerous of all the scavengers is the house crow. This is a remarkable bird, for it seems to be unable to live apart from man and his habitations. It is apparently the only species of bird entirely dependent on man for its existence, and it is always found within a short flying distance of a village, town, or city. Toward the north of the Indian subcontinent, in the foothills of the Himalayas where settlements are sparse, the house crow is replaced as the major city scavenger by the jungle crow.

In suburban gardens and city parks in India and various parts of Southeast Asia, bulbuls, drongos, rollers, sunbirds, and babblers are all prominent. At night the cosmopolitan barn owl hunts for rats in most Asian cities, and several other owls are also often common, particularly in parks: the collared scops owl (*Otus bakkameoena*), the spotted owlet (*Athene brama*), and the spotted wood owl (*Strix seloputo*).

As a family group, pigeons have been remarkably successful in adapting to the urban habitat. The rock dove (town pigeon), is so successful that it is best considered as a pest. In Southeast Asia and India, a widespread species is the spotted dove, which, like some of the species mentioned above, has been widely introduced in other parts

A house crow joins a cow to hunt edible treasures in this Kashmir rubbish pile. House crows—the commonest airborne scavengers in southern Asia—may depend upon man for survival.

Above: street pigeons (descended from wild rock doves) are at home in the city. Its tall buildings afford them man-made counterparts of the cliff ledges where rock doves lay their eggs.

Below: clustered mud nests of house martins under the eaves of a house at Albufeira, southern Portugal. The species still nests on cliffs in a few rural areas, but generally favors buildings.

of the world. It is a small dove, often seen in groups running along roadsides, where it is a frequent casualty. In Malaysia, an even smaller species, the peaceful dove, also occurs in parks and gardens, and its range spreads southward to Australia, where it is known as the zebra dove.

Another common species of dove is the palm or laughing dove, which ranges from India westward into Africa, where it is characteristically found in cities and other man-made habitats. In eastern and northern African towns, the namaqua or masked dove is also common. In the New World, several small doves have adapted to life in villages and cities. The tiny, sparrow-sized ground dove, which ranges from the southern United States and the Caribbean islands down to northern South America, is increasingly a bird of the urban environment. In South America, the bare-faced ground dove, the Picu dove, the black-winged ground dove, the Inca dove, and several other species all commonly occur around villages, and sometimes in towns and cities.

One of the largest members of the pigeon family that has adapted to city life is the wood

pigeon. This is a species that is found over most of Europe, and that extends eastward to India. It is a major agricultural pest in many places, and so persecution by farmers has made it extremely timid and wary of man. However, in some European cities—and also Baghdad—it has become well-established as a bird of city parks. In the last few years it has even been observed to abandon its tree-nesting sites in favor of scaffolding (a sort of artificial tree, as far as a bird is concerned). In the past, it was always dependent on trees for survival in the heart of cities, but if increasing numbers of wood pigeons take to nesting on artificial sites, an increase in urban wood-pigeon populations can be anticipated.

Of all the doves occurring in European cities, the collared dove is probably the most famous. This species does not just *survive* in towns and cities; it is truly an invader—which is another chapter in the changing story of city wildlife.

The weavers and sparrows belong to a family that includes several highly successful species, notably the locust bird (*Quelea quelea*) and the house sparrow. Both of these are so successful as to be regarded as pests over most of their range. Several other related species have been adapted to urban environments for such a long time that they can be considered as survivors rather than invaders.

In Africa several species of weaver occur in suburbs and parks, but it is in Asia that the sparrows have diversified. In Central Asia, several species are found in cities and villages, though few seem to be extending their range. The snow finch, which breeds at high altitudes, often seeks out human habitations during hard weather, and in some areas of Central Asia snow finches nest right in the center of cities, mixed in with house sparrows. The rock sparrow is another mountain species. Rock sparrows have also been observed in the same regions, nesting in old house martins' nests as well as under the eaves of buildings; their colonies may comprise as many as 100 pairs.

The house sparrow is very closely related to several other species, notably the Spanish sparrow. The latter is far more widespread than its name suggests, for it is found throughout southern Europe and North Africa, and even eastward to the Himalayas. It often nests away from man and is rather nomadic, but it may also find a home in urban areas, where it has been known to nest alongside house sparrows. In

Mongolia and adjacent areas, Saxaul sparrows nest in buildings. In the Himalayas and eastward to Japan and Korea, russet sparrows are common in villages and occasionally on the outskirts of cities; they may also turn up in the center of towns when they are migrating.

In many towns of Central Asia, China, and other parts of the Far East tree sparrows are common, whereas the house sparrow is absent. In Central Asia generally, the tree sparrow is often found in the city centers, with the house sparrow nesting on the outskirts—the reverse of the situation in southern and central Europe.

In Europe, swallows and martins have long been associated with man. Today, swallows usually breed in barns and other outbuildings in fairly rural areas, but when horses were the normal mode of transport, they were undoubtedly far more widespread in urban areas, where they could nest in stables. One of the last recorded instances of swallows nesting near the heart of London was of a few in the antelope sheds in the Regent's Park Zoo. The house martin, as its name suggests, is even more closely associated with man. This species breeds in Europe and Asia, and, like the swallow, migrates south for the winter. Over most of Europe, the house martin builds its nest almost exclusively on man-made structures, usually under the eaves of houses. On some large apartment houses in the

center of Bucharest, I have seen a row of nests beneath practically every balcony. In Moscow, martins nested on theaters in the center of the city until some time in the 1960s—but no longer. Because of the lack of suitable building mud, the birds are now forced to nest elsewhere.

The house martin's nest is a shell of mud mixed with saliva, and with a small entrance hole. The original habitats of these birds were cliffs and gorges, as they still are around the Baltic, in eastern Asia, and in some other parts of the birds' range. At first, house martins, like American cliff swallows and other cliff-nesting birds, found the brick and stone of man's cities to be a hospitable environment, because the tall buildings were not unlike natural cliffs. As cities everywhere have expanded, however, the birds' survival has become precarious, for they need a ready supply of mud—preferably a shallow muddy stream—for use in rebuilding their nests each year. They also need man's tolerance, and modern urban man is often obsessively tidy; he cleans and drains muddy streams, and he may even destroy the martins' nests because he finds them unsightly.

Superficially similar in appearance, though unrelated to the house martin, the swift is a species that has retreated from many towns, but it appears to be holding its own in Moscow. In East Berlin, Rostock, and Dresden, architects have deliberately encouraged swifts to nest in modern apartment buildings by using hollowed-out bricks in the upper stories.

Another martin whose survival is connected with city man is the sand martin. This species

Kittiwakes nesting on a factory window ledge. Some coastal cities attract this and certain other kinds of seagull. The gulls evidently look upon rows of seafront buildings as continuations of the sea cliffs where their kind traditionally breeds.

rarely nests in the heart of cities, though it often passes through them on migration, but in suburbs and outlying areas it excavates its burrows in sandpits, railway cuttings, and the like, or it may even nest in man-made holes such as drainpipes without doing any further digging of its own. Sand martins have been known to nest in walls in Germany and in drainpipes in England. The species has a precarious foothold in city suburbs, but with a bit of encouragement it could perhaps become a characteristic bird of European cities. Artificial nesting colonies (sand martins are gregarious) could be built from a stack of drainpipes and erected in gardens.

Several other species of Old World martins and swallows occasionally nest in villages and suburbs, and it is possible that these and others may one day become true city birds.

The New World, too, has its urbanized swallows and martins. Two North American species that have adapted to man-made nest sites are the tree swallow and the purple martin. Both will use nestboxes provided for them, and one multiple nestbox may contain several dozen nests. In suburban and rural North America, the erection of multiple nestboxes for purple martins has become almost competitive, with some colonies numbering several hundred nests. The American cliff swallow sites and builds its nest much as does the Old World house martin.

Urbanization and industrialization can have benefited few birds as much as the chimney swifts of North America. Before the existence of cities they lived in hollow trees, but they soon adapted to a completely artificial environment. They now live in factory chimneys and other vertical shafts, where they glue their nesting material to the walls with saliva. Several thousand birds may nest in one high colony. Most of the world's swifts, however, live in the Old World, where, although they are not so completely urbanized as the chimney swift, their survival is nevertheless very closely linked with towns and cities. The Alpine swift, common swift, pallid swift, house swift, little swift, and white-rumped swift are all species that commonly nest in buildings, often almost exclusively so.

The palm swifts are closely related to the other species of swift. Although they do not nest in buildings, palm swifts are often found in cities and suburban areas. In towns in Jamaica, the Antillean palm swift often nests in the palm trees that grace the streets and gardens.

Nest colony of house swifts located beneath the rafters of a dwelling. The Chinese erect wires to support such colonies, because they believe that the house swifts will bring them luck.

We have seen that the wildlife that survives in a city is both diverse and ever-changing. Often the survivors are about to retreat and need man's help if they are to be encouraged to stay. The parks and open spaces that city man provides for the more beautiful and obvious forms of wildlife, such as birds, also help the more secretive and less obvious mammals. As soon as man encourages the wildlife he likes, then a whole host of opportunists benefit—reptiles, mammals, plants, and insects. However small our garden or even window box, given the slightest chance, wildlife *will* survive in the city.

Wildlife Retreating

The retreat of wildlife from a city is related to the spread of that city; the more rapidly the city spreads the more likely it is to destroy wildlife, because indigenous plants and animals will not have time to adapt to the new environment.

Under normal conditions, wildlife can adapt to new or unusual environments with remarkable speed, and this is particularly true of species that manage to survive in the unstable environment of a city. The North American skunk, which often makes itself at home under buildings, is one such example. Before the Industrial Revolution, many species, such as the kites and ravens of medieval European cities, managed to keep pace with the relatively gradual changes that occurred. During the last two centuries, however, those species unable to evolve fast enough to keep pace with the expansion of factories, office buildings, apartment houses, shopping districts, and traffic-laden roads, have disappeared, to be replaced by other species better adapted to a niche in the new ecosystem. Thus, the brown rats, which replaced the black rats in many places between 300 and 100 years ago, are themselves being replaced in Rangoon, New Delhi and many other Asian and Southeast Asian cities by little Burmese house rats.

The rapidity with which animals and plants can evolve to meet environmental changes is perhaps best illustrated by those species that live in isolated, oceanic islands, where the physical characteristics of birds, mammals, reptiles, plants, insects and other wildlife have been known to change enormously during the course of only a few hundred years. Cities, also are, "island" habitats, surrounded by contrasting agricultural or natural landscapes. As an illustration of what can happen, the house mice in some modern South American cities are so unlike their Asian ancestors that earlier in this century a mammalogist commented that if we didn't know its history, "the South American animal would be classed by many zoologists as belonging to another genus." Few modern zoologists would go quite as far, but most zoologists would agree that the success of the house mouse everywhere is largely the result of its ability to evolve rapidly over a comparatively short time.

In the period since the Industrial Revolution there has been a continuing drift of people away from the land and into the cities, as well as a worldwide rise in population associated with better health. For instance, according to the 1961 census, 22.5 per cent of the British population lived in the London metropolitan area, as compared with only 8.1 per cent in 1800. Similarly, whereas only 1 per cent of the population of the United States lived in the metropolitan New York City area in 1800, the percentage had risen to 8.2 per cent by 1960. Such increases must somehow be accommodated; and so, as the centers of cities become crowded, people move out and make their homes in the suburbs, thus extending the boundaries of the city even farther. It is probably reasonable, therefore, to consider the suburban environment, despite its extra tinge of green, as a natural extension of the city, equally inhospitable to certain kinds of wildlife while tolerant of others.

This would be true, generally, only for the urban reaches of the so-called developed countries. In Latin America, as in other poor regions, the typical form of urban development brought about by the drift from the land is the formation of surrounding *callampas*, *villas de miseria*, *barrios*, or *ranchos*, as the shantytown slums are variously known. In contrast to the affluent suburbs of North America and Europe, the shantytowns of Central and South America, parts of Africa, and southern Asia are havens for very little wildlife other than such vermin as rats and cockroaches. The shantytown type of city growth is nothing new. Medieval towns had their shanties outside the city walls. Only the scale is different.

Urban man's impact on wildlife is not just confined to the city and its suburbs. In fact, most of the native wildlife of any built-up area is bound to have retreated well in advance of the spread of towns, driven off by farmers cultivating the land. Even in fairly remote places wildlife may be at risk from urban families seeking recreation. A century ago, there were extensive swamps and coastal heathlands near Melbourne, Australia, and these habitats teemed with living creatures. A hunter who supplied the Melbourne

Building a bypass. Every year new road-building and housing schemes designed to relieve population pressure upon existing urban areas destroys millions of wild plants and animals. Many are directly killed by the construction operations. Many more die because they lose the habitats essential to their survival.

markets with fowl in the 1850s recorded emus, bustards, red-tailed cockatoo, corella cockatoo, ground parrot, and many other bird species that are no longer to be seen in those parts. Hunters, whether for business or sport, along with amateur naturalists who watched birds down gunbarrels, observed insects on pins, and stuck flowers onto paper, were part of a destructive force that ensured the eradication of any wildlife that could perhaps have coped with the changes in habitat brought about by the expansion of Melbourne.

Pressure on the wildlife of the countryside, then, is to a certain extent proportional to urban population and the amount of leisure time available to the city dwellers. Obviously, some forms of pressure—trapping, for instance—are controllable and have, in fact, declined. Others, though, are very much on the increase. Common

meadow plants, for instance, have drastically declined in grassland areas adjacent to the world's major conurbations and this is at least partly due to the visiting hordes of fresh-air seekers, who either trample down the flowers or pick them. Overpicking has caused many of the prettier flowering plants to disappear from suburban and city parks. During the Victorian era, a fern craze swept Europe and America, and ferneries sprang up in living rooms everywhere. Even today, wild ferns are often dug up and transplanted to pots and gardens, where they rarely flourish. In New York the maidenhair fern, a particularly attractive species, has almost disappeared, and the once-abundant Christmas fern, which is green even in mid-winter, has been drastically overpicked by Yuletide gatherers.

Recent research indicates that the effect of people walking over grassy hillsides and meadowland is very similar to that of grazing. This means that public grasslands, with their attractive wild flora, can be maintained in all their beauty only if access to them is regulated and limited by

Shacks roofed by loose sheeting form this shantytown on the fringes of São Paulo, the fastest growing city in Brazil and arguably in the entire world. At their best, modern cities discourage much wildlife. In dense shantytowns like this almost the only wild survivors are hardy pests such as rats and cockroaches.

such things as keep-off-the-grass and no-picking rules. Among the first plants to suffer, once their habitat has been discovered by the public, are the various wild orchids, whose beauty makes them irresistible to picking by collectors. Uncontrolled human pressure can lead eventually to denudation and erosion problems of the kind that exist today in any city park where people have unrestricted use of short cuts between the various laid-out paths.

Most European cities are so old that their beginnings are difficult to date accurately, and so we have few dependable records of what sort of creatures inhabited them in their earliest days. Even in the New World, cities were usually fairly well established before naturalists began to study their flora and fauna; but we do have some interesting indications of the abundance of wildlife in certain areas that later became great cities. In 1628, for instance, soon after the first Europeans settled on Manhattan Island, trappers there sent nearly 7000 beaver skins to Europe, and deer and bears abounded in the island's woods. In 1670, an account of Manhattan and the surrounding countryside written by a certain Daniel Denton and published in London noted that in Long Island's Jamaica area (which is now, of course, very close to the center of the city of New York) there were bears, deer, foxes, wolves, heath-hens, cranes, geese, and ducks. Denton also reported that whales and seals were common in the sea to the south of Long Island. Much of the island was wooded, with red and white oak, walnuts, and chestnuts among the commonest species, as well as maples, cedars, beeches, holly, many fruiting bushes, raspberries, and strawberries, "of which last is [in] such abundance in June that the field and woods are dyed red."

Alas, this abundance of wildlife in the western part of the island (now part of the big urban complex of New York City) was destined to

51

disappear. As late as 1903 The American Museum of Natural History published a leaflet that named 45 species of hawk moth occurring in the metropolitan area. By 1935, however, when Dr. Frank Lutz made a survey of the insects in nearby Ramsey, New Jersey, 20 miles from the center of New York, he could find only 10 species of hawk moth. Even the little remaining "natural" landscape of New York has been altered by the introduction of exotic plants from all corners of the globe. Something like 40 per cent of the plant life in modern New York City is European in origin, and the decline in numbers of the native moths could well be connected with the loss of the indigenous plants on which hawk-moth caterpillars feed.

Over and above all the human activity that directly harms the native wildlife and forces it to retreat, there is the indirect menace of the city itself and its by-products. Around most major cities, industrial complexes exert a steri-

lizing effect on the surrounding countryside, and this in turn influences the animals that survive in, retreat from, or invade the city. Each year some 350,000 tons of lead are burned in internal-combustion engines in the Northern Hemisphere. Most of this poison from car exhausts is in urban areas, and it would seem reasonable to expect it to have a harmful effect on wildlife.

Pollution is nothing new. It has always been a feature of the city environment, and long before our time, man has not only been conscious of it but has tried to combat it. In the Middle Ages, for instance, statutes were passed in some parts of Europe that attempted to control the pollution produced by coal fires, but the statutes seem to have had little effect. It was not until the Industrial Revolution, however, that pollution became a major factor in the decline of wildlife from around the cities.

Somewhat surprisingly, the atmospheric pollu-

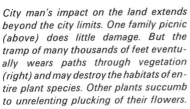

City man's impact on the land extends beyond the city limits. One family picnic (above) does little damage. But the tramp of many thousands of feet eventually wears paths through vegetation (right) and may destroy the habitats of entire plant species. Other plants succumb to unrelenting plucking of their flowers.

tion that creates the mixture of smoke and fog now known as "smog" is mainly produced by smoke from domestic fires rather than from industry. This is certainly true in Britain, at least, as was demonstrated in the 1950s when the Clean Air Acts drastically reduced the number of big-city smogs by controlling domestic smoke pollution. Although there is still atmospheric pollution in Britain's cities, as in all others, the famous pea-soup fogs Hollywood used to enshroud London in are now a thing of the past. But even when cities have managed to curb domestic smoke pollution, there remains a long and depressing list of pollutants that affect

wildlife. The most significant pollutants affecting plants (and consequently the animals that feed on them) are, in order of importance, ozone, sulfur dioxide, nitrates (particularly peroxyacyl nitrates), hydrocarbons (particularly ethylene), fluorine, pesticides, chlorine and hydrochloric acid, nitrogen dioxide, heavy metals, and solid particles (soot, etc).

Water pollution, of course, is a major urban problem. Many of the world's cities are situated on rivers, and at the time of their foundation they usually got a good deal of food from the water. With the passage of time, however, most rivers in urban areas have become so polluted

Urban wastes poison much wildlife otherwise able to survive in the city. The smoke from chimneys (above) and the smog produced by the exhausts of cars (below) pollute the atmosphere. Sewage and chemical wastes released into such rivers as the Thames (seen here at London) can kill fish stocks, although a purification program for the Thames proved that exiled species may return when the water is cleaned.

that they are more or less devoid of life.

Until the Industrial Revolution, a wide variety of fish were found in London's River Thames, but most of them disappeared in the course of the 19th century. In the Middle Ages, a polar bear kept in the royal menagerie at the Tower of London was taken to the river daily on a leash, and allowed to eat its fill of salmon. Even during the first quarter of the 19th century, over 7000 pounds of salmon were caught there. Since then, the Thames has lost most of the life that used to flourish in it, although from time to time small numbers of a variety of species have turned up, and eels have managed to survive through thick and thin. In recent years, to be sure, increased public awareness and concern over pollution has led to efforts to clean up the river and as a result some species have begun to return.

In 1654, in a letter to his home country, a Dutchman living in New Amsterdam (as New York was then named) wrote that the waters around it were alive with perch, sturgeon, bass, herring, mackerel, weakfish, stone bream, eel, and various other species. Most of these have now gone from the New York rivers and coastal waters, although on the cleaner Atlantic coasts fish are still to be found. In this case, though, we cannot totally blame pollution for the disappearance. In the rivers and seas around Manhattan, the fish have been affected not only by the massive pollution that the city produces, but also by climatic changes that have caused some species (particularly in the cleaner salt water) to shift their range northward as the New York area has become warmer.

One New York fish that has undoubtedly disappeared almost entirely because of pollution and overfishing is the sturgeon. In New York the sturgeon fishery, which was once worth $6 million in a single season, is now totally defunct. Shad, eels, and some other fish do still manage to survive, however, even in the murkiest waters around the city. The Federal Water Pollution Control Administration recommended the widening and deepening of the inlet connecting Moriches Bay to the Atlantic, which will help to flush pollution out to sea, and it also recommended that wastes from duck farms be discharged at least one and a half miles out to sea. With the millions of dollars now being spent on cleaner rivers, the decline in fish populations is being arrested—and may eventually even be reversed.

Our increasing concern for the deteriorating

environment has led to a considerable interest being taken in lichens. At first glance, these strange rather insignificant plants, an association of particular species of fungi with single-celled algae, look like a moss or liverwort. More than a century ago, botanists noticed that certain lichen species seemed unable to survive in city centers. Since then, close observation of lichens has taught us that some of them are peculiarly susceptible to urban pollution, and we use their presence or absence as relatively accurate indicators of pollution levels in metropolitan areas.

Lichens are especially sensitive to sulfur dioxide. With millions of tons of sulfur dioxide being pumped into the world's atmosphere each year as the waste from power stations, it is hardly surprising that many lichens are disap-pearing even in rural areas. As for towns and cities—look at the spot-encrusted sulfuric-acid-eaten facade of almost any European cathedral and see how much damage the polluted air has done to the fabric of buildings upon which lichens would otherwise flourish. If you wander through any big city with your eyes wide open, you will notice that lichen coverage becomes increasingly sparse, with the number of species decreasing as you approach the center of the city, where the atmosphere is drier and more heavily polluted. In the central districts of both New York and London today, you will find only one species. Lichens were first studied in the London area in the late 18th century, when 200-odd species appear to have lived within 16 miles of the city center; in recent years, only 62 species have been recorded within the same area.

A particularly interesting study was carried out in 1970 in the churchyards of London and its suburbs. Gravestones provide an ideal habitat for certain species of lichen that thrive on limestone and similar alkaline substrates. Such species are not killed off by atmospheric pollution; it simply inhibits their spread and colonization of new sites. And an examination of the dated gravestones of the area studied has produced plenty of evidence in support of this fact: some 90 per cent of the stones dating from 1750 to 1775 are inhabited by a species called *Caloplaca heppiana*, as against only 25 per cent of those dating from 1875–1900, and none at all after 1900.

You may well ask whether the loss of lichens matters. The answer, of course, is that lichens are not just isolated plants, they are part of an ecosystem about which we know very little. Some animals feed on lichens—for instance, snails, mites, and a wide variety of insects including springtails and moths. The bark lice that feed on lichen are preyed on by bugs, which in turn provide food for many other animals, as do most of the other lichen-feeders and *their* predators. Some insects have evolved cryptic coloring that mimics the lichenous patterns; without the real lichen background they become blatantly obvious to predators such as birds, and so they tend to disappear along with the lichens.

Among the other plants that suffer from atmospheric pollution, conifers come off especially badly, because, since they do not shed their leaves, they cannot rid themselves of the accumulation of noxious dust. In a study made near the city of Sudbury, Ontario, it was found that spruces appear to be less affected than pines, and that the white (or Weymouth) pine is the most sensitive of all. The young white pines, it was found, do not grow well, or in some cases do not grow at all. The older ones die off. Larches, which are deciduous conifers, can tolerate much higher levels of pollution than can the others. And accumulations of soot appear to have more serious effects when they are deposited during daylight rather than nighttime hours—probably because the pores (stomata) of the plants are open only when the sun shines. The extent of pollution is often far greater than the city dweller realizes. Few Londoners, for instance, are aware of the fact that the pinetum of the Royal Botanic Gardens, which is located in Kew, nine miles away from the center of London, has had to be moved some distance from the city because it has proved impossible to grow pines at Kew.

For the wildlife that manage to survive the disturbances and pollution of city life, there are yet more obstacles to overcome. Telephone wires and power cables present a serious hazard to birds, particularly to such large species as swans and other waterfowl. In summer, melting tar on roads can foul the feet of birds and small mammals and can ensnare them just as effectively

Yellow and gray lichens grew like stains spreading in slow motion across the limestone surface of these gravestones. But some lichens stop growing if the air becomes polluted. Studies of dated London gravestones show that these lichens flourished in the mid-18th century but ceased spreading by 1900— proof that London's atmosphere had become considerably worse.

57

Power lines, deceptively resembling threads of gossamer, swing across the countryside in northern Spain. Where such cables converge on a city, birds run a serious risk of colliding with them, and thus suffering major injury or death.

as it did other creatures thousands of years ago at the tar pits of Rancho la Brea, the famous paleontological site in California. Airplanes coming down to land often kill birds, too, though it is doubtful if this affects the overall population. What does affect the population, however, is the action taken by airport authorities against "bird strikes" (the descriptive name for collisions between birds and planes), which are much more common, and can be much more disastrous, than many people realize. The wide, flat expanse of airport areas has a great attraction for wild creatures such as gulls, starlings, bustards, and hares, all of which can cause

accidents. So they must be got rid of somehow— and a whole host of techniques, from scarecrows to detonators to flashing lights have been used to keep airports free of "pests." The most successful of such techniques, ironically enough, is a relatively natural one: flying trained falcons over the airport just before an aircraft lands, in order to frighten other birds off the runways. Inevitably, wildlife populations rarely flourish in inhospitable environments of this sort.

One of city man's most effective destroyers of indigenous wildlife is the motor car. In the past the slow-moving horse-drawn vehicles used to provide food for a wide variety of creatures; with the permanent retreat of the city horse, many insects and the animals that fed on them also retreated. Sparrows and other birds used to eat the spilled grain of horse feed. Vast numbers of flies used to breed in the manure. Insects and plants used to be carried into the big cities in horse feed, and they often managed to gain a foothold in the urban environment. Thus, the horse's food and manure formed the basis of an important food chain. Now the automobile has broken the chain irreparably.

The motor car is, moreover, a killer in more direct ways. Everywhere in the world it takes its toll of birds, mainly the smaller passerine species. In Europe and adjacent areas and in New Zealand, hedgehogs are a common casualty. In suburban areas of North America, skunks and turtles are among the casualties; in Australia it is possums that suffer most. Dark, heat-absorbing road surfaces attract reptiles, and in warmer climates snakes and lizards are common road fatalities. Frogs and toads migrating to their breeding ponds also get crushed by interurban traffic. Insects, too, are attracted to the heat-retaining road surfaces, particularly at night, and both insects and road casualties attract predatory and scavenging animals, which may themselves end up as highway victims. Indeed, the urban predator (the nonhuman variety, at least) leads a precarious life, delicately balanced between successfully living off the rich pickings of the roads and being itself destroyed.

As with horses, other domestic animals were once abundant in the Western World's cities. Nowadays, most town animals are kept as pets, but chickens and pigs used to be common in urban backyards, and their general disappearance has led to the disappearance of the fauna associated with them—their parasites, flies, and large numbers of rats and mice.

As I have already emphasized, one of the most important factors governing the kind of wildlife in a city is the degree of tolerance shown to it by man. Some species seem to us to be either too huge or too dangerous to have living alongside us. Thus, bison, tigers, lions, and other large mammals have never really had a chance to thrive at liberty in city streets. Some surprisingly big animals do, however, manage to hang on in towns. Hyenas scavenge on the outskirts of thickly populated areas in Africa, foxes and coyotes raid garbage cans in Europe and North America, and jackals and other canids are a common sight in the suburbs of many Asian and African cities.

Where wildlife is traditionally tolerated, as in many Oriental countries, it will often be remarkably abundant, but a change in attitudes can have drastic consequences. China is remarkable for the dearth of wildlife in most of the country's populated areas. Until very recently, the Communist Chinese regarded practically all animals as competitors for the food that the human population required. There was, for instance, an all-out attempt to rid the country of

Horse-drawn vehicles crowding London's Oxford Circus in 1875. The horses' fodder and manure enabled swarms of sparrows and flies to breed in the city, and insects and wild plants moved in, hitching rides in horse feed. Thus horse fodder and manure created an urban food chain, broken by the coming of the car.

sparrows—an attempt, incidentally, that resulted in the slaughter of countless other small birds as well as the offending species. Modern visitors to China have commented on the fact that even flies seem rare there. This can be accounted for by the fact that national campaigns to clean up breeding places, and then kill, with every available means, the flies in cities were carried out with the greatest possible efficiency.

There are numerous other reasons why individual species disappear from the city and its environs. One, of course, is the felling of trees. Rooks once nested in many European cities, but they have disappeared from nearly all the larger ones. Because rooks need large, mature trees in which to nest, it is likely that when their rookery is chopped down to make way for city growth, they have no alternative but to retreat. Similarly, birds of prey are forced out by a lack of food in city streets or by pollution of one kind or another.

Birds of prey used to be a familiar sight in practically every city in the world. Now, although a handful of species can still be seen flying over New York, Berlin, Paris, and most other major cities, the variety and number have been drastically reduced. Just after World War II, about 15 square miles of Warsaw lay in ruins, and hordes of rats and mice throve in the rubble. The rodent population provided ample food for sparrowhawks, goshawks, kestrels, peregrine falcons, and barn owls, and so the predatory birds also throve. Today, however, the only species that still flourishes in rebuilt Warsaw is the kestrel, which is the most adaptable of such birds. The others have flown away in pursuit of better pickings, or—as has happened with birds everywhere in recent years—have fallen victims to poisoning. (This may be deliberate in a few cases, but it is mainly due to the accumulation of pesticides in the small mammals and other creatures on which the big birds feed.)

Among the birds particularly affected by poisoning is the peregrine falcon, which has disappeared from all the city habitats where it once flourished. Peregrines are known to have bred in New York City as recently as a generation ago, when, having found an abundant food supply in the form of pigeons and starlings, they were able to rear their young in nests on upper-story hotel and skyscraper ledges. Even more recently they were nesting in Moscow and other Russian cities. (An interesting fact that emerged when such big-city peregrines were studied was that nests built on bare ledges had poor drainage, and so young birds reared in them became soiled and fetid, whereas nests made on piles of dirt and gravel kept the baby birds clean and healthy.) It seems likely that peregrines would have become firmly established as urban-dwellers had it not been for the accumulation of poisonous pesticides in the bodies of their prey. By now their in-city numbers have shrunk to a level from which they will probably never fully recover.

Even the European white stork, which has been protected on the continent for centuries, has been losing ground. To have a stork nesting on one's house is considered lucky in most northern European countries, and householders encourage the birds to nest by placing artificial platforms—often old cartwheels—over chimneys and on roofs. Earlier this century, storks were still quite common in towns in Alsace, The Netherlands, Switzerland, Denmark, and Germany. Some 150 pairs, for example, were counted in Switzerland alone—but by 1950 they had all disappeared. The outward expansion of cities has meant that urban storks must fly farther and farther away to feed, and telephone wires, electric cables, and rooftop aerials make such flights increasingly hazardous. Even in the open countryside, the storks have trouble finding food, for the demands of human populations have meant the filling in of ponds and the draining of marshes, with a consequent reduction in the number of frogs (a staple in the stork's diet). In addition, changes in agriculture and the use of chemical pesticides have reduced the edible insect population and contaminated those that are left. Finally, such storks as still survive in Europe are subjected to intense pressure during the winter months when they migrate to Africa, where significant numbers are shot by the proliferating and ever-hungry human population.

The movement of wildlife as it is affected by modern urban man should not, however, be viewed as an entirely one-way affair. As certain species decline and disappear, others take their place. Thus, while kites and ravens, the classic scavengers of medieval cities, are no longer to be seen in 20th-century Western towns, gulls and crows have colonized the urban habitat and are spreading rapidly. Much the same thing is true of plants. For instance, the London rocket, which is said to have colonized the waste ground created in central London by the Great Fire of 1666, is now a very rare plant—the last recorded sighting was near the Tower of London; but the Oxford ragwort has, to a certain extent, taken its place, along with a close relative of the rocket, the wall-flower, which has escaped from cultivated gardens to colonize waste ground. So, in spite of all the changes and upheavals, life does continue in the city.

We must always be wary of over-simplifying trends. The species we regret to see retreating from our cities this year may in a few years be considered as pests. Those we think of as pests today may vanish within a decade (as did the not-at-all-regretted black rat). The reasons for the ebbing and flowing are so complex that no single answer can be given to the question of why urban wildlife is ceaselessly changing. The only thing that is certain is that we can expect the variety of wildlife in a city and its close-packed suburbs to change constantly—and, indeed, to change more rapidly than do the flora and fauna of practically any other habitat.

Many wild species have grown scarce in and near the cities, but others (and domesticated animals) have multiplied. Right: white storks nesting in a tire put on a chimney by Dutch citizens, who think storks bring good fortune. But nest sites are no use without a food supply; drainage and insecticides have slashed the frog and insect population that these storks depend upon, and their kind is becoming rare throughout Europe. Below: chickens thrive as a species under human management.

Wildlife Invading

Although many of the wildlife species to be found in urban areas are survivors of the original forest-edge habitat, there are other, very important—in fact, often dominant—forms of city-dwelling wildlife: the invaders. These are the species of plant and animal that find the urban environment so hospitable that their success in colonizing regions to which they have previously been alien is often such that they become pests.

The ability of wildlife to colonize virtually any city habitat is best demonstrated by what happens on a piece of ground that is temporarily left derelict after being cleared for building. Within a few weeks it will be swarming with life, both plant and animal. This life can be very roughly grouped into three categories: the natural invaders that spread of their own accord, such as willow herbs, nighthawks, and collared doves; the temporary invaders that never become permanent residents, such as the rare insects that drift in and, more particularly, the migrant birds that pause to rest before continuing their journey; and the invaders that are helped along by man, such as mynahs, parakeets, and garden plants.

During World War II, when bombs devastated large areas of such cities as Düsseldorf, Coventry, Dresden, Belgrade, Leningrad, Warsaw, and London, a profusion of vegetation sprang up in the burned-out sites within weeks or even days of the bombings. Such sites gave botanists an unprecedented opportunity to make uniquely large-scale studies of the succession of flora on disturbed ground.

London, of course, was one of the most frequent targets for bombers; in 1940 and 1941 an area of just over 100 acres was laid waste in the heart of the city, and parts of this large tract of derelict land remained undeveloped for up to a quarter of a century or more. Plant life quickly invaded the exposed ground. By 1955 botanists had re-

Wild plants flower where people used to kneel in prayer. German bombs laid this London church open to the sky. Soon, tiny plants and animals were colonizing the rubble that remained, and if man had left the site alone, trees would have sprouted amid the ruins. Where man moves out, wildlife rapidly moves in: forests can cover entire abandoned cities in this manner.

Among the species that seeded themselves on European city sites exposed by shells and bombs were dozens of types of cultivated plants escaped from gardens. Blooms that concealed the harshness of war damage include those of the plants pictured here. Left: the parchmentlike pod partitions of honesty, a plant with white or lilac flowers. Below left: wallflower clinging to a stone wall. Below right: the usually purple flowers of Buddleia bushes attract butterflies—hence the popular name of butterfly bush.

corded 342 plant species on land that had probably supported far fewer than a quarter of that number, mainly in a few small gardens, in prewar days. The botanists who carried out surveys of the bombed sites grouped the invading flora under a number of headings, which for convenience can be reduced to eight major groups: plants whose seeds were dispersed by wind; those whose seeds were brought in with horse fodder; those whose seeds were brought in by birds; plants from seeds of edible fruits discarded by human beings; plants with burrs that had been brought in stuck to clothing, fur, and so on; those that had already existed in local gardens; deliberate introductions (including garden plants from elsewhere); and plants of unknown origin.

The most numerous group of invaders were 68 plant species from gardens in the area, and 26 of these had become truly naturalized. They in-

Japanese garden on a site at Covent Garden, in central London. In this case plants colonized a site exposed by demolition for a project that was later shelved. Local residents used the respite to create central London's first new public garden in more than a century. The land lacked topsoil, but the property company owning the land supplied earth-moving equipment to make good the deficiency and a designer created a sense of spaciousness by contrasting areas of land and water. Trees were deliberately planted, but the garden's temporary nature encouraged an informality that gave scope for small wild plants to get a footing. Developers, however, have now also built on nearly all of the city's bombed sites dating from World War II. Naturalists have thus largely lost the opportunity of seeing the stealthy process by which nature begins to retrieve the land that industrial man had taken over.

cluded honesty, sweet alyssum, wallflower, evening primrose, butterfly bush, greater snapdragon, asparagus, and Peruvian lily. Most of the remaining garden plants occurred only in small numbers, and although some lasted for several seasons, they never became established. It is probable that many of the garden plants were introduced deliberately by civic-minded Londoners in an attempt to bring a note of hope and rebirth to the ravaged landscape. However,

once established, certain of the species, such as those I have named, proved quite capable of propagating themselves.

Although after a decade or so garden plants had become the most numerous category of invaders on the bombed sites, they were by no means the first to colonize. The very first arrivals to be recorded were those with wind-dispersed seeds. Botanists swiftly noted 53 species of them, including some that are familiar on waste ground

in almost every corner of the world. Perhaps the two most characteristic groups of wind-dispersed flowers are the rosebay willow herb and the ragwort. Willow herbs, which have purple-pink flowers, are also known as fireweeds—not for their color, which is not at all fiery, but for their rapid colonization of burned-out ground. After a forest fire in the temperate regions of the world they are always among the first colonists; and because a single plant can produce 80,000 or more seeds a season, each of which is airborne on a fluffy parachute, they spread with amazing rapidity. The blitzed areas of all the bombed cities of Europe provided an ideal habitat for willow herbs, and it was often only just a matter of weeks before the first seedlings were pushing up through the rubble and ruins. But it does not take a war to encourage these plants. Today the great willow herb is among the first colonists of any land where a building has been demolished

or of the verges and embankments of newly constructed roads.

Not far behind in colonizing ability is the ragwort. There are several species of these bright yellow flowers, but perhaps the classic waste-ground example in Europe is the Oxford ragwort. This plant is thought to be a native of Sicily. At any rate, it appears to have been carried to Oxford in the 18th century by someone who found it on the slopes of Mount Etna. The specimens were planted in Oxford University's Physick Garden (a garden where medicinal plants are cultivated), and it was from there that some seeds, blown on the winds, managed to colonize walls elsewhere in Oxford. By 1800 the ragwort had evidently become naturalized in several parts of the city, but for many years this was as far as it spread. Then in 1879 it was seen growing on a railroad outside the city. This was to be a feature of the Oxford ragwort's spectacular spread; in the days of steam trains, clinkers and the frequently scorched railway embankments provided a habitat not so very different from the rocky, volcanic slopes of Mount Etna. Eventually, the plant adapted to a broader variety of environments, and it has now spread to every city in Britain and across the water to France. In the cities of North America, its place is taken by another yellow-flowered member of the daisy family; the similarly named ragweed.

Another plant that flourished in London's bombed sites was bracken. During the 19th century it was seldom found in England's great cities, and it remained rare right up to 1940. It came into its own during the war, however, and is now extremely common in London as well as in other urban areas where the bombs fell freely decades ago. As a schoolboy, soon after the war, I used to visit the still extensive bombed sites during summer holidays, and I can remember my first impression being one of brilliant color: purple rosebay, sunny yellow ragwort, bright leaf-green bracken, interspersed with splashes of garden flowers and less familiar plants, with the occasional brown tree trunk seemingly growing out of a wall. There might even be a clump of

pale yellow evening primroses—a relative of the willow herb—that had no doubt escaped from someone's well-kept garden. Or perhaps my eye would light on two other spectacular species that had escaped from gardens to become characteristic plants of the new-found habitat: purple-petaled, yellow-centered Michaelmas daises, and curved, golden-flowered goldenrod. One of the commonest of the larger plants was the butterfly bush (*Buddleia*), which grew halfway up, or actually on top of, walls left standing in the ruins.

Just as on any temporary waste ground of today, most of the plants that invaded Europe's bombed sites had wind-dispersed seeds. Along with the rosebay, there were such other willow herbs as the great hairy, the dull-leaved, and the broad-leaved willow herb. And among the wide-

Rosebay willow herb's tall, purple-pink flowers are a familiar sight on burned-out ground, in forests and in city centers alike. The plants can drift deep inside a city in the form of seeds wafted along by means of their light, fluffy parachutes.

Abandoned industrial sites on the edges of cities are favorite bridgeheads for advancing nature. Here, masses of yellow-flowering tree lupines beautify a derelict railroad siding at Lowestoft, in eastern England. These plant invaders originated in California and escaped from gardens. Tree lupines thrive in open sandy soil that many other plants find unsatisfactory.

Ferns and other epiphytes cloak the outline of an old wall in Thailand. Bricks and mortar and the organic debris lodged between them provide nourishment adequate for plant growth, especially when the atmosphere is usually warm and damp.

spread colonists that blew in on the wind were also the male fern, birch tree, sallow and willow, coltsfoot, Canadian fleabane, thistle, and dandelion. But, as I have said, there were several other ways in which plants could make their way to new places.

In the 1940s, for instance, there were still some working horses in London and other European cities, and some of the flora that invaded the bombed sites grew from seeds brought in with horse fodder. Numerous grasses, as well as a wide selection of cereals and the weeds that grow among them, were able to colonize waste ground in this way but this source has virtually disappeared along with the working horse from the big cities of the developed world. A related source of fresh plant invaders does survive, however, in birdseed: from time to time, corn hemp, or rape seed, either discarded from the cage of a budgerigar or canary or deliberately set out for wild birds, takes root and spreads.

Other invading waste-ground colonists grow

Wherever there is the light, warmth, moisture, and freedom from disturbance, plants secure a roothold. Above left: a young hazel tree and bracken lay claim to the abandoned interior of a decayed railroad building. Hazels and bracken are plants that thrive in open woodland settings, of which this gutted building offers a kind of urban equivalent. Left: stunted willow herb keeps alive on the meager quantity of soil lodged in this curiously formed pouch. Sagging lead and asphalt on roofs and sidewalks can leave cracks where windblown dust collects and provides nourishment for any windblown seeds that happen to drop in. If the streets and buildings of a city are infrequently cleaned and repaired, plants find places to push down roots that, given time, will split apart the city's very brick and concrete fabric.

71

An insect and a flowering plant represent two of the various ways in which nature colonizes city habitats. Left: elephant hawkmoth, a handsome species with big, spectacular caterpillars. These feed upon the willow herb that often lives on neglected urban building sites. Center: dandelions that have gained a roothold in the side of a brick wall. Each dandelion seed has its own little parachute. These particular plants no doubt sprang from seeds that had been blown into crevices in the wall by some conveniently timed breeze.

from the seeds tossed away or spat out by human beings eating fruit. The wild flora to be seen in an empty lot is likely to reflect—in part, at least—the local popularity of various kinds of fruit. In the tropics, for instance, one finds wild date, palm, or melon plants; in temperate regions, perhaps plums, apples, blackberries, and cherries.

Most of London's bombed sites have now disappeared. Not a few naturalists would have liked to see some of them preserved but, with the increasing value of land in central urban areas, preservation for the sake of the biological sciences has been out of the question. Instead, naturalists must continue their studies of how wildlife invades city places by observing the temporary open spaces that are left whenever buildings are demolished. One interesting discovery has been that modern building-site waste

ground attracts some species notably different from those that settled in the bombed sites. Changes began to take place, in fact, very soon after World War II. When botanists carried out a survey of the wild plants on a site near St. Paul's Cathedral in 1947–49, for instance, and then again in 1952–55, they found that by the 1950s the male fern, common persicaria, goldenrod, and beaked hawksbill, none of which had been spotted in the earlier survey, had colonized and were becoming common. By contrast, the red goosefoot, fat hen, and many-seeded goosefoot, all three of which had been abundant in the earlier survey, had become quite rare. From this one sample, a microcosm of the whole city, the characteristic fashion in which the balance of the ecosystem changes can be clearly seen.

In an earlier chapter, I pointed out that many

Blue tit at a birdhouse on a birch tree. Tits are the Eurasian counterparts of North America's chickadees. These groups of birds include bold species that inhabit city gardens, where they enjoy the fat and peanuts put out by suburban bird lovers.

of the plants that successfully colonize the modern city are exotics (that is, not indigenous), and that they are either introduced deliberately as garden or city-park plants or have invaded the new territory by accident. South American species such as the gallant soldier and the shaggy soldier are now common in Europe, whereas the European garden chrysanthemum grows wild in Buenos Aires. The American golden rod has found new homes all over the world—it is a naturalized citizen of Paris, London, Tokyo, and Delhi—whilst Paris and London have exported the wallflower to San Francisco. And so the list goes on. I anticipate an almost cosmopolitan city flora in the not too distant future, with the more successful invading species pushing out so many of the native species that only a few of these will remain in the home ground. The list of cosmopolitan plants will probably include rosebay and other willow herbs, Oxford ragwort, ragweed, butterfly bush, touch-me-not, cotoneaster, wallflower, dandelion, goldenrod, Michaelmas daisy, evening primrose, Canadian fleabane, and various umbellifers (flowers whose stalks all spring from the top of the main stalk to produce a flat, umbrellalike head), together with a hardy selection of fruit and vegetables.

A few years ago studies carried out on the composition of the flora of the Polish city of Posnan found that well over half the total of more than 550 plants were of exotic origin. In all, there were 311 aliens, 40 per cent of which originated in western Asia or southeastern Europe, with nearly 27 per cent coming from Mediterranean Europe, 18 per cent from central Asia, a few from America, and a single species from Africa.

The wealth of plant life on waste-ground sites soon attracts insects and other invertebrates. The little animals arrive in some of the same ways as the plants; the first colonists are either flying species (flies, moths, beetles, bees, wasps) or windblown (plant bugs, aphids, lacewings, spiders). The hay that brought in grass seeds may also harbor a common grasshopper or two. The brown silverline moth, a species often associated with bracken, colonizes derelict land after the host plant has become established. Various species of butterfly are attracted by the rich variety of vegetation and can soon be seen sunning themselves on the appropriately named butterfly bushes. Workers who take their sandwiches to an empty lot in London for a bit of lunch in the late-summer sun may well see large, spectacularly marked caterpillars crawling around in search of a place to pupate. These are probably the larvae of eyed hawk moths, which feed on the Salix bushes, or perhaps of elephant hawk moths, which feed on willow herbs. Also feeding on the Salix bushes may be the bizarre-looking larvae of the puss moth. The abundant ragwort plants have their share of brightly

colored insects, too; the black and yellow larvae of the red and black cinnabar moth and the "woolly bear" caterpillars of the garden tiger moth both feed on Oxford ragwort.

A few aquatic species of insect also manage to colonize waste ground, although the aridity that tends to prevail in big cities in spite of most of them being near water (moisture evaporates from cement and brick fairly quickly) prevents most such species from gaining more than a temporary hold. However, water beetles and mosquitoes and other insects with aquatic larvae sometimes manage to invade flooded basements of demolished buildings and to stay there until forced out by new construction.

Perhaps most surprising of the insect colonists on waste ground, though, are the beetles that feed on carrion, such as old bones thrown out as rubbish. Like the aquatic insects, these carrion-feeders have an amazing ability to find new habitats and take advantage of them.

Black redstarts (cock right, hen left). This Eurasian species of mountain bird provided wartime London ornithologists with their most exciting experience of invading wildlife. Once one of England's greatest rarities, this bird nested in the London area in 1926 but became almost common in the city center during World War II, when blitzed buildings provided clifflike nesting sites, and homes for the redstart's insect prey.

Birds colonize cleared city sites in a particular order that may reflect the sequence in which particular kinds of vegetation moves in. Goldfinches (near left) were among the first arrivals on wartime bombed sites, where they fed upon the seeds of thistles—thistles are among the earliest plants to flourish on waste ground. Once bushes were established, the European blackbirds (far left) took territories and built nests.

One of the next links in the food chain that starts with vegetation and goes on with plant-eating insects is bird life. Birds, of course, eat both insects and the seeds of plants. To return once more to the bombed-out areas of World War II London, which provide such excellent examples of the way wildlife invades every possible urban habitat, it was their crops of thistle, ragwort, and other plants that attracted passing finches, such as goldfinches and linnets. Then, as soon as bushes were established, a few blackbirds took up territories in these areas and started nesting. But the biggest reward for bird watchers in the London of the mid-1940s was the increase in numbers of the black redstart—not a remarkable bird to look at, but in a quiet, discreet way a very attractive species. The body plumage of the male is dark slate and black, with a brownish-red tail. The female is rather similar, though duller in color.

Since the middle of the 19th century the black redstart had been expanding its range from its original home in Asia and southeastern Europe. In its "natural" state, its habitat is rocky hillsides, mountains, ravines, gullies, and other such barren spots. But as it spread across Europe it often adjusted to man-made substitutes; in France and Germany, it frequently nested in nooks and crannies on the elaborately carved exteriors of Gothic churches, cathedrals, and other large buildings. Occasional pairs began to nest in similar places in England from the 1920s onward. The ruins left in the heart of London by the blitz provided an ideal habitat for the birds, since the conditions were almost identical with those of their native southeast European and Asian homelands. The jagged basements and walls were not unlike rocky cliffs, screes, and gullies, and they were covered in ragwort, willow herb, and other colonists of disturbed ground, which flourished in spring but were already past their peak in the dry days of summer. The tall buildings surrounding the ruins provided ideal cliff ledges from which the tiny black redstart cock could guard his territory. And so more than 20 males could be heard singing over the noise and clatter of war-torn London.

In the years following the war, as bombed sites were gradually cleared and developed, the black redstarts were squeezed out, but they did not completely disappear; instead, they found new areas to colonize. Black redstarts in many parts of western Europe have now become associated with large industrial buildings such as power stations and railway yards, where plant—and consequently insect—life often flourishes on untended ground or in walls and crevices.

Poland is the only other country where the wildlife invasion of bombed sites was studied to anything like the same extent as in London. By the end of the war about 80 per cent of the buildings in Warsaw had been destroyed, leaving

close on 15 square miles of abandoned ruins. It was not until the mid-1950s that the center of the city began to resume its main functions, but its redevelopment thereafter was rapid, and by 1965 nearly all traces of the havoc had vanished. The vegetation in the ruined areas was much the same as that found in London, but because of the greater extent of the devastation and the slower pace of subsequent disturbance, the ground cover often became very much denser than in the British capital. Probably as a direct consequence, bird life was also much richer and more varied than that of London's ruined acres. For instance, the crested lark, a species absent from Britain, found the open ground of derelict railway yards and the vast spaces of flattened rubble a suitable substitute for its natural habitat of dry open country in Poland, and it became a common bird in wartime and postwar Warsaw. Sand martins

excavated their burrows in the heaps of exposed soil and in craters and pits left by the bombs, and wheatears nested in cracks and crevices in the piles of bricks.

Soon after the war blackbirds started nesting in Warsaw, and mallards suddenly increased on park lakes. These species have continued to increase, unlike many of the other birds, which disappeared with redevelopment because their fortunes were closely tied up with the existence of the ruins. Polish ornithologists have pointed out that both the blackbird and mallard have undergone a degree of "urbanization," and this urbanized population has been spreading eastward across Europe. A similar trend in adaptation to city life has been noted in gulls and, as we shall see, in the starlings of both Poland and Russia. It has been predicted that song thrushes and jays—species that are well established in

in all but the most secluded parts of Moscow's suburbs—the large, leafy grounds of hospitals were one of the more common sites—but the crows have gradually increased and now form one of the most abundant species of resident birds, nesting in the larches that line the streets in the heart of Moscow. They even nest in a poplar tree right beside Kiev Station and in a mature birch tree opposite the Ukraine Hotel near the busy Lenin Prospect. In the evening the hooded crows and jackdaws gather together to roost, often in vast numbers. At one time there was a large roost in Red Square, but now most of the roosts are in cemeteries; one cemetery alone has about 10,000 birds, two thirds of which are crows, the rest jackdaws. These roosts have also attracted what is undoubtedly Moscow's most spectacular feathered visitor: the eagle owl. In recent years this large nocturnal predator has twice been seen in the city, where it was undoubtedly feeding on roosting crows. Not long ago, too, a long-eared owl moved in to the botanical gardens of Moscow University to feed on roosting sparrows.

In places that have been cleared for redevelopment, just as on bombed sites, wildlife has to start from scratch. Trees of the tree sanctuary in the University's botanical gardens were planted in the bare soil of a bulldozed area. After only 20 years a total of 30 species of bird, including such rarities as golden orioles, were nesting there. But the nesting bird that has perhaps the greatest appeal for the city dweller is the nightingale, and this species successfully invaded the botanical gardens as recently as 10 years ago. By 1973 the voices of 10 singing males could be heard. Soviet scientists who have studied the birds of the botanical gardens believe that one of the most important reasons why nightingales have been successful in colonizing the gardens is that these are not located near a residential area, and so there are almost no cats in the neighborhood.

On the outskirts of Moscow, some startling discoveries have been made about the way bird life, and indeed all wildlife, is affected by the indiscriminate use of pesticides, particularly insecticides. Insecticides appear to kill off insect species at random; but although this may be initially true, the recovery period of insect

western European cities—will colonize Warsaw within a few years. Other birds have also increased in Poland since the war, for a variety of reasons, not least of which is the fact that Polish people have formed the habit of putting out food for birds. The species that have particularly benefited from this include jackdaws, collared doves, and, of course, titmice.

In Moscow in recent years many areas have undergone massive redevelopment. At the same time there has been an actively promoted, and largely successful, campaign to encourage birds. In the case of the hooded crow, the campaign has been rather too successful, for this species is now one of the most significant predators of small birds. It has even adapted its behavior to the point of actually lifting the lids of man-made nest boxes in order to get at the young! Earlier this century hooded crows were rare as nesting birds

species is variable, and so the population of certain species builds up faster than that of others. In the case of aphids, the problem is that they feed on the sap of plants by inserting their tube-shaped mouthparts, and so they can often avoid insecticide residues on leaf surfaces. Apart from annoying horticulturists the resultant build-up of large aphid populations has had two quite dramatic effects on the wildlife of Moscow and other Russian cities (similar phenomena probably occur elsewhere, too, but they have so far been studied only in the USSR).

The first and most immediate effect has been the massive explosion of the population of ladybugs, for which the Russian name is "God's little cows," and whose larvae feed on aphids. In 1973 ladybugs appeared in vast numbers in Moscow and in many towns on the Volga. In city streets, their squashed remains were to be seen everywhere, and birds soon began to feed on the corpses. This was particularly interesting, since birds do not normally eat ladybugs. As a result of this new food source, Moscow's bird population also increased enormously. (As a personal postscript, I found the accounts of the aphid/ladybug plague interesting when I read them nearly two years after the event, because in the late summer of 1973 I had witnessed thousands upon thousands of ladybugs arriving on the Danube Delta in Romania from the north; this was presumably a lemminglike migration from the Volga River area.)

The other effect of the increase in aphids, according to Soviet scientists, has been a rise in the number of great spotted woodpeckers. This woodpecker has developed a special technique for collecting aphids: it draws an aphid-covered leaf or sprout through its bill, collects a ball of insects on one side, and takes the hazel-nut-size dollop of aphids back to its nestlings. In cool, wet summers, when the aphid population is at a low level, the woodpecker (largely deprived of its wood-boring prey by tidy-minded city dwellers who destroy dead wood) has to look elsewhere for sustenance. It becomes predatory, feeding on

nestlings, particularly those of birds breeding in artificial nestboxes. This change in eating habits has also been helped by the fact that Muscovites have put up thousands of nestboxes to attract small birds.

Because of the nestboxes and the food put out for them, an enormous number of small birds, particularly titmice and starlings, have invaded Moscow. An annual National Bird Day has resulted in up to 10,000 boxes being put up each

The common nighthawk (not in fact a hawk, but a nightjar) normally lives in open country, but has taken to nesting on flat gravel roofs in North America's eastern cities. After sunset the bird begins a high, bouncing flight in search of insects.

year, mainly for starlings. The starling is still invading new territory. Its expansion into urban areas over the last few hundred years is difficult to plot, for isolated populations often existed in the vicinity of cities and towns before the built-up areas spread out and engulfed them. In most parts of the world where starlings are common, the birds tend to be despised as rather messy pests, but there are many places where they are welcome, and still others where they remain very rare. They used to be extremely rare in winter in Moscow—so much so that ornithologists were astonished when seven of them spent the winter of 1958 in a Moscow park. Then, in 1960–61, four starlings spent the winter at the opposite end of the city, and thereafter the birds became regular all-year-round residents; by the winter of 1973–74 many hundreds were roosting in the fir trees of the Kremlin. A similar situation exists in Poland: for some unknown reason, having invaded the cities of eastern Europe, the starlings—or, at least, great numbers of them—no longer feel the need to migrate to avoid the cold winters.

Perhaps one of the most unexpected birds to have invaded Western World cities is the common nighthawk of North America. The family of goatsuckers or nightjars (which includes the nighthawks, whippoorwills, and pauraques) are not particularly adaptable, and in Europe they are often among the first species to retreat as the city encroaches on the surrounding countryside. However, the common nighthawk appears to be an exception. In its natural state, it nests in open country, preferring gravelly areas, barren rocks, and open land unobstructed by trees and shrubs. It also nests on cultivated land, in plowed and stubble fields. But its most remarkable association with man is actually in the heart of towns. In some cities of America, flat roofs are a very common habitat for the nighthawk—a fact that was already being noted a century ago.

One of the first reports of roof-nesting nighthawks came from Philadelphia in 1869. By the 1870s their presence had been recorded in Boston, Cleveland, and Montreal, and it was not long before they had invaded many other cities in the United States and Canada. Nighthawks are either crepuscular or nocturnal, and they feed largely on mosquitoes, moths, flies, and other insects that are active in and after the twilight hours. But their spectacular increase in cities is prob-

ably linked not so much with the amount of food available as with the suitability of the habitat. The flat rooftops are perfect for the birds, for on them they are safe from practically all predators. There was a time when people occasionally persecuted these attractive birds because of the "hawk" in their name, but now they are protected and permitted to flourish.

In Europe, the most notable recent wild-bird invasion of towns and cities has been made by the collared dove, which originally inhabited the continent of Asia as far east as Korea. Today it can be found in association with Western man—often in cultivated areas and suburban gardens, and increasingly in thickly populated cities. The beginning of its expansion westward is too long ago to be known, but it had reached Constantinople by the 16th century, and by 1834 it had got as far as what is now the city of Plovdiv in Bulgaria. By the beginning of our own century it had not spread much farther west and was more or less confined to the Turkish Empire and adjacent territories. In the 1930s, however, its spread suddenly accelerated, and just before the outbreak of World War II collared doves were being spotted in Yugoslavia, Austria, and southern Germany. By the end of the war they had reached Italy, and today they are a familiar

Collared doves have recently proved immensely successful invaders of European city parks and gardens, where they are safe from hunting. This century birds originating in the Balkans have occupied all of central and much of western Europe.

sight all over western Europe, including Scandinavia and the British Isles.

Another dove, the palm, or laughing, dove, also shows signs of spreading its range, again in association with man. It has been introduced into various parts of the world, including Australia and Malta, and its continental European populations have spread from Turkey westward to city after city.

Mammalian invaders are much rarer in the city than birds and insects—with, of course, such obvious exceptions as rats and mice. Generally speaking, however, urban mammals, particularly the larger ones, tend to be native species that have survived the growth of the urban area by retreating to parks and gardens, rather than invaders. Two notable exceptions are the hedgehog and the European red fox. For many years foxes were seldom seen in the suburbs of English towns and cities, but from the late 1950s sightings became more and more frequent until, by the mid-1970s, the red-fox population had built up to a perhaps dangerously high level, and foxes were venturing into some of England's largest cities. I use the word "dangerously" because foxes are potential carriers of rabies. Rabies has been spreading north and westward across the continent of Europe at a rate of around five miles a year, and the British Isles are protected only by the Channel. If the disease were to be carried across this narrow stretch of water—perhaps by a smuggled pet—it could spread throughout the fox population and wreak havoc on foxes, dogs, human beings, and all other mammals in and around Britain's cities.

For the time being, however, Britain's urban foxes provide a rare opportunity to study a large wild mammal in an urban environment. City foxes are usually less healthy than their rural counterparts; they frequently suffer from mange and a variety of other canine diseases, mainly because of their poor diet. They are primarily scavengers, feeding on the contents of garbage cans, raiding poultry yards, and stealing pet rabbits if the rabbits' owners are unwise enough not to keep them locked up. Occasionally they may even take a cat; most stories of cat-killing are untrue, but foxes will certainly pick up any dead cats that have been run over on roads.

Birds, rats, and hedgehogs are all frequent road casualties, and they, too, form an important part of the foxes' diet. (The motor car is also one of the most frequent killers of the fox.)

For all their abundance, foxes are rarely seen by most city dwellers, since they do most of their hunting at night. Hedgehogs are much more often sighted. Even the most unobservant European city dweller is likely to come across one or two from time to time, and many people must have seen their squashed corpses on urban roads. Like the fox, the hedgehog has adapted particularly well to "suburbanization." In several parts of Europe, it is more abundant in suburban gardens than in any other habitat.

Another surprisingly big mammal that has invaded suburbs in recent years—notably those of Copenhagen—is the marten. Although marten populations have declined in most parts of the Northern Hemisphere as a result of persecution by furriers and gamekeepers, this group of mammals could well flourish in suburban habitats almost anywhere. Martens feed to a large extent on birds, and birds are often superabundant in city suburbs and parks.

Wherever man has gone, he has taken animals

Some creatures that come to live in cities do so freely; others are imported against their will. Above: pine marten in a beech wood. Martens have recently invaded the suburbs of Copenhagen and some other cities, where the birds that largely form their prey abound. Left: Canada geese, coot, mallards, and tufted ducks share a pool in London's Kensington Gardens. The waterfowl in city parks are often pinioned, captive birds. But Canada geese derived from captive North American birds today feed and breed by choice on urban lakes in three continents.

83

and plants with him. Just as primitive nomads took their flocks, and primitive slash-and-burn agriculturists took their seed, so Western post-industrial man literally transports species from zoological and botanical gardens around the world. Many such animals and plants cannot survive without man's care, but there are quite a few that are able to thrive if they escape.

Of the city wildlife of captive origin, perhaps the most common are the several kinds of water-fowl. In many parts of the world, tame ducks, geese, and swans populate ornamental lakes in city parks. For hundreds of years waterfowl have been transported all over the globe to meet the demand, and in time great numbers of these have escaped. Thus, for example, Canada geese are no longer confined to North America but are now well established in New Zealand, Scandinavia, and the British Isles, where they have developed new migration patterns as well as frequently nesting right in the heart of cities. You can sometimes see them flying in the evening over busy shopping centers. Similarly, mandarin ducks, American wood ducks, Bahama pintails, greylag geese, ruddy shelducks, scaups, widgeons, and a host of other species can be expected to have found habitats on practically any city lake in the world.

In most cases, the waterfowl seen in parks are purely captive, and they are usually pinioned (that is, an end of one wing has been mutilated so as to prevent flight), but as they often breed, the young may start new colonies of freeliving birds. The captive waterfowl will also act as decoys for wild ones on migration and will attract them down. In mid-winter, too, large concentrations of these birds may gather to feed on bread and other bits of food tossed to them by bird-lovers. So their numbers have multiplied to a point where few people think of them as wild creatures. Wild they are, however, no matter how comfortably they have adapted to the urban habitat.

Among other species of captive birds that have successfully taken to city life as a result of being introduced into cities by humans are the mynahs, natives of India and southeast Asia,

Escaped pet birds of certain species have formed wild populations in some cities. Above: an Indian mynah (a noted mimic) on a houseboat in Kashmir. Mynahs now haunt parks and gardens in North America, Hawaii, and Australia. Right: ring-necked parakeets on an acacia tree in a London garden. London and New York have wild colonies of these colorful South Asian birds.

Cities provide huge markets for animal traders supplying all kinds of mammals and birds as pets, or for less obvious reasons. Left: cages crammed with twittering and squawking birds fill this Indonesian bird market. These captives are sold as pets, for use as food, or to fight each other. In some Southeast Asian markets pious Buddhists buy and then free birds to gain merit. Huge quantities of colorful finches and parrots also pass through Asian markets on their way to the pet stores of European cities. Right: gray parrots and a young hyena form part of the stock of this animal dealer at Kano market in northern Nigeria. African as well as Asian cities do a considerable trade in animals. In both continents, the result is often the same: the captive creatures are so poorly treated that they die soon after purchase. Each year thousands perish in crowded boxes consigned to the cities of the West.

which are now at home in the cities of western Canada, Hawaii, Australia, and elsewhere. In the parks and gardens of some places, they have flourished so well that they are on the verge of becoming a pest. Ring-necked parakeets are also world travelers. Common in the urban centers of southern Asia and India, where they nest in cavities in buildings, they are popular in the West as cage birds—but like other captive birds they sometimes escape. Among the new areas colonized by escaped parakeets are several places in and around Greater London and New York, where small colonies of these exotic creatures have managed to survive.

India and Southeast Asia are the places of origin for enormous numbers of wild birds sent into captivity all over the world, and the bird markets of Delhi, Bangkok, Singapore, and other such cities are a conservationist's nightmare. A major function of the bird markets in Thailand and other parts of the East is to provide specimens for pious Buddhists to purchase and release —an act that is considered very virtuous indeed. Unfortunately, though, the released birds are usually too weak to survive in the open. They

flutter away in the midst of Delhi or Bangkok, many to die, many others to be recaptured and transported back to market to start the cycle all over again.

Rather surprisingly, one of the most successful groups of city invaders are reptiles: the geckos, which are members of a lizard family. Most species of gecko are small, with the large eyes and vertical pupils characteristic of nocturnal animals. Many geckos also have pads of various sorts on their toes, which enable them to climb very smooth surfaces and help them to adapt well to city life. In addition, they are often among the most common species of lizard on islands and in coastal areas, which makes them liable to be transported accidentally around the world on cargo boats. There is, however, one limitation to their ability to survive in a variety of urban habitats: they can live only in warm climates. Different species of gecko have now colonized cities in all five continents. For example, the so-called Mediterranean gecko, which was probably a native of southwestern Asia originally but has long been established in maritime cities around the Mediterranean, has spread to the Canary

Islands, the West Indies, and such American cities as New Orleans, Brownsville, Miami, and Key West.

Over the last century or so, man has also taken to moving fish all over the globe, for the benefit of anglers and to exhibit in aquariums. Canals, rivers, and city-park lakes are stocked with a wide variety of fish that may or may not be native to the region. Various species of trout and bass are among the commonest kinds to be transported. The forecourt of a modern hotel, the smaller lakes in parks, and the little pond in your own garden are the likeliest places to be stocked with ornamental fish—none of them native, of course. The most familiar of these are goldfish, a species domesticated many hundreds of years ago by the Chinese. Many of the goldfish found in park lakes originated as unwanted aquarium

pets that have been given their freedom; within a couple of years of being released, they revert to their ancestral greenish color. Aquarists have been responsible for the spread of several other species of fish, but as a rule fish have fairly precise habitat requirements, and so, even if they do not die in a strange environment, they may fail to breed.

A remarkable exception to this general rule has been recorded in the case of guppies. Guppies are native to northeastern South America and are popular in tropical aquariums, where they breed with almost incredible facility. In recent years two colonies of these tropical fish have been discovered in, of all places, Britain. Presumably, the ancestors of one of the colonies, which inhabits a river in a London suburb, were released by an aquarist suffering from over-

Collectors have scoured the world to decorate city living rooms with colorful fish that survive well in captivity. Above: the goldfish, a brightly colored species of carp, domesticated in China for centuries. Goldfish thrive and breed in garden ponds but are often kept in tiny overcrowded bowls where many suffocate or die from other causes. Left: the veiltail guppy, a pretty tropical aquarium variety, stems from the less colorful wild guppies of South America. These fish need heat and rarely survive outdoors in northern winters.

population problems; because they appear to have been dropped into the outfall of an electricity-generating station, the warmth of the water was sufficient to enable the little creatures to survive. And they have continued to survive in a section of the river that has been diverted to the power station, where the water temperature never drops below about 60°F. Obviously, this particular type of colonization under highly favorable—and artificial—conditions, is fairly unusual, but it shows how, given the *right* conditions, the appropriate species can make use of them.

In the past the main reason for keeping fish in cities was for food. Carp, in particular, were once kept in the ponds of larger houses, although rarely in towns. In recent times increasing attention is being paid to the idea of making use of the urban situation itself to provide fish as an additional source of food for the city dweller. Biologists, for instance, have been experimenting with feeding fish on the products of waste sewage. In the tropics, they have experimented with farming the freshwater fish *Tilapia mossambica*; in temperate regions, with rearing carp. In the future we can expect to see a lot more of such

fish in urban fish markets. Fish have also been introduced into urban waters for another reason: insect control. The most important such species is one of the guppy's relatives, the mosquito fish, a small fish that, as its name suggests, eats mosquito larvae and pupae, and is now widely dispersed in many tropical and subtropical regions, where it also occasionally appears in urban ponds and ditches.

Although they are hardly typical urban animals, many of the species that man has transported across the world are often abundant—in fact, too abundant—in cities. For instance, a giant snail, originally from east Africa, now has a very wide, man-made distribution in the tropics. During a particularly severe plague of the creatures 400 giant snails were collected in a garden in the Javanese city of Jakarta in a single night. A similar example is the giant South American toad, which was introduced a few years ago into practically every country that grows sugarcane, in order to control the sugarcane beetle. The giant toad made an efficient job of controlling the beetles, but in many places it became an unwelcome predator, killing a wide variety of attractive native wildlife.

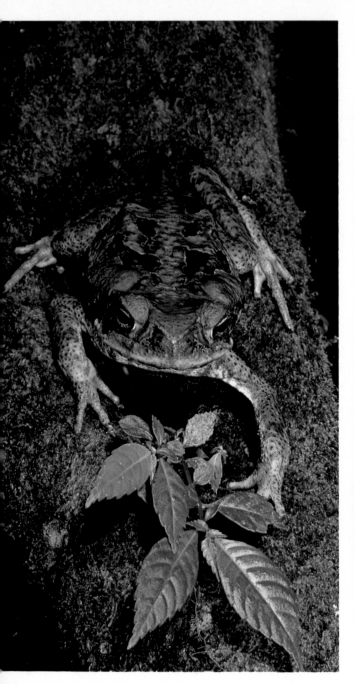

Giant South American toad. Imported to curb farm pests, this large amphibian now hunts beetles, mice, and birds in city suburbs of the Philippines, West Indies, Florida, and Hawaii.

These are only two examples of a great number of cases in which the introduction of an alien animal or plant has had disastrous results. It is strange that in the light of such past experience, thoughtless, ill-considered introductions are still going on all over the world. It is one thing for wildlife to invade a habitat on its own; it is quite another for man to transport exotic forms of wildlife from one place to another without first considering the consequences.

Of all the invasions of cities, the annual migrations of birds often provide the most fascinating spectacle. Even a city that normally has little bird life can suddenly become alive with hundreds of thousands of birds. Migrating birds usually try to avoid built-up areas, but in adverse weather conditions they need to take shelter, and the city is often their only possible refuge. Some cities are actually focal points for migrant birds. These are mainly, though not

Birdwatchers gaze at flights of white pelicans migrating near Lake Van in eastern Turkey. Even more spectacular is the autumn bird migration across the Bosporus in northwest Turkey. Many thousands of storks, eagles, and other birds that are better gliders than fliers rise above Istanbul on warm morning air currents, then wheel on stiff wings from Europe out across the water gap to Asia.

exclusively, cities on islands, peninsulas, and promontories, such as Gibraltar, Istanbul, and Singapore.

Perhaps the most fascinating of all bird migrations is the one passing across the Bosporus at Istanbul. From about August 20 every year, birds of prey, storks, and others gather over the city every morning and circle around waiting for the air temperature to build up sufficiently to provide the thermals they need to give them enough uplift for their flight across the Bosporus. It is well worth going to Turkey just to see the wonderful spectacle of them finally taking off. Sadly, the numbers and variety of species to be seen today over Istanbul are far less than they once were. Ornithologists of the 1860s reported "thousands and thousands" of eagles, buzzards, kites, hawks, harriers, and falcons flying in the skies above the city (then known, of course, as Constantinople). In 1870 several hundred pairs

of Egyptian vultures were breeding in the city, but they began to die out soon afterward; there were then thousands of black kites, too, but by 1966 only 20 pairs remained. Of the 37,000 birds of prey recorded as migrating over Istanbul in 1966, the most abundant species were the nearly 13,000 buzzards, followed by almost 9000 honey buzzards. In 1968 a survey during a three-day period in September recorded 8000 buzzards passing over the city, and nearly 5000 lesser spotted eagles, and on one day alone 6000 honey buzzards. The other species recorded in 1968 included Egyptian vulture, griffon vulture, imperial eagle, booted eagle, spotted eagle, sparrowhawk, Levant sparrowhawk, red kite, black kite, short-toed eagle, hobby, lanner falcon, saker falcon, kestrel, and lesser kestrel.

The main reason for the occurrence of such vast numbers of birds over Istanbul is that the city happens to be situated at a strategic point on a migration route. Many other cities are likely to be on the birds' route, but the sight is less awe-inspiring in most places because the birds are not usually as easy to watch as they are in Istanbul. Pioneer studies of visible migration were carried out in the late 1950s in London's Regent's Park, and ornithologists found that large numbers of birds were flying over the heart of London, using traditional flyways that followed natural river and land contours. Finches, crows, thrushes, pigeons, larks, and pipits were among those most frequently observed. Many such birds however, migrate at night, and so their flight is not as visible as the daylight activity over Istanbul. On an overcast night in October it is quite possible to hear—and even see in the street lights—redwings migrating through London, but such glimpses are fleeting.

In Canada, the Toronto Dominion Center, a group of buildings that includes skyscrapers rising to 600 to 740 feet, has proved a serious hazard for birds migrating through downtown Toronto. By studying the casualties, scientists have been able to establish some data on the nocturnal migrants. During a recent three-year

Skyscrapers of Toronto's Dominion Center pose shadowy threats to birds migrating over the city at night. Low cloud tends to keep the birds below roof level, and dazzling lights in the buildings increase the risk of collision. Birds hit the skyscrapers and drop dead, or flutter, injured, to some nearby resting place, perhaps to fall prey to patrolling saw-whet owls. More than five dozen species figure in the death toll, among them ovenbirds, kinglets, and several kinds of sparrow and warbler.

study of autumn migrations, 470 individuals of 64 species were found dead around the skyscrapers. The highest mortality level for any one night was 21 birds of four species; another night, 21 birds were again killed, but this time 10 species were involved. The most common casualty was the white-throated sparrow, with 60 killed; closely followed by 59 yellow throats, 45 ovenbirds, and 43 tree sparrows. Other species that were quite frequent migrants were the golden-crowned kinglet, the brown creeper, the slate-colored junco, the black-throated blue warbler, the myrtle warbler, the magnolia warbler, the yellow-bellied sapsucker, and the swamp sparrow.

Small birds such as these sometimes dash themselves against skyscraper walls because they generally keep below the cloudline when migrating. At the same time, the internal lighting of the buildings has a dazzling effect, similar to that of coastal lighthouses. Experiments with lighthouses have shown that floodlighting the *exterior* considerably reduces bird mortality, but this would be impracticable for most skyscrapers. And so birds continue to die. Not all of the skyscraper casualties are killed, however; many, merely bruised, settle on ledges or nearby trees in a state of exhaustion, exposing themselves to another danger: predators. In Toronto, saw-whet owls that have been seen in the vicinity of the Dominion Center have undoubtedly been preying on exhausted migrants. Rats also frequently feed on the birds that are actually killed.

Central Park in New York City has long been a favorite haunt of bird watchers studying migrant birds. More than 260 species have been listed as seen in the park (over 100 have been recorded in one day alone), most of them migrants. In autumn there is the challenge (or excitement) of the "fall warblers," which, as every American bird watcher knows, are among the most difficult of all birds to identify. Twenty-nine different species have been recorded in a single day.

Invading wildlife—plants, insects, birds, reptiles, mammals—is remarkably persistent. We should have no illusions about man's ultimate dominance in the cities: it does not exist. If man left his cities tomorrow, the flora and fauna, assisted by wind, sun, and rain, would immediately begin to take over. Within a decade all that would be recognizable would be the shells of buildings. The details would have disappeared beneath grass, weeds, shrubs, and trees.

Pests and Vermin

A scorpion and a giant Achatina snail on a garden wall in Bangkok. Both scorpions and snails can be pests: scorpions can inflict painful stings on man; snails eat up his plants. In fact pests are any wild creatures able to share man's environment so effectively that they actually compete with him for food or living space. Pests make up a large proportion of the wildlife in any city.

What makes an animal or plant a pest, vermin, or a weed? Basically, the terms are used of any forms of wildlife that are so successful in adapting to the man-made environment that they actually compete with man for parts of the environment or its products. As one definition of plants puts it, "a weed is only a flower growing in the wrong place." However hard he tries, man is usually unable to eradicate these unwelcome cohabitants completely; indeed, most of the

time he appears to be fighting a running battle to control them.

Although, as we have seen, a vast amount of wildlife is threatened in modern industrial cities, there are some plants and animals that actually thrive in the crowded conditions of a city and are dependent on man for food and shelter. We know that all animals are capable of producing more offspring than they require to replace themselves. In a balanced ecosystem the surplus will be kept in check, but in the artificial environment of a city without these natural checks, populations may increase enormously. It is only when these species proliferate and get out of control that they become pests. In various parts of the world, just as Michaelmas daisies, bamboo, and horseradish can become weeds, so pigeons, sparrows, mynahs, possums, and countless other kinds of fauna have been introduced by man only to become so well established that they become regarded as pests.

Anyone wanting to study city wildlife could well start by studying its pests and vermin. In most cities, there is a government or city administration department with responsibility for controlling pests and vermin. These departments frequently publish leaflets and identification guides, and by writing to the local pest officers, Ministry of Agriculture, or medical and health officers, it is possible to gather a considerable amount of information about the commonest forms of wildlife in a particular city. The study of a city's mammals, insects, and birds is often a study of its vermin.

Pests and vermin fall into two broad groups: the economic pests, which compete for or destroy man's food and property, and those animals and plants that carry disease. Some animals—for instance, rats and pigeons—are both competitors for food and carriers of disease.

Insects are by far the most numerous pests, both in quantity and in variety. There are thousands of species, many of which are of minor or only local importance, and to enumerate those regarded as pests throughout the world would be an impossible task. Insect pests occur in a wide variety of forms: the order Diptera alone includes mosquitoes, midges, horse flies, tsetse flies, house flies, flesh flies, dung flies, fruit flies, and several other families that are health hazards and often occur in cities. Termites and wood-boring beetles do countless millions of dollars' worth of damage to buildings; beetles, weevils, cockroaches, and other insects despoil man's stored foods. The larvae of some of the

Left: enlarged view of a brown spider, a species found in houses in Missouri and neighboring parts of the United States. The spider subdues prey by ejecting poison from a special gland through a pair of clawlike fangs. Brown spiders are one of the species capable of inflicting a nasty bite on any human being unlucky enough accidentally to arouse them.

Flies and beetles include species that rank high among the pests that plague our cities. Above: head of a house fly, much enlarged. Antennae and huge, compound eyes help the fly to find food. It salivates on such solids as bread and sugar and sucks up the nourishing liquid product. Because flies also feed on excreta and other filth they are liable to spread serious diseases that include typhoid, cholera, and dysentery. Below: granary weevils and grains of wheat punctured and scooped out to satisfy their appetites. Stocks of corn and barley also suffer from their onslaught, but rice and various dry-food products fall to many different kinds of weevils. Altogether there are some 50,000 weevil species, each with a long, distinctive snout or rostrum, and most with larvae specialized for devouring one part of a plant of one species or of a limited group.

Termites are superficially antlike insects that cause tremendous damage to wooden buildings in the tropics. Above: soldiers of the snouted harvester termite, a South African species. Right: part of a wooden building in Trinidad. Termite galleries have so perforated this piece of wood that it might crumble at a touch.

Lepidoptera — clothes moths in particular — attack fabrics as well as garden plants. In addition to the insect pests of cities and towns, there are thousands of others that attack crops and trees in rural areas and are, also, the bane of suburban gardeners. The more successful a species is in the city environment, the more likelihood there is of its becoming a pest. Although we may not like them, insects are the most influential wildlife of the city—more so than the birds recorded by city birdwatchers.

The scale of the problems involving insect pests can be gauged by examining a few in some detail. Termites, for instance, are a largely tropical group of insects but a few species do occur in temperate regions. It was estimated that in 1961 in the USA alone, termite-control measures and termite damage cost somewhere in the region of $250 million. By the early 1970s this figure had doubled. Termite damage occurs largely in country areas, but termites are also major pests in cities in the warmer parts of the world, particularly the older established cities that used wood in the construction of buildings.

Clothes moth (enlarged) on cloth. The adult females lay eggs on furs and silk and woolen fabrics, which the resulting larvae devour. Clothes moths are pests found all over the world.

Altogether, around 2000 species of termites have been identified. They are most abundant in Central and South America, Africa, and Australia. Only two species are native to Europe, and Paris seems to be their northern limit. An introduced species, originally from North America, has been found surviving in small colonies in warehouse basements in Hamburg.

Superficially, termites look rather like large white ants, though in fact they are probably more closely related to cockroaches. Like ants, they live in large and complex structured communities with up to several million termites in a single colony. The termite colony is divided into castes, and at the center of each colony is a queen many times larger than the other termites. She is virtually an egg-laying machine, capable, in some species, of laying an egg a second for several years. The great majority of termites, however, are the so-called workers carrying out the various functions of the community: nest-building, foraging for food, making fungus gardens, building tunnels to the food supplies and to the queen and her attendant king. Others develop into soldiers, whose job it is to protect the colony.

In their natural environment, termites play a wholly useful role essential to the proper maintenance of the forest ecosystem, particularly in the tropics. They have no such useful role in the unnatural world of man's cities, and do untold damage not only to wood but to various other materials, particularly plastics. The damage to plastics can be very serious if underground communication cables are attacked and destroyed. No one knows why termites attack plastics, because the food value is virtually nil; the most likely explanation is that they simply move obstacles that block the routes between their nests and food supplies.

The order Coleoptera (beetles and weevils) is another very large and diverse group of insects causing countless millions of dollars' worth of damage to crops, food, and property, as well as occasionally spreading disease. The largest group in the Order are the beetles, with around 300,000 species described to date, and probably several thousand more not yet identified. In fact, they are the most numerous group of all insects and make up about one third of the animal kingdom. A great variety of species occur in a wide range of habitats in our cities and towns. Of those beetles that rank among man's enemies, perhaps the best known are the Anobiidae. This family of wood-borers (and "woodworm" larvae) includes furniture and death-watch beetles, which cause widespread damage to furniture and, more usually, to the actual fabric of buildings. They attack mainly hardwoods and cause extensive damage, particularly to such historic buildings as London's Westminster Abbey whose roof was recently in serious danger of collapsing after being attacked by death-watch beetles. In the same family as the wood-borers are other pest species of beetle—for instance, the drugstore or bread beetle (*Stegobium*) as it is sometimes called, which is a common pest of dry stored foods, attacking considerably more than bread.

However, not all the insects commonly found in a city are harmful. Some have acquired reputations not wholly deserved. Cockroaches have been domestic pests for centuries, occurring wherever there is warmth and food, especially in kitchens and boiler rooms. An unpleasant feature of cockroach infestation is the distinctive odor that lingers on food and anything else they touch, and they are universally regarded as pests. Although cockroaches are undoubtedly capable of spreading disease, such as bacterial infections causing food poisoning, typhoid, and other intestinal disorders, in many environments they do little or no harm. Cockroaches have been

transported by man all over the world, so that it is difficult to know where their original home was. This diversity is suggested by their common names for example: the Oriental cockroach, German cockroach, American cockroach, and Australian cockroach, all of which are in fact cosmopolitan species; the first three probably originated in Africa, the latter in Asia.

Two of the most familiar insect pests, silverfish and firebrats, are among the most primitive species, although, because of their rather crustaceanlike appearance, many people do not realize that they are insects. They are both cosmopolitan species found in city households throughout the world. Silverfish are common in food cupboards, larders, and around sinks, where they feed on food scraps, glue-sized paper, and mold. Firebrats feed on similar substances but, as their name implies, they are generally found in warmer places, such as kitchens and bakeries. Both the firebrat and silverfish belong to the order Thysanura, the bristletails, which in the natural state live in soil litter, under tree bark, in beach debris, and so forth, feeding on rotting vegetation. Like cockroaches, firebrats and silverfish sometimes carry disease, but very often they do no harm,

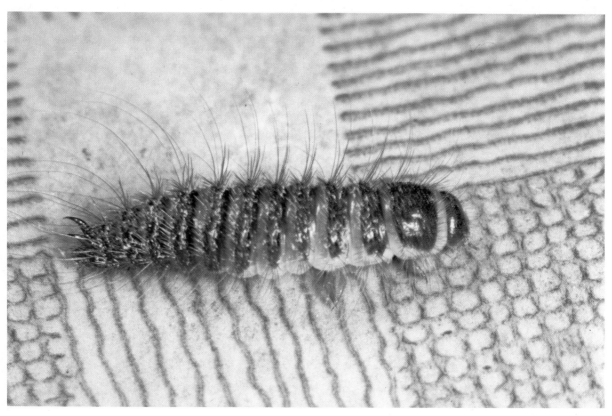

Enlarged views of beetles that attack the structure and contents of man's homes in city and in country. Right: a furniture beetle beside the hole from which it has emerged after many months of larval tunneling. Furniture beetles tend to mine in softwoods, whereas one so-called deathwatch beetle eats oak—a hardwood. The furniture beetle is a particular threat to softwood chairs, tables, and cupboards, but the death-watch beetle can bring about the collapse of old oak beams supporting roofs. Below left: larva of a larder beetle, a pest in food stores. Below: carpet beetle larva at home in the miniature jungle of hairs or fibers on which it feeds. Carpet beetle larvae eat some kinds of car-peting, and furs, feathers, or woolens that they find in closets. In contrast to these pests, the adults lead harmless lives, feeding on pollen.

and merely indicate that food is available.

It is not only man's habitat that attracts a host of unwelcome creatures, however. Man himself, especially when he is found densely packed in cities, provides an ideal habitat for a very wide variety of parasites. These and the other animals that go to make up the fauna actually living on man, I shall be discussing in more general terms in Chapter 6. Most of these parasites do remarkably little harm to their hosts, in any case, although occasionally some of even these lesser animals can reach pest proportions. Far more serious are those insects that carry such diseases as malaria, yellow fever, and bubonic plague, for these can devastate the densely packed urban areas.

The flea is just one of the parasites of man and animals. Of the 500 or so varieties known, many parasitize a particular bird or animal. One flea, however, is intimately bound up with the many "plagues" that have swept various parts of the world throughout history, and it is therefore relevant to examine both it and plague in some detail.

In the natural state, the bubonic plague bacillus (*Pasteurella pestis*) is carried by, and affects, many species of rodents such as ground squirrels, marmots, and mice, as well as the fleas that parasitize them. The plague causes death among these mammals and occasionally among

Cockroaches and silverfish are among primitive insects that infest buildings, especially where people leave food scraps in bakeries, and restaurant and household kitchens. Above: magnified view of an American cockroach—a worldwide species that probably evolved in Africa. Below: silverfish (much enlarged). This tiny creature hides in food cupboards and around sinks.

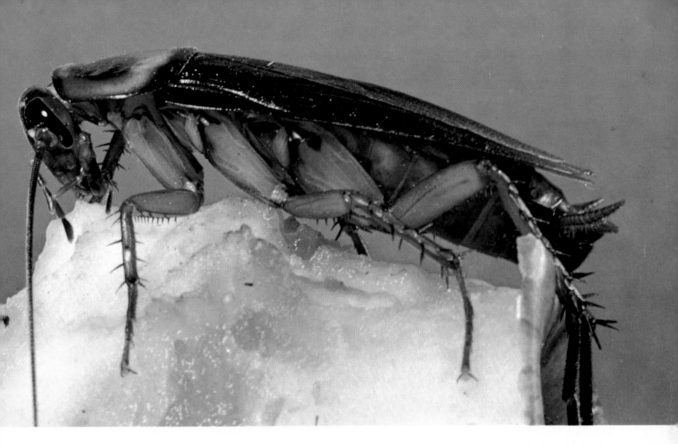

people infested by their fleas. But this usually happens in the countryside and thus rarely reaches epidemic proportions. However, when these fleas come into contact with a population explosion of rats, such as may occur in or near a city, the situation can change rapidly.

In densely populated cities, where rat populations are often high, the flea population is correspondingly even higher. The rat fleas affected by the plague bacillus do not succumb as rapidly as their hosts, so that when the rats die the fleas, which feed only on warm blood, leave the corpses in search of other hosts. Because rats live in such close proximity to humans, it is the human body that is the most obvious choice. When an infected flea bites and tries to suck the human blood, its gut, by then often blocked with the multiplying plague bacilli, rejects the meal and so regurgitates it, complete with bacilli, back into the human bloodstream before the flea dies.

In this way the rat flea spread the bubonic plague that scoured Europe and many other parts of the world at regular intervals over the centuries. It could be said to be one of nature's ways of checking overpopulation in the human species, particularly among city dwellers. The Black Death that overran Europe in the 14th century, the plague of which Pericles wrote, and the Great Plague of London recorded by Samuel Pepys were probably forms of bubonic plague.

Thucydides in Book II of his *History of the Peloponnesian Wars* describes in detail the plague that ravaged Athens in 430 B.C. He tells how the first symptoms of the disease in healthy people were burning headaches, soon followed by red and inflamed eyes, bleeding from throat and tongue, unnatural breathing, unpleasant breath, and painful coughing. The stomach was affected next with aching, retching, and vomiting. By the seventh day the body was wracked with pain and "internal" fever. The skin was reddish and covered with small ulcers and pustules, yet was not hot to the touch. Many of those that survived the fever died at the next stage when the disease descended to the bowels causing ulceration and continuous diarrhea.

The few who survived could still be affected by loss of memory, blindness, or loss of the use of the extremities as a result of the disease. Thucydides says that even the birds and animals that ate the unburied bodies during the plague died. Plague is still endemic in many parts of the world, although an understanding of the disease has led to a reduction in its occurrences.

To the urban naturalist the plague is a striking example of one of many epidemic diseases that

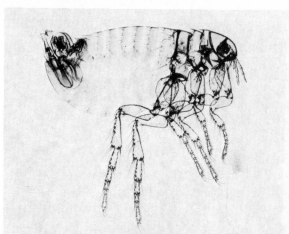

in the past limited population growth in cities. Disease in general has until very recently been one of the main factors in checking urban population growth: as the population grew, so did the mortality rate. In New York, the death rate rose from 1 in 46.5 persons in 1810 to 1 in 27 persons per year in 1859, due to the congested and unsanitary conditions prevailing in the city. Yellow fever which, like malaria, is carried by mosquitoes, carried off about 10 per cent of the population of Philadelphia in 1793, and in 1852 killed over 8000 people.

If asked to name the most prominent pests among city wildlife, most people would probably

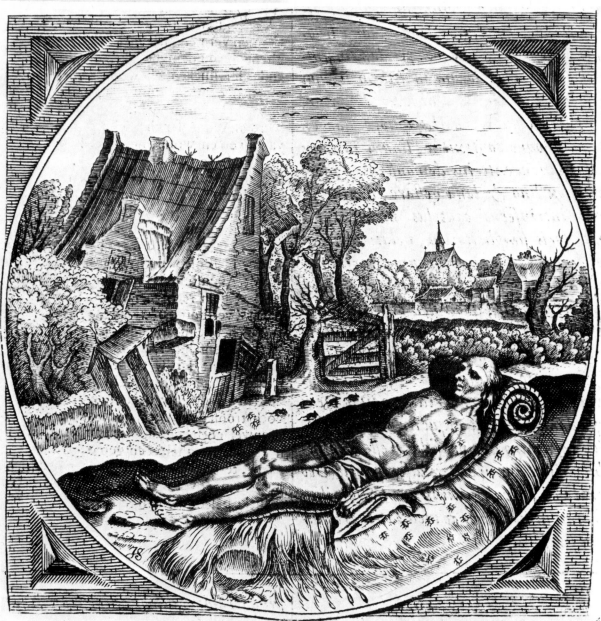

mention rats and mice. Throughout their recent history the black rat (*Rattus rattus*), the brown rat (*Rattus norvegicus*), and the house mouse (*Mus musculus*) have been closely associated with man, and in particular with city dwellers.

The exact origins of these three rodents will probably never be known with any real certainty; they have been transported all over the world wherever man has gone and have nearly always become serious pests. Their survival is usually fairly closely linked with that of man, so much so that when man abandons a city or village, these *commensals*—animals that "share" our food—lose their major source of sustenance and also disappear. This was demonstrated in the 1930s when the island of St. Kilda in the Scottish Outer Hebrides was finally abandoned by its human inhabitants: almost immediately its unique subspecies of house mouse — *Mus musculus muralis*—became extinct. The same would probably happen in most cities.

The house mouse, like the rat, is generally assumed to have originated in Asia. Its association with man is very ancient and was mentioned by ancient Greek and Roman writers. In the warmer parts of Europe, Asia, and in other parts of the world, house mice live in fields and hedges quite independently of man's habitations. But in cooler, temperate regions, they are nearly always closely linked with man and his dwellings.

Like most successful pest species, the house mouse is extremely adaptable and in many parts of the world has developed quite well-marked and distinct subspecies. In the Americas, Australia, and other parts of the world where there are no closely related mice to compete with the house mouse, it often fills a wide variety of niches in the ecosystem but is usually closely linked with man, and usually most abundant in cities. Perhaps the most famous adaptation is that of house mice living in meat cold stores. They have developed thicker and longer coats than those of normal house mice, to protect them in the constantly sub-zero temperatures.

In recent years the scale of house-mouse infestations in many cities has been reduced, mainly due to improved poisons. But mice (and rats) often develop resistance very rapidly.

In what is presumed to be its original home in India and Burma, the black rat is a largely tree-dwelling species found in open country, often far away from human habitation. Its spread to the cities of the world was much later than that of the house mouse, and it was not until the Middle Ages that it reached pest proportions in Europe. The spread of the black rat is traditionally associated with the Crusades; the returning knights are alleged to have brought the (plague-infested) rats on board ship when they returned from the Levant. The truth behind this tradition can never be known, but the spread of both rats and the plague is traced to that time.

As the black rat spread farther north the harsh winters of the northern European countryside forced it to move into the warmth of men's houses more and more, and it gradually became very much a city-dwelling animal. The accompanying plagues spread and increased, ravaging Europe until the 18th century when the black rat's numbers began to decline. This was due not to the work of man but to the spread of the larger, more aggressive, and even more adaptable brown rat. The black rat had meanwhile spread to the far corners of the world, and was particularly numerous in the East. Although still the dominant species in many tropical cities, especially in Asia, in most of the temperate regions the black rat is now found mainly in the older parts of the older cities, where it inhabits the upper stories and rafters of buildings. Its climbing abilities also give it a natural advantage over the brown rat on board ship. In many temperate-zone cities, dockyards are often the sole remaining habitats for the black rat. Usually the stock survives only because its numbers are constantly being added to by immigrants from abroad. The black rat may well become extinct in many cities—but I doubt if even the conservationists will shed many tears!

The brown rat, which is the ancestor of the pet white and "hooded" rats and the laboratory rats, also had its origins in Asia, but in more temperate regions than either the house mouse or black rat. Its original home was probably in Central Asia near the Caspian Sea and Lake Baikal. Early in the 18th century it suddenly started a spectacular and rapid advance, spreading first across Europe, and then throughout most of the rest of the world. Largely because the

Left: 17th-century engraving of a plague victim. Fleas, black rats, and a tumbledown cottage help to tell the story of his death. Rats living in the man's home died of plague. Rat fleas abandoned the corpses and hopped onto the man, infecting him with plague bacilli from the rats. Black-rat fleas transmit plague far more easily than the human flea (above, enlarged).

brown rat breeds faster than the black rat, it quickly became the dominant species.

Although we may regard plague and many of the other diseases such as typhus, rabies, and food poisoning carried by rats as largely things of the past, it is as well to realize the fine balance that keeps rats, mice, and other pests in check. We know that the black rat suddenly expanded across Europe and then the rest of the world in the Middle Ages. And we know that the brown rat suddenly changed its habits and spread over the world. But what about the next rodent pest?

Perhaps it is in what we believe could have been their original homeland, India and South-east Asia, that we must look for the key to future trends in the movements of these rodents. In Rangoon, for instance, there are five species of rats and mice that infest houses. A survey showed that out of the total number of rats and mice, the brown rat, which inhabited mainly dockland areas, constituted only about 10 per cent of the total; the black rat found mainly in the better class of suburban houses made up another 10 per cent; whereas the house mouse, which, although widespread, amounted to only 5 per cent of the total. The commonest species were the little Burmese house rat (*Rattus exulans*) and the lesser bandicoot or Indian mole rat (*Bandi-*

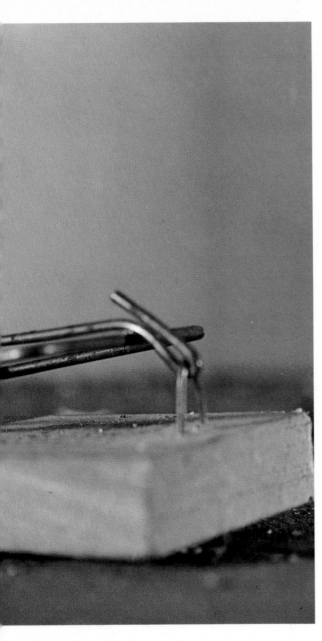

the same trend in the rat population structure has been observed: the black and brown rats are decreasing, and the little Burmese house rats are rapidly multiplying. A small change in the genotype, such as occurred in the black and the brown rats in the past, and enabled them to expand their range explosively, could create a new pest species of frightening proportions.

Pests can seemingly evolve almost overnight. Some of the plants and animals discussed in the last chapter had remained confined to a small area for century after century and then, for no immediately apparent reason, they started to expand. Probably a new mutation enables the species to take advantage of the man-made environment. Such was the case with rats and mice, and the same might be true of golden hamsters. The golden hamsters so familiar as pets are all descended from a single pregnant female found in the Syrian desert earlier this century. Selective breeding has already produced an enormous variety of colors, even long-haired forms, and present-day hamsters are possibly hardier than their wild ancestors. From time to time hamsters have escaped and shown that they can still survive in the wild. Fortunately, pet hamsters are strongly territorial and are normally kept singly, so that unless the escaped animal is a pregnant female it is unlikely to found a colony. There have been instances in the cities of Bath and Bury St. Edmund's in England, however, where several individuals have escaped from pet shops and become established in the wild. Once this happens it requires well-planned efforts to exterminate them because they hibernate and store food, making poisoning difficult.

One of the most successful groups of birds in urban areas are pigeons. In nearly all parts of the world, one or more species usually nest in the centers of towns and cities. The town pigeon *par excellence* is the feral descendant of the domesticated form of *Columba livia*, the rock dove. From ancient times pigeons have been kept for food, for carrying messages, for sport (racing and trapshooting), and purely for ornament. Before the days of winter-feed (such as turnips) for cattle and sheep, pigeons were an important

cota bengalensis), the former constituting nearly half the total rodent population.

In Bombay, on the other hand, the lesser bandicoot is now the commonest species, but in 1912 98 per cent of the rats were black rats, whereas the lesser bandicoots were very rare. During the course of this century the black rat has become highly resistant to plague, while at the same time it has dropped in numbers to a mere 32 per cent of the total. On the other hand, it has been discovered that the lesser bandicoot, which has taken over as the dominant species, is very susceptible to the disease.

In other Indian and Southeast Asian cities,

The black rat, at first a tropical tree-dweller, moved west through Europe in the Middle Ages, colonizing city dwellings as it sought protection from the cold. With it came the bubonic plague.

source of fresh meat during the winter months, and most large estates in ancient and medieval times had substantial brick or stone-built dovecots, often holding several thousand birds. It is the descendants of these birds, augmented by others, that form today's city pigeon populations.

No longer normally a source of food, pigeons are now classed mainly as pests and vermin, though, surprisingly, most people treat them with considerable affection. I am sure that tourists in London's Trafalgar Square, New York's Central Park, or outside St. Mark's in Venice would not feed the pigeons that confidently settle on their heads and shoulders if they knew a little more about the birds. Town pigeons are often infected with, or carriers of, a wide variety of diseases

including some, such as avian tuberculosis, that can be transmitted to man. London pigeons also carry a fungus that causes not only skin disease in human beings who come into contact with them but also, by infecting the lungs and nervous system, causes a form of meningitis. Another disease carried by pigeons is ornithosis (a form of psittacosis), which, when it infects man, causes chills, fever, headache, intolerance to light, loss of appetite, sore throat, nausea and vomiting.

The brown rat—a large and aggressive species—has colonized the world since spreading from Central Asia in the 18th century. It usually displaced the black rat, but they may coexist.

At the time of the outbreak of ornithosis among the citizens of Chicago in the mid-1940s it was found that 45 per cent of the city's pigeons were infected. In Paris, over 60 per cent are infected, and the disease has also been recorded at similar levels in most other cities.

Like many other birds, pigeons also have lice, fleas, and a number of other parasites living on their skin and among their feathers, as well as internal parasites, such as worms. Although the town pigeon is not unique among birds in carrying disease and parasites, it is usually far less healthy and more heavily infested than its wild counterparts.

The other major urban bird pest, the now ubiquitous house sparrow, undoubtedly had a very much more restricted range at one time. Sparrows are close relatives of the weavers, which inhabit dry grassland areas, and as such probably evolved in Africa—but their recent history has been closely linked with that of man. The sparrows were first taken to America in 1850 and released in Brooklyn. Using our knowledge of their breeding habits, a simple piece of arithmetic shows that a decade later, with no predation, there would have been 275,000 million sparrows in America. Such a number could have consumed the world's annual wheat output in one week! Yet, when they were first introduced into the USA, Americans used to shoot shrikes and other birds that preyed on the sparrows, as it was hoped that the latter would feed on the canker worms that were devastating the orchards of New England and the park trees of New York. By 1900 sparrows had spread across most of North America and were everywhere regarded as unmitigated pests, and today it is the shrikes that are officially protected.

In China, sparrows are regarded as such pests that they have been ruthlessly slaughtered, although never completely exterminated. English "sparrow clubs" of the 19th century attempted a similar extermination but, although tens of thousands were killed (31,000 in one village alone in the period 1819–35), the sparrow still survived, and in cities it proliferated. Over much of its original range the house sparrow is now less abundant, due partly to changes in agriculture and to changing transport in towns, but although there may be fewer house sparrows in northern

Left: female golden hamster and young. Hamsters are rural animals that thrive on cultivated land, where they eat field crops, and collect grain in underground larders. But golden hamsters abound in cities in the form of pets. Sometimes, several golden hamsters escape and establish a breeding colony. Hamster colonies in food stores could create even greater problems of eradication than rats or mice, because the hamster habit of spending long periods hibernating and living off hidden food supplies makes these little rodents difficult to trap or poison. Right: hordes of pigeons rely upon the food offerings from the tourists visiting St. Mark's Square, Venice. Vacationers taking snapshots of their loved ones festooned with hungry pigeons are usually unaware that many of the birds carry disease organisms transmissible to man. Avian tuberculosis is one such bird ailment, aspergillosis—a fungus infection of the lungs—another. There is also a type of psittacosis that produces a whole battery of very unpleasant symptoms in human beings.

Europe than there were a century ago, it has since spread over most of the Americas, South Africa, Australia, and New Zealand.

The story of the starling is rather similar to that of the house sparrow except that it did not start to expand its range and become a pest until much later. In fact, in Europe its status as a pest is questionable; it causes a considerable mess in its urban roosts and tends to displace other nesting birds, being rather aggressive in its search for nesting holes, but otherwise, with its largely insectivorous diet, it is beneficial to man. In America, the other places where it has been introduced, it is also often responsible for the local extinction of native birds in city parks and suburbs. However, overall, the starling can at present be regarded perhaps as a nuisance rather than a pest.

As I pointed out earlier, it is often the introduced wildlife that become serious pests, and this is certainly true of birds. In Australia and New Zealand the ancient and distinctive fauna and flora were largely unable to compete with the highly adaptable introduced species. Nearly all the bird pests, including sparrows, were deliberately introduced into these countries in the period between about 1860 and 1930, in the hope that they would be beneficial to the farmer. Twenty-two pairs of house sparrows were brought to New Zealand in February 1868, but by 1875 they were being shot as vermin. They became such a plague in the cities that permission was sought (unsuccessfully) to put down poisoned corn within the city of Christchurch.

Although pigeons, sparrows, and even sometimes starlings are regarded almost universally as bird pests, several other bird species have moved into cities and urban areas and in some places, at least, they, too, must be considered as pests. Bulbuls, which are common garden birds in Africa and Asia, have been introduced into Australia, where they often cause extensive damage to flowers in suburban gardens and parks. Asiatic mynahs have been introduced into places as far apart as Canada, Australia, New Zealand, and Hawaii. The mynahs are popular birds except with those people who cultivate

fruit trees, because their diet consists largely of fruit. They are, however, a danger to native birds because of their aggressive competition for nesting holes.

The city environment, then, is particularly vulnerable to the rapid and sudden spread of insect, bird, and mammal species that find conditions right. For just as the cultivating of large areas of a single crop enables pest populations to explode, so man's sprawling, overcrowded cities have become, in effect, vast "monocultures" ripe, in an era of mass transit, for the rapid spread of new pests. With our armory of scientific and technological know-how we should be able to control them—these "flowers in the wrong place"—and the diseases they may carry.

Black-headed bulbul, trapped for banding. Bulbuls are Asian and African songbirds. The black-headed species is one of many that are common in suburban and even urban Asian gardens.

Gray squirrel at a feeding station. Among the most invasive and persistent of introduced pests, gray squirrels originated in North America, but now also thrive in Britain, where they sometimes eat the seeds and shoots of trees in city parks.

City Man

Urban man is, relatively, a very recent phenomenon. In socio-economic terms he is only just
emerging from being a hunter-gatherer and a
pastoralist and it is far too early to say whether
or not he is more than a transient evolutionary
experiment. He still retains many of the behavioral patterns of his ancestors, modified to
some extent by the conditioning of city life, and
he also tries to preserve some sort of contact
with his wild "natural" past through his gardens
and his pets. He is also himself a habitat, acting
as host to numerous lesser animals.

It is only very recently that so-called civilized
man has begun to rid himself of the rich and
varied community for which he acts as host.
Even today, the majority of human beings in the
world carry parasites of some sort and, although
medical services are usually better in cities,
particularly of the so-called developed world,
poorer urban areas everywhere make perfect
breeding grounds for a whole host of parasites.

Fleas, bugs—including the well-known bedbug—and lice are the most obvious, feeding as
they do on the blood of their human hosts.
Bedbugs can inflict painful bites but do not carry
disease. The bloodsucking assassin bug, found in
Mexico and South America, and occasionally in
the United States, transmits the often fatal
Chagas' disease. Fleas are now becoming rare
in many cities, partly because of better personal
hygiene, which is also the main factor in reducing
bedbugs and body lice; but in the United Kingdom there has been an increase in the reported
cases of head lice. The disappearance of fleas and
lice is due in large measure to modern housing.
Homes today are generally drier and warmer than
their counterparts of a century or so ago, conditions that fleas do not like. Floors and carpets
are usually cleaned at regular intervals, getting
rid of flea pupae.

Fleas, lice, and bugs are large enough for us
to see, and therefore easy to destroy. But man
is parasitized internally as well as externally.

*Rush-hour crowds help us to grasp what New York City's multi-
million population means. Man was not designed for life en
masse, but began as tiny bands foodgathering in a wilderness.
His biological adjustment to city life is far from complete.*

Bedbug, much enlarged. Bedbugs infest dirty city dwellings, hiding in mattresses and bed frames, and emerging in the night to suck their hosts' blood.

Louse (enlarged) on hair. Head and body lice may infest people living in crowded conditions, and can transmit the terrible disease typhus. Washing may not eradicate lice, and their numbers are increasing as the insects acquire resistance to insecticides.

Parasitic roundworms that may invade man's body include Trichinella spiralis *(above, encysted in heart muscle)* and the tapeworms *(below, part of one shown much enlarged)*. Both are absorbed by eating underdone meat, and the former can be fatal.

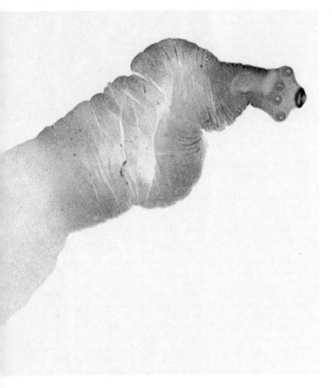

Most people at some time in their lives are infested by one or other of the 50 or so parasitic species of nematodes, commonly called roundworms. Most of these are harmless to man, but a few can cause serious illnesses such as epilepsy, blindness, or liver disease.

The largest of the nematodes can grow over 12 inches long. A mature female will lay as many as 200,000 eggs a day. In modern cities this worm has become rare, but it still occurs, particularly on salad vegetables grown in parts of the world where human feces are used as fertilizer. The worms live in the intestine of the host, feeding on partly digested matter, but normally they cause little harm—even with infestations of 5000 or so—although as few as 100 can block the gut or move into other parts of the body and cause the death of the host. Another unpleasant nematode is the hookworm *Necatos*, which burrows into the intestinal wall of the host and feeds on the blood.

Perhaps the most dreaded of all roundworms, however, is the one that causes trichinosis. When pork—the source of so many of man's parasites—is not thoroughly cooked, adult trichina worms will survive. These do little harm to their human hosts, but the larvae, which may number over 100 million, bore through the flesh, causing excruciating pain and, in many cases, death. It is thought that it was trichina worms and various other parasites that led to the Jewish and Muslim religious laws banning the eating of pork—a wise precaution when one realizes that a single infected pork sausage may contain as many as 100,000 worms!

Even more serious are the trematodes, or flukes, which are flatworms. Because part of their life cycle is in water, they are found mainly in rural areas, but flukes such as the liver fluke are often transmitted to urban man when he eats mollusks or raw or undercooked freshwater fish. The fluke makes its way from the gut to the liver, via the bile duct. Once in the liver it feeds on blood, and can cause serious anemia.

Perhaps the best-known of all man's internal parasites are the cestodes, or tapeworms. Practically every vertebrate animal is at some time during its life parasitized by a tapeworm of some sort. Tapeworms are among the most perfectly adapted of parasites: they do not have digestive tracts or mouths, and simply live attached to the guts of other animals by suckers or hooks, absorbing food that has already been digested.

The dog devotedly gazing at the boy could be a carrier of tapeworms. If a dog licks someone's hands or face, tapeworm eggs in the dog's mouth may be transferred to the person's body. If the eggs find their way into the person's mouth, that individual may—unaware—become an unwilling host for this particularly unpleasant parasite. Large populations of urban dogs mean that even the cleanest cities harbor tapeworms.

Two very common tapeworms are found in beef and pork, and ingested by man when he eats under-cooked or raw meat. Regular meat inspection and careful cooking have eliminated or drastically reduced the incidence of the beef and pork tapeworms in most of the developed parts of the world, but another, possibly even more dangerous, tapeworm can occur in even the cleanest cities. This is transmitted to man by dogs: when dogs lick the face or hands of a human being there is a risk that they will pass on the tapeworm's eggs. The larvae that hatch from these eggs form cysts that, if located in the brain, can cause blindness and even death.

Living in the blood and digestive tract of most humans are vast numbers of single-celled animals (protozoans) that feed on bacteria and food particles. Most of these protozoans are harmless, but some cause diseases such as dysentery. It is interesting to note, however, that in Britain, the amoebic-dysentery protozoan found in a large percentage of the population does not give rise to the disease.

Another type of protozoan, a microscopic sporozoan, is responsible for malaria, which until very recently was one of the most devastating and widespread diseases in the world, killing millions of people a year.

The connection between the veritable zoo that lives on and in man, and the diseases to which

these creatures gives rise, was only understood after the invention of the microscope. A Dutchman, Anton van Leeuwenhoek, was the first person to see the microscopic life that existed inside his own body. A draper by trade, he experimented with lenses in his spare time and managed to achieve a magnification of 270 times with a resolution of 1.4 microns—which means that through his lenses it was possible to separate two objects only 0.0014 mm apart. In 1681, after suffering an attack of diarrhea, he examined his own feces and discovered the protozoan now known as *Giardia lamblia*. He accurately described its shape and the way it moved. Leeuwenhoek then went on to describe an even

Part of old Lagos, Nigeria. Market stalls and flimsy, shanty-town structures are typical of the crowded living conditions in which disease organisms may spread unchecked. Urban epidemics have hitherto helped limit world population growth.

smaller organism, the first known bacterium. He continued to describe microorganisms from a variety of sources, and in 1683 wrote to the Secretary of the Royal Society in London a letter that has become a classic of bacteriological literature. In his letter, Leeuwenhoek described an assortment of microbes that he had collected on a toothpick from between his own molar teeth.

The importance of disease in controlling man's

119

population growth is sometimes overlooked by historians. This is particularly true in the case of urban areas throughout the world, which have always been very vulnerable because of their density of population. In the last chapter we discussed some of the diseases carried by city wildlife that, in the not too distant past, were major factors controlling man's population.

One of the best-documented diseases is bubonic plague, transmitted to man by the fleas of rats and other rodents. In A.D. 542, during the reign of the Roman Emperor Justinian, a pandemic (world epidemic) broke out and raged around the Roman Empire for over 50 years. The 18th-century English historian Edward Gibbon estimated that during that time some 100 million people were killed by it in Europe alone.

The next pandemic, known as the Black Death, started in the 1340s in Central Asia, spreading throughout Asia Minor, Arabia, Egypt, North Africa, and Europe, reaching Britain in 1348; it killed about 25 million people throughout Europe. Other epidemics arose in the 15th, 16th, and 17th centuries. This particularly virulent form of the disease then gradually died out, with the last epidemics sweeping the East toward the end of the 19th century. From about the middle of the 19th century the disease ravaged China, where nearly all the outbreaks were traceable to a marmot known as the tarabagon. From the East, a milder form of plague reached California in 1900, where small outbreaks, including *pneumonic* plague—where the disease is spread from the breath of an infected person— were recorded in Oakland in 1919 and in Los Angeles in 1924.

Although rarely since then as devastating as at the time of the Black Death, the plague nevertheless still needs careful monitoring. In India, where epidemics have been recorded from the 11th through to the 20th century, a check is kept on the rat populations as an indication of possible outbreaks of the disease.

Even if city man is gradually ridding himself of the portable zoo he has been carrying around since long before he lived in cities, he still retains most of his ancestral behavior patterns.

For thousands of years, as early man evolved, he developed behavior patterns that helped the species to survive. These patterns have analogies in the behavior of other animals, as, for instance, in the case of territorial behavior. In the wild, many animal species established areas that the male defends against others of his own kind. A territory provides a place where the animal can mate or feed in peace. When an animal is outside its own territory it seems to be at a disadvantage. As an intruder, it never reacts as strongly to threats as an owner of a territory does; and when two rivals clash, the established holder of the territory almost invariably defeats the interloper. So it is with city man; on his home territory he is king. In an argument with a neighbor across a garden fence, neither side is likely to achieve satisfaction, because both are on home territory. Should one or other cross into his neighbor's territory, however, he is then immediately at a disadvantage and is likely to retreat at the slightest threat of violence.

Modern man's instinctive defense of his own property and family is as pronounced as it was in his ancestors. In fact, it might be argued that this behavioral pattern is more marked than ever. Because the city evolved—in part at least—to protect the wealth that had been won from the land or from other tribes, one might expect city-dwellers to tend toward materialism. It is therefore not surprising to find modern man defending with his life the pieces of paper we call money. In the first cities, granaries were the equivalent of banks, and in some primitive societies still surviving today a man's wealth is measured in cattle, sheep, corn, wives, and so on, all of which have a real and immediate survival value. From what we know of early man, he had few luxuries, unless we count his necessary tools and implements, some of which he decorated with such obvious care. When we come to urban man, however, the pursuit of wealth and sheer abundance become ends in themselves, so that the more he accumulates, the higher his position in society.

In ancient cities defense and trade were a normal part of life and did not perhaps radically affect the mental or physical state of the inhabitants. Also, of course, the urban units were usually fairly small. Whenever they began to grow too large, as we have seen, natural selection, in the form of disease and war, would reduce the population to a level that would

On his home territory, city man is king. His apartment or his house is civilization's equivalent of the territory needed and claimed by man's apelike ancestors for foodgathering and for mating. Like them, modern man instinctively defends his home. He also defends property that has become an extension of it.

As people learned to live in villages, then towns, then cities, the biological urge to possess a family and land to live on became expanded to a desire to acquire a mounting and increasingly sophisticated mass of possessions. Above: for the townsfolk of Dogondoutchi in south-western Nigeria, a food surplus is a highly prized possession in a country where crop failure can cause famine. Thus Dogondoutchi's granaries on stilts are the equivalent of city banks, and their grain is as valuable to local people as is cash to a Western city-dweller. Right: a Bakhtiari Moslem in Iran measures his wealth largely by the number of wives and children he is able to support. Left: this large, expensive automobile in Washington, D.C., represents the kind of possession that Western city man most covets. For his society, however, the pursuit of material possessions has become an end in itself.

stabilize with its environment. Since the Industrial Revolution, however, man's physical evolution has increasingly fallen behind the pace of his technological evolution. He can fly from Tokyo to New York in a few hours only to find that, having got there, his body has not adjusted to the speed with which he has traveled; we call this condition "jet-lag."

Man can build tower blocks and skyscrapers and provide homes for hundreds of families in his cities, homes far more luxurious and comfortable than any in which his predecessors lived. Yet the rate of mental breakdown appears to rise with the height and number of these buildings. Man's emotional adaptability is simply not sufficient to adjust to such intensive urbanization. The stresses imposed on man in a major city induce reactions similar to those of animals, particularly primates, in a badly run zoo. This is the theme of Dr. Desmond Morris's book *The Human Zoo*. Just as overcrowded monkeys savage their offspring, so their human counterparts, the Naked Apes living in tower blocks, are more likely to ill-treat their babies.

Millions of years of evolution prepared the emergent humanoid ape that became *Homo sapiens* for life as a hunter-gatherer on the prairies and in the forests. The enormous change to becoming a pastoralist or settled farmer was spread over a long time; and the few centuries that then elapsed before man became urbanized were not enough for him to throw off the old behavioral patterns and develop new ones. The basic unit of "natural" man is the tribal unit, a small community with a well-ordered hierarchy, and man's behavior has evolved accordingly. But when the tribe developed the "super-tribe" of the city, man no longer recognized all the other inhabitants of the city, and found it difficult to adapt his behavior. Man's unique success as a species is largely due to his adaptability, and he did manage to cope with many of the new, urban problems by forming castes, guilds, classes, and so forth. In fact, the larger and more cosmopolitan the city, the more there is a tendency for people to form themselves into close-knit racial groups, even ghettos, in which minority groups live because of social, legal, or economic pressure. In the last 150 years or so, however, the pace of city life has accelerated faster than man has been able to adapt, and it is possible that his species is failing in the city environment.

In sixth-century Byzantium, after the Western Roman Empire had collapsed, there developed a behavioral phenomenon that is clearly paralleled in modern cities. The city formed two functions: the "greens" and the "blues." These were chariot teams whose following grew out of hand, creating a situation verging on anarchy.

Byzantium was a declining, overpopulated city, with enormous social differences between its inhabitants, and its resources stretched almost to the limits. The analogy with modern cities in the Western world is obvious. The behavior of man in this situation is the same today as it was nearly 1500 years ago. In many cities rival factions dress ostentatiously in their uniforms, be they Capulets, Hell's Angels, Skinheads, or Orangemen. Football fans adorn themselves in their team's colors, and develop war cries, and if two rival groups meet, open battle may break out. Just like their chariot-supporting forebears in Byzantium, they rampage and vandalize, terrorizing the city's inhabitants.

Such behavioral trends suggest that the supercity is ultimately an environmental failure. However hard he tries, I do not think that Desmond Morris's Naked Ape will ever overcome the problems that large cities inevitably create. The fact that more and more city-dwellers dream of a second home—a cottage in the country, a shack in the hills, or a chalet in the mountains — suggests that man instinctively realizes the inadequacies of city life. And the people who *do* "escape" are not just the dropouts, the hippies, and the "eco-freaks" who claim to have completely rejected civilization. They are ordinary men and women.

Man did make some positive attempts to overcome the problems of city living before admitting defeat and retreating from the urban environment. Apart from the provision of social and other services, throughout history he has brought the countryside and animals from his "natural" past into the towns and cities.

In the past most animals kept in towns were reared either for food (doves, chickens, guinea pigs, rabbits, cows, goats), as guards (dogs), as working animals (horses, llamas, donkeys,

Inhabitants of the many unsightly and unhealthy slums often have a strongly developed sense of community. Biologically adjusted to life in small tribal units, man tries to recreate such units (in the form of social classes, racial ghettoes, guilds, and so on) within the city's "super-tribe."

camels), to keep down rats (cats, mongooses), or because they had religious significance (monkeys, apes, crocodiles, cows). Nowadays most animals kept in cities are there purely as pets. Pets fulfill several functions, but in particular they provide companionship (cats, budgerigars, parrots) or are ornamental (tropical fish). They may also be status symbols (pythons, lions, alligators) and they can be of educational value to children, teaching them about living creatures.

Of these various categories of animals, horses and other draft animals have all but disappeared from most urban areas in the developed world, although a wide variety of them are still used elsewhere. In the mountain cities of South America, llamas still bring produce to market, and in the High Andes they will probably remain superior to any wheeled vehicle for a long time to come. But in the oil-rich countries of North Africa and the Middle East the Landrover, truck, and car are rapidly ousting the camel.

The authorities in an increasing number of modern cities are introducing regulations that make it difficult for people to keep animals, on the grounds that they cause a public nuisance, but in cities and towns of the nonindustrialized

areas of the world, backyard farming of animals up to the size of pigs is common. When the Spanish Conquistadores overran the Inca Empire in the 16th century, they found that guinea pigs (domesticated rodents derived from wild cavies) were kept for food. Guinea pigs can still be seen scampering around the gardens of suburbs and villages in the Andes. In Europe and the parts of the world colonized by Europeans, the domesticated equivalent of the guinea pig is the rabbit. Although not widely kept now, rabbits have been very popular in the past, particularly in times of economic depression and war, because of their food value. Poultry such as chickens, ducks, and geese often figure highly in the backyard farm. In the Far East especially bred cocks, fitted with razor-sharp spurs, are also kept for fighting.

In the developed world man's love of domestic pets has meant a high density of dogs in towns and cities (in New York alone there are over 275,000 dogs with licences) and the consequently high volume of feces in streets and parks is alarming many medical authorities. Many of the parasites and diseases that affect man have their origin in his canine friends. New

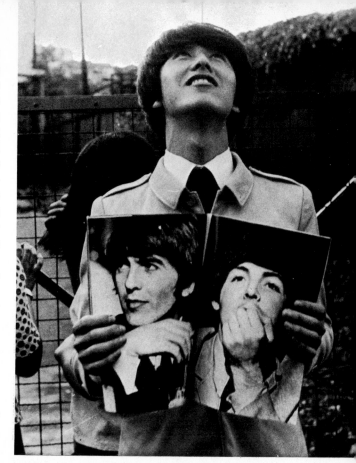

York's Environmental Protection Administration estimated that each year the city's dogs deposit somewhere up to 20,000 tons of excrement and up to 1 million gallons of urine on the streets—a frightening thought to the layman, but an interesting field of study to a biologist. Apart from possibly transmitting worms to man, dog feces provide a source of nourishment for a number of creatures, such as flies, which, in turn, are food for songbirds and other attractive denizens of the city.

In many parts of the world stray dogs are a problem. In cities that require dogs to be licensed, dog catchers are often employed to round up strays, but elsewhere, quite large numbers of dogs can live in a semiwild state.

In the early 1970s, a study was carried out on the dogs living in the city of Baltimore, Maryland. It was found that the packs, of up to 17 dogs, were very loosely structured, and often included pets that had been let out by their owners for exercise. The dogs seemed to find enough food to satisfy them in garbage cans, and many people in the city put out food for the strays. Particularly interesting are the findings on the population structure and mortality of Baltimore's dogs: some 17,000 a year were collected dead off the streets, the majority killed by cars, and some 6,000 strays were humanely killed each year. Out of an estimated total population of only 100,000 dogs, this is a very significant toll. It means that few of the stray dogs of Baltimore live to see old age and that the population is, on average, young. Young dogs are more prone than older ones to infestation with tapeworms, to dog diseases, and—most alarming of all—to rabies. This last fact could be very serious should any of the dogs become infected, because some 7000 cases of dog bite are reported annually to the City Veterinarian of Baltimore; the real total is probably double this figure. Most of the victims are children. From this one study alone, it is obvious that dogs

To a thoughtful observer, both of these seemingly unconnected scenes reveal man's reluctance to immerse himself entirely in the artifical environment of the city. Above: a tiny park on New York City's East 51st Street. Open areas between buildings, with trees and an artificial waterfall, bring an illusion of the natural world into one of our planet's most densely built-up areas. Left: milking a goat on a rural commune. Increasing numbers of young people disenchanted with the artificiality of urban civilization are drifting out into the countryside, and trying to live by simple, rural self-sufficiency.

play a very important part in the urban eco-system, acting directly on the health of man in the city.

Cats do not present quite the same problems as dogs, although large numbers are often kept as pets or exist as strays in cities. Unlike dogs, they always try to bury their excrement and, being primarily predatory carnivores (dogs have become largely scavengers), often perform a useful function by destroying rats and mice. On the debit side, however, they are also notable predators of songbirds and are probably the main reason for the absence of ground-nesting birds in suburban areas. Cats probably also account for the rarity of lizards and frogs in such areas. Cat populations in cities are generally higher than those of dogs, but they are also considerably more difficult to estimate. In New York City it is believed that there are about 300,000 cats. But the cat population is very much subject to fashion. In London in 1951 there was approximately one cat to every five households. In 1961, when budgerigars had become popular pets, there was one cat to every 12 households, but by 1971 it had climbed again to one cat to every eight households.

Although dogs and cats are the most popular pets of the city-dweller, there are a wide variety of other animals for sale in pet shops. The commonest pets after dogs and cats are probably birds and fish, followed by mammals such as gerbils, hamsters, rats, and mice, then land turtles, terrapins, chipmunks, and an assortment of snakes, monkeys, and other unusual pets. Nor are these animals a relatively insignificant part of city life. An examination of import and export figures soon shows the volume of the world trade in wildlife.

Few countries keep detailed or accurate records of mammals, birds, and fish in captivity, but available statistics give some idea of the scale of the trade. Japan alone imports at least 1 million wild birds each year, and in 1971, before the imposition of strict controls, nearly 1 million birds were imported into the United States. Schiphol Airport near Amsterdam handled some 17,000 consignments of wild animals in 1970, among which were over 7 million birds; more than 250,000 birds are sold each year in the "Sunday" market in Bangkok, and in 1969 one German state alone imported about 400,000 birds. In 1972, the USA imported 1 million live fish, and the UK imports up to

One way in which city man preserves links with the countryside is by keeping animals: for food, as pets, or for their entertainment value. Above right: hog on a string in Otavalo, Ecuador. Dwellers in Andean towns and cities still keep hogs and guinea pigs in their back-yards as living larders. Left: pet hare on an apartment carpet, where it seems strikingly out of place. Many kinds of pets imported into city dwellings live in surroundings entirely different from those for which they are adapted in the wild. Above: caged goldfinch in a town on the Spanish island of Majorca. City man has long kept small songbirds for companionship, and their tuneful voices recall the freedom of the fields and woods. Unfortunately for the birds themselves, their owners often occupy small apartments and are unable or un-willing to spare the birds more than a bare minimum of living space. Far right: this organ-grinder's monkey wins sym-pathy — and cash — from passersby. Monkeys and circus animals including lions, elephants, and sea lions all find themselves forced into the alien urban environment to satisfy city man's taste for exotic wildlife entertainment. In most cities, only food and draft ani-mals are scarcer than they used to be.

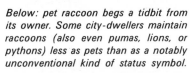
Below: pet raccoon begs a tidbit from its owner. Some city-dwellers maintain raccoons (also even pumas, lions, or pythons) less as pets than as a notably unconventional kind of status symbol.

250,000 land turtles a year and about 600,000 birds. Most of these animals are destined for city apartments, where they find themselves in totally alien environments compared with their state in the wild.

In the course of this book, we have already discussed mammals and birds that originated as pets but have since escaped to become features of our "natural" city fauna: mynahs, parakeets, guppies, and hamsters, for instance. If the world trade in wildlife were to continue at its present level, we could certainly expect more escaped pet species to become established in the wild. But the public is gradually becoming aware of the dangers of allowing pet populations to get out of hand and in the near future we shall probably see tighter control on the trade in wildlife.

Most pet animals, apart from cats and dogs, are kept within the confines of their owners' property, and are only rarely seen by the outside world. The main places where city man comes into contact with more exotic wildlife are special parks and zoos.

From earliest times man has collected and displayed animals in his cities; these first menageries were probably a mixture of domesticated animals, tamed wild animals, and a small number of caged wild animals. I have seen such collections in North African towns on the edge of the Sahara, where camels, goats, sheep, ducks, and geese mix with gazelles that have been captured when young, and then hand-reared. Also displayed in grim and squalid cages are hyenas, desert foxes, snakes, and small birds.

The Ancient Egyptians, although by no means the first people to introduce menageries into their cities, certainly outshone their contemporaries. In fact, some of the menageries have yet to be surpassed in scale. They kept oryxes, gazelles, other antelopes, cheetahs, lynxes, wild cats, geese, hares, giraffes, monkeys, ostriches, and many other animals, some being bred in captivity. Menageries gradually became part of the trappings of royalty, and from Egypt through the Middle East to China most courts had elaborate collections, the like of which the world has seen again only very recently.

Cats and dogs are among the most numerous of the beasts that keep man company in the city. Left: dogs fouling city streets may spread disease but also provide food for flies that go to feed songbirds. Right: the city cat's ecological role is keeping down populations of rats, mice, birds, frogs, and lizards.

By the time of the fall of the Roman Empire, menagerie-keeping was in a general decline. Animals had been slaughtered in vast numbers in the Roman arenas, and for the next few hundred years Europe could claim only a handful of miserable menageries attached to the courts, although Marco Polo recorded that they still flourished in the Far East. And when Cortes and his Conquistadores entered Tenochtitlan in 1519 they found a menagerie comparable to many modern zoos. It was a vast, well-ordered collection with a staff of 300 keepers; but there was also a grisly side to this collection. The larger carnivores, such as jaguars, were fed on the remains from the almost daily human sacrifices in the temples.

During the Renaissance in Europe there was an awakening of interest in menageries, and the wealthy patrons of the arts and sciences began forming private collections. In 1752 the Holy Roman Emperor Francis I erected special buildings to house a collection of animals in the beautiful gardens at Schönbrunn in Vienna for his wife Maria Theresa, which can perhaps be described as the first real zoo (which is the shortened form of zoological garden). Although it has kept abreast of developments in the zoo world and has expanded and altered, parts of the original building still exist. In 1765 Schönbrunn Zoo was opened to the public, but it was many years before public zoos existed in more than a handful of cities. America's first zoo was founded in Philadelphia in 1859; another was opened five years later in New York's Central Park, by which time there were nearly 50 zoos open to the public in cities throughout the rest of the world. London Zoo was founded in 1828, and soon became established as the prototype of a new type of zoo: the modern scientific zoo, run by a zoological society with interests often

Since ancient times, people have kept collections of exotic animals in cities. But modern public zoos date only from the 18th century, and since then have gone through several transformations. Below: an engraving of people at the bear pit in the London Zoo in Regent's Park in 1835. In those days, big fierce animals were given pitifully small and often poorly lit enclosures, and some were always visible only through bars. Right: polar bears in a more natural setting in the London Zoo today. Unimpeded by bars, people can gaze at the bears across a pit or can look down upon them from a walk above and behind their enclosures. This allows room for the bears to exercise, and contains a pool in which they love to take a bath. Even so, lack of space means that zoos in city centers often cannot give their animals pens as large as they need. Largely for this reason, some spacious, parklike zoos have been set up outside, but within easy reach of, major cities.

quite different from those of the earlier menagerie-owners. The education of visitors and the scientific study of the inmates of the zoo gradually became the order of the day and are still features of all good modern zoos.

As we have seen, urban man needs some contact with the wildlife that was once so much part of his life, and in the modern zoo it is there in a convenient, easily obtainable form. Since 1907, when Carl Hagenbeck opened his zoo in the

No barrier separates these ostriches from the spectators who watch from automobiles cruising through a safari park. Typical of many modern zoos, this one in southern California has beasts in natural settings, and is near a city (Los Angeles).

suburbs of Hamburg, zoo architects have attempted to give their animals a natural background, as much for the sake of the visitors as for that of the animals. Hagenbeck built artificial mountains and hills, features that have been copied in most of the world's zoos, so that today the modern urban hunter can take a cab in the Champs Elysées or Fifth Avenue and in a few minutes, equipped with telephoto lenses, "shoot" a lion or tiger at a distance of only 20 feet. Zoos also enable children reared in an urban environment to learn about wild animals that otherwise they would probably never see.

The most recent trend in zoos is the establishment of so-called "safari parks," which carry the idea of the natural setting one stage further. Much of their appeal is based on the fact that they are usually situated within reach of large

cities and thus accessible to nature-starved townspeople seeking the excitement of a safari.

Although the term "safari park" has been used only recently, the idea is an old one. In the early 19th century, Lord Derby kept herds of eland and other animals on his estate near Liverpool, and a little later the Duke of Bedford started keeping herds of deer, including the very rare Père David's deer, on his estate at Woburn, north of London.

Even before modern zoos were developed in Europe and America, most major cities cultivated "physick" gardens, which—as their name suggests—were created in order to grow plants for their medicinal properties, and as such played an important part in the development of modern experimental biology. Many of these gardens survive today under the more familiar name of botanic gardens.

The need for green plants, as well as animal life, is a strong one and, considering the value of land in cities, it is amazing how many homes still have gardens, however small. City man needs

something closer, more immediate than the publicly owned "nature" of city parks and squares. He needs, in fact, a garden—even a window box will do—to keep him in physical and spiritual contact with the natural world of his ancestors.

All cities have some trees, and most of the inhabitants welcome them, but the prize for tree-consciousness must surely go to London, Ontario. Virtually every street in the city is lined with trees, with altogether over 400,000 trees officially owned and maintained at the taxpayers' expense, as well as thousands of privately owned trees in gardens. Over 50 varieties have been planted by the City Park Department since protection was first given to trees in 1870. The trees include gingkos, sugar maples, tulip trees, Russian olives, and an avenue of elms planted when the city was founded in 1855.

Gardens fulfill two functions: they produce food in the form of fruit, vegetables, and herbs, and they give aesthetic pleasure through flowers and decorative plants, such as ferns. City-

The gaudy blooms of modern flowerbeds do not appear here in London's Chelsea Physick Garden, founded by apothecaries in 1673 for the study of rare herbs and other plants. Today's botanic gardens are the direct descendants of such research collections.

dwellers put enormous effort into maintaining their gardens and allotments, which seems to show how necessary is some sort of contact with the natural green world that man left so long ago. This poses some interesting questions, such as: Is there a correlation between the unrelatedness of a man's work and the amount of effort he puts into his garden? If vegetable gardens, lawns, rambling flowerbeds, pools, and fountains are just a few of the ways in which city man recreates the countryside, then what sort of man creates each type? One generalization seems to be true: most active field naturalists have ill-kept gardens, or concentrate their efforts on vegetables. This suggests that by escaping to the countryside and seeing genuine wildlife, the need to imitate it in the city is suppressed.

As we have seen, gardens all over the world

have been responsible for the spread and encouragement of a number of flowering plants in the city. If we now look at the vegetable garden in detail, we can see just how cosmopolitan are the origins of the food plants that are commonplace in any city garden.

Until the Middle Ages the kitchen gardens of European cities would have contained a far smaller selection of plants than they grow today. Two of the commonest and most widespread garden food plants, potatoes and tomatoes, hail from the New World and were unknown in the Old World until the 16th century. Peppers, paprikas, hot peppers, and chillies, now so much a part of Oriental and Asian food, were unknown in these areas before the discovery of the New World. Brussels sprouts, cauliflower, broccoli, asparagus, beets, turnips, and other European garden vegetables were taken to many parts of the world by European colonizers. From the Middle East have come rhubarb, artichokes, and honeydew melons; from India and adjacent areas have come carrots, cucumbers, gherkins, and eggplants (aubergines); and from China, certain onions and radishes. In the last few decades

dozens of less familiar vegetables have been moved around all over the world. Many city-dwellers experiment with growing or eating new and exotic fruits and vegetables. As with any introductions, there may be problems. The climate may not suit one of the new plants, or a local fauna species (itself perhaps introduced) may find it a very suitable food. But gradually, as adapted strains are developed, we can expect a cosmopolitan distribution for most garden plants.

The trend toward the cosmopolitanization of people, plants, and wildlife in cities is merely echoing what is happening to the cities themselves. The newer parts of most great cities in the world are tending to become more and more alike. The same cars and shops are duplicated in every city. The people dress in the same fashions and, because of the speed with which news travels, there is a tendency for their behavior to become similar, as we see in the periodic outbreaks of hijackings and kidnappings by urban guerrillas. We can see, then, the emerging patterns of cities and city life today. We should perhaps look briefly at future trends.

In 1968 the US Department of the Interior published a report entitled *Man . . . an endangered species?* It is a question that every environmentalist must ask time and again, and that every ecologist studying city life must ask. The answer, I am fairly certain, is "No," but for city man as we know him it may well be "Yes."

The American report states right at the beginning: "The two specters facing him (*Homo sapiens*) are overpopulation and unbridled technology—both self-induced!" Paleontologists have found that throughout prehistory, and for that matter throughout history also, the extinction of animal species has been caused by three main factors, some of which have occurred in combination: overspecialization, changes in climate or geological catastrophes, and direct competition with another species.

Anthropologists tell us that man's success and rapid evolution is due to his adaptability. This should allow him to overcome most climatic and geological upheavals. Alternatively, urban man's downfall could be brought about by direct confrontation with his own species, such as would be likely in a global war. If we rule this

out, there still remains the first factor, a much more realistic threat to urban man's downfall. Paradoxically, man has become overspecialized in being adaptable, and is now caught in his own technological trap. Ask almost anyone in any of the world's cities how he could solve any of the problems connected with the overcrowding of our cities—transport, for instance—and the answer will invariably involve such things as monorails, hovertrains, and helicopters, thus leading us further and further into the technological trap. There is a dangerous tendency for people to give technology, in the words of Admiral Rickover, "a momentum of its own, placing it beyond human direction or restraint— a tendency more pronounced in some countries but observable wherever there is rapid technological progress."

If cities are to survive into the 22nd century A.D., or even into the 21st, then city councils must learn to control and use man's technological achievements to improve his natural environment. This will mean reversing the current trend for technology to take over and dominate both man and his cities.

In their plants, animals, and buildings, and in the dress and manners of their human inhabitants, cities become increasingly cosmopolitan in character. Left: typical of many vegetable gardens in temperate countries, this English garden is largely stocked with plants derived from other lands. Its cabbages are European, but its rhubarb hails from the Middle East, its corn from the Americas, and so on. Much of this grand mix-up dates back to the Age of Discovery, when European explorers brought home the potato and tomato from the Americas. Right: traditional Scandinavian architecture still helps to identify this as the main shopping street in Copenhagen. But the clothes and customs of the people passing by are almost indistinguishable from those of any other Western city.

Index

140

Picture Credits

Key to position of picture on page: (B) bottom, (C) center, (L) left, (R) right, (T) top; hence (BR) bottom right, (CL) center left, etc.

Acknowledgments

I would like to thank the following people and organizations for their help in preparing this book: Judith K. Walker, Dr. Vladimir M. Galushin, USA Agricultural Research Service Plant and Entomological Sciences Staff, Rentokil Laboratories Ltd., The Department of the Environment Building Research Department, John Bayliss, Dr. A. S. Malchevsky, Dr. Blagosklonov, and Sally Heathcote.